Additional praise for *On Course for Business* . . .

"This book is a must for anyone who wants to get ahead in business and understands that golf is an indispensable tool in succeeding! As a financial advisor, I use golf to network and meet new clients. And as president of the Los Angeles chapter of Executive Women's Golf Association, I especially advocate knowledge of the game of golf for women. At corporate outings, get out of the spa and out on the course where the decisions are being made! You'll have more fun, and get ahead at the same time!!"

> —Kathrine Russell
> Morgan Stanley Financial Advisor and
> President of Los Angeles Chapter of EWGA

"As the former National Sales Account Manager for the #1 soft drink company in the U.S., I wish I had known the business golf strategies that Suzanne shares. I know it would have been a huge factor in deepening my client relationships and fostering even greater career success."

> —Corene Mathias
> Business Executive

"Suzanne Woo blows away every excuse a woman has for not playing golf and reveals the personal and business triumphs that make it essential. Her book is a must read for every woman who has ever passed up the game— men and women alike can benefit from her methods to maximize the game for optimum results!"

> —Kimberly Barton
> President, Kinetic Group, Inc. International

On Course *for* Business

Women and Golf

....

SUZANNE WOO

JOHN WILEY & SONS, INC.

To Melissa Courtney, Ryan Alexander, and Reggie,
for your unique ways of sharing your love and joy with me

Published by John Wiley & Sons, Inc.
Published simultaneously in Canada.

This publication is designed to provide accurate and authoritative information in regard to the subject matter covered. It is sold with the understanding that the publisher is not engaged in rendering professional services. If professional advice or other expert assistance is required, the services of a competent professional person should be sought.

Library of Congress Cataloging-in-Publication Data:

Woo, Suzanne, 1962–
    On course for business : women and golf / by Suzanne Woo.
      p. cm.
    Includes bibliographical references and index.
    ISBN 0-471-44297-6 (pbk. : alk. paper)
    1. Women executives—Social networks.   2. Women in the professions—Social networks.   3. Business networks.   4. Golf for women.   I. Title.

HD6054.3 .W677 2002
650.1'3'082—dc21

                                                                    2001046965

Printed in the United States of America.

10 9 8 7 6 5 4 3 2 1

Acknowledgments

Writing this book has been a solitary act—me with my laptop or PC. However, it has not been a solitary process. As I write, I'm still hearing the whispers of those who have shared their thoughts, feelings, and wisdom with me about golf and life.

I have learned valuable lessons from every presentation that I have given. I especially give thanks to those clients, corporations, and associations who enthusiastically responded to sharing my passion for the game of golf. You confirmed my belief that I have something unique to share. My hope is that you've enjoyed the pleasures and rewards from this great game as much as I have.

I give special thanks to Sally Richards—author extraordinaire—for knowing I had a "book in me" and for introducing me to Linda Mead of LitWest Group. Of most importance, Sally, thank you for rescuing Reggie and bringing him into my life. Thank you, Linda, for your persistence in finding a home for this book with John Wiley & Sons.

While writing this book, I was fortunate to have the generous support of many people. Barry Salberg has always championed me, personally as well as my business. Tim Polk, thank you for your wordsmithing and for being a fabulous writing coach. Much appreciation to Scott Garey for sharing your healing skills that enabled me to write this book. Special thanks to Susan Schwartz, Eve Ogden, Gayle Uchida, and Denise Qualls for always believing in my success.

Thank you to Debra Englander, my editor at John Wiley & Sons, for your vision and belief in this book—you are a true professional. A hearty thank you as well to Elke Villa, Felicia Reid, and Paul McCarthy for your diligent work on the book's cover, as well as to Michel Bohbot for the cover illustration. Special thanks to Bernice Pettinato at Beehive Production Services.

To the many people I interviewed, thank you for sharing generously your business golf experiences—your stories provided inspiration for this book. Helen Conroy, many thanks for introducing me to your amazing network of professionals. Thank you to those who reviewed drafts: Shawn Greene, Susan Fornoff, Sheila Navis, and, especially, Linda DeWitt.

v

Special thanks to Reggie's other family for welcoming both of us into your family—Dorrie Jorgensen, Linda Jorgensen, and, especially, Georgiana Hawxhurst. Thank you, Georgi, for making sure that I ate well and kept sane with our walks with Tiramisu and Reggie along the marina.

I couldn't have made the journey from being a highly stressed real estate attorney to following my passion as business golf speaker and author without the help of many in my life. To my parents, James and Vivian Woo, thank you for always believing that I could accomplish whatever I set my mind to and for wanting me to have a better life than you have had. Wes and Zita Woo, thank you for letting me share in the lives of your two special gifts—Melissa Courtney and Ryan Alexander. Take good care of them.

John and Nancy Woo, your belief and help in realizing my vision are much appreciated. Grandma, when that special man appears in my life, I hope we can share that day together. Ken Tong, thank you for your Excel expertise. Thank you to all of my other family members and friends who have given me your support in your own ways, especially Jeffrey Tong.

Bobbie Krueger, my heartfelt thanks for your friendship, insights, and for always listening without judgment.

Phyllis Greene, my deepest gratitude for your compassion and wisdom. It has been a tremendous honor to have you in my life.

Jacqui "Zocko" Zock, special thanks for helping me "lighten up" and our many laughs. I am sure there are many more laughs to come—on and off the golf course.

Finally, Jack, I, too, hope you can see my life unfold. Indeed, our friendship was fated. I miss you dearly and I know we will meet again.

Foreword

You're standing in the midst of a crowded business reception in your best suit. Many of the people you most need to talk to are milling about holding drinks and exchanging business cards. It's your job to get out there and network. If you're already getting queasy just thinking about it, then I don't have to tell you much about why I love the game of golf. Throughout my career, golf has offered instant common ground—an intangible commodity that is worth its weight in gold, both personally and professionally.

As the founding managing partner of Andersen's Growth and Retention of Women (GROW) initiative, a program designed to help women advance professionally, I have spent a great deal of time looking for ways to help women become more visible as leaders. That connection is one of the reasons I'm so supportive of the message of this book. However, I must make a critical point. To me, golf is not about helping women "fit better into a man's world." Golf is simply an extraordinarily effective relationship-building tool. No professional of either gender will become a business leader without superior relationship-building skills. While sharing your enthusiasm for the game as an instant icebreaker, and an invitation to play golf is a tried-and-true vehicle for business hospitality, golf's greatest benefit is how it helps you relate to other people.

Relationships are built on trust, connection, and reconnection—not a five-minute exchange over hors d'oeuvres, trading business cards, or even doing lunch. My experience has been that golf affords a uniquely valuable opportunity to spend four hours of uninterrupted time with someone, to really get to know that person. What makes him or her tick? How does he or she make decisions? Does he or she play fair? What else do we have in common besides golf? I remember one afternoon on the course that taught me more about my client than I had learned in all of the previous year.

Spending time on a golf course teaches you about your playing partners, but it also offers insight into yourself. When I was getting started, I was not as experienced as some of my golfing colleagues, but I had developed a knack for chipping and putting. When I entered best ball tournaments or scrambles,

I was able to participate and feel like a team player because I was able to contribute what I do best in a way that helped my team.

In addition, as women work side by side with men, there are real and important boundaries about what constitutes appropriate interaction. Where dinner or out-of-town travel might be less comfortable or unsuitable in some cases, golf is always appropriate.

In my work with GROW, we have always emphasized the importance of networking with other women, with clients, and with colleagues—male and female. One of the insights Andersen has gained from GROW research is that women need to be connected to formal and informal networks. Golf offers ideal networking opportunities. Across the country, GROW has sponsored many golf events, including lessons on a course owned by a female client. Golf also provides fertile soil for another cornerstone of career development—mentoring. Senior men and women can take protégés out on the links for some time together—to share ideas, advice, friendship, and, of course, fun.

In our 24/7 world, work and life integration is a top priority for many women in business, and getting out to a beautiful spot for a few hours not only helps refresh and restore the spirit, but it's also great for problem solving or squeezing in some exercise.

As the working mother of twin girls, I look forward to sharing the game of golf with them. I know I will appreciate having such an enjoyable way to stay connected with my daughters as I learn about who they are and they get to know me better. My husband and I have enjoyed golf for the same reason over the years. Before we had children, we were able to play more often, but that's what's so wonderful about this sport. You don't have to play like an expert to enjoy it, and you can always come back to it. There's always room for refreshing your game or for improvement. It's a sport you can enjoy all your life, however your life evolves.

I've gained so much from playing golf over the years—from miniature golf with my family as a child and golfing with friends in college to corporate golf outings as an Andersen partner. While the game of golf is not some magic bullet for professional success, I look at it as one more "club in my bag"—and, frankly, it's just plain fun.

Thanks to Suzanne Woo's wonderful book, women intimidated by golf's seemingly arcane rites will quickly see how simple it is to get in the game. Once they do—as Suzanne and I know firsthand—they'll be hooked for life.

Karen L. Kurek
Founding Managing Partner
Andersen's Growth and Retention
of Women (GROW) Initiative

Contents

....

Introduction

Don't Be Left Out

I had just finished a presentation on the benefits of playing business golf to a Silicon Valley-area Chamber of Commerce when a well-dressed, twenty-something woman named Lisa rushed up and thrust her business card at me. "I need to learn how to play golf!" she said in a determined, even desperate voice. "Tell me when, where, and how much, and I'll be there!" Although I strive to motivate audiences to learn to play business golf, I was taken aback by her urgency. It was gratifying to know that I had truly connected with one audience member!

I later learned that Lisa was a financial consultant with this country's largest investment banking firm. She had noticed that every Wednesday after trading hours, four to six male financial consultants in her office would leave as a group while she was left behind, often having to handle her colleagues' paperwork for their clients. Annoyed with these newfound administrative duties, she learned her colleagues were headed to the golf course, often with prospects and clients.

"I need to be out there with them on the golf course, not in the office doing their paperwork," she said. She was missing out, she realized, on the benefits of playing business golf—the bonding among co-workers, prospects, and clients, and learning about personal backgrounds and the latest industry information. And, perhaps even more important, missing out on decisions made about which financial consultant would handle a prospect's account.

Perhaps, like Lisa, you have been left out of the action on the golf course. You may have learned of deals sealed on the golf course while you were sitting at your desk. Or, you awkwardly stop speaking when the business conversation turns to golf. Thousands of businesswomen who have attended my presentations and seminars have admitted that they don't know how to respond or

1

react when weekend golf tournaments or their clients' golf games are discussed. Other than Tiger Woods, you probably don't know the names of the top golf professionals or how to react when a client boasts, "I shot a birdie on this dogleg left, uphill par 5." Is this animal cruelty or should you congratulate your client? After reading this book, you will know exactly what to say and much more!

How I Got into This Great Game

I remember when I was nine or ten asking my father about the white bumpy balls and wooden sticks poking out of the worn leather bag in the corner of our garage.

Then, as I got older, I would watch a few minutes of the weekend professional golf tournament on TV. I used to think golf was a silly game. Hitting a little white ball that isn't moving and then chasing it until you hit it into a hole—how difficult could that be? I don't have a defender flailing his arms in my face to block my shot, or a ball speeding at me that I have to return over a net and inbounds.

And then I wondered what fashion statements the players were making—grown men dressed in electric lime green or outrageous hot pink shirts with matching slacks, no less. I assumed that they'd never wear those outfits on the street and somehow the golf course was their acceptable place of poor taste. I never imagined that I would be playing the game.

However, after my second year of law school I began taking swing lessons at a local golf course. I soon realized that I was wrong to think golf was an easy game. Even though the ball just sits there, it takes some doing to hit it. Also, I was thrilled to see that the loud clothing colors had evolved to khakis and polo shirts.

I decided that I wanted to specialize in commercial real estate and land-use law. I intended to represent large real estate developers in their business dealings. I also wanted to achieve the highest success in the world of attorneys and law firms, which is to make partner after seven or eight years with a firm. To achieve this, I knew, besides being an excellent attorney, I had to be a "rainmaker"—someone who continually attracts new clients to the firm and develops long-term relationships with clients and colleagues.

As a young Chinese-American woman, I was looking for an edge on how to help create those relationships. In addition to handling clients' legal matters, I needed to find something that we had in common. I didn't have pets or children to talk about. And then I realized that given the demographics of most law partners and real estate developers—wealthy, older, mostly Caucasian males—they would likely play golf.

After a series of golf lessons, I was pleased that I could hit the ball, and my hunch about golf paid off even before I became an attorney. Prior to my graduation from law school, I began interviewing for an associate position with California law firms. When appropriate, I mentioned that I played golf and intended to use the game as a business-building tool with clients.

One San Francisco Bay area law firm partner, who later offered me a position with his firm, asked, "What has playing golf taught you about yourself?" On quick reflection, I responded, "Temperance and patience." He gave a smile of recognition and nodded as he said, "Yes, golf can be a humbling game."

My Journey to Helping You

I fulfilled my goal of practicing real estate law with a prestigious San Francisco law firm for several years. Looking back, however, it is now clear that my life was just work. I was consumed with the definition of a "billable hour." If I saw a bad movie, I was annoyed and resentful because I had wasted three billable hours. I missed months of my newborn niece's growth even though we lived only thirty minutes apart. I wasn't enjoying what I was doing or the people I was meeting. I didn't know what a toll this constant focus was taking on my life until I was forced to take a period of time for soul searching that I had never planned for or expected.

One day, after six hours of sleep, I woke as usual at 6 A.M., got dressed in my so-called power suit, and was ready to leave for my office across the bay. I was in my newly purchased house on the eleventh fairway of my golf club. Although I fell in love with the house the first time I stepped inside, now it was a dusty, torn up mess, with construction in every room. Suddenly I sat on the corner of my bed and was overcome by exhaustion. I sat there wondering what I was feeling. By 7:15 A.M., I realized that I wasn't going to make it to work.

I called my mother and said, "I'm coming over to sleep. I don't feel well." I got to her home and slept until 3:30 P.M. In a groggy state, I clicked on the TV and will never forget seeing authorities wheeling out blue barrels of Jeffrey Dahmer's cannibalized victims. As I clicked off the television, I remember saying, "This is a nightmare." I didn't realize it was the truth for the victims and their family, and, in a much smaller way, a start of my awakening from the nightmare of what my life was like then.

After nearly twenty-seven hours of sleep over a two-day period, I visited my doctor thinking there must be something physically wrong with me. After a routine examination, he told me to get dressed and to meet him in his office. When I arrived at his door, I was afraid I was seriously ill. Never in the three other visits during the prior six months did he close the door to his office.

He said, "I've seen you several times over the last few months. There's nothing wrong with you physically. But whatever you're going through, it is taking a toll. You need to take a look at your life." He then gave me the name and phone number of a counselor.

As you can imagine I resisted the notion of seeing anyone. I was on my way to success: was graduated from law school, had passed the California bar, and had joined a prestigious law firm. What could possibly be wrong? After some persuasion from longtime friends and even my secretary, I made my way to the office of the counselor for what I thought would be a visit or two.

I worked with the counselor on a variety of complex and painful issues over several years. I think of it as the time that I first truly met myself, the person who was, sadly to say, a stranger to me. I discovered what I liked, what I wanted, and how I wanted to live my life. It was time to leave the prestigious law firm and try to gain some balance and sanity in my life. I started my own legal practice, but worked in a less stressful and more mindful way. I also worked for a start-up company in sales and marketing.

This downshift in my work gave me some needed time to play more golf with friends at my club. In fact, I credit playing golf with helping me to make so many deep life changes. While playing golf, I often watched how I behaved and reacted on the golf course and realized that was how I responded to situations in my life. The golf course was a revealing mirror of my life. For example, a friend asked why I had white knuckles when gripping the club. Instead, I should have gently held the club as if I were cradling a bird. I realized it was a metaphor for how I lived my life—uptight and strangling the breath out of myself. I now look out for that grip on and off the course. I know I've lost balance when I'm using what I call the GOD grip—the grip of death.

Then, during several months in 1995, my understanding of how to live my life changed dramatically. One day in March, a close friend of eleven years called to ask me to visit her. Jackie (she preferred "Jack") was an insightful, wise woman eighty-eight years young. Initially a customer of my gift shop in my prelaw school days in Placerville, California, a quaint town in the gold country of California, Jack later became someone who taught me how to live my life and regrettably how to say goodbye to a loved one. If you know the story of the friendship that went beyond boundaries in *Tuesdays with Morrie*, then know that Jack was my Morrie, and I fortunately had much more than just Tuesdays.

In the five months after Jack told me she was dying of lung cancer, I was on a path of taking an emotional and psychic pummeling. In addition to going through the dying process with Jack, I grieved with close friends during the loss of six others in their lives. During this painful time, the golf course was again a special place where I could be with friends and escape from the hurt. This period helped clarify what is important to me. I had to find a passion that I could share with others.

Two weeks after Jack died, I took my niece to the local library. In thirty incredible minutes of furiously writing (or taking dictation), I had the topics and material that I wanted to tell the world, and especially women, about golf. Right then, I decided to focus my life on hitting a golf ball rather than law books. Out of my passion and tremendous gratitude for the game, I founded GOLF 101, now BizGolf Dynamics, a California-based business golf consulting and public speaking company.

Several factors affected my decision to form BizGolf Dynamics. I recalled at networking functions how I enjoyed talking about the game of golf. Most women were shocked that I knew how to play. They would ask me all kinds of questions. Why did I learn? How did I know where to start? Was golf as difficult as it looked? Most seemed envious that I could play the game or at least talk intelligently with clients and colleagues about it.

In addition, while golf publications said more women were playing the game, the statistics also showed women were dropping the game just as quickly. I understood why women were quitting the game. Although I was strongly motivated to learn for business reasons, I remember how awkward I felt when I first arrived at the golf course for my lessons. I was in unfamiliar surroundings. I saw different colored flags, which clearly were the targets, but I had no idea the distance to the flags. I tried to swing my arms and turn my torso like my golf swing instructor said, even though I had never moved my body in that way before.

I also remembered how uncomfortable I felt when I eventually made my way to a golf course with my brother and father. I didn't know how far I could hit the ball. I didn't know where to stand when they were taking their swings. And I'll never forget seeing a score card and the sea of numbers, thinking to myself, "I'm not an accountant. I'm an attorney because I don't want to deal with numbers." After learning—mostly by osmosis and by making mistakes— eventually my golf swing and knowledge came together as I played with family and friends.

Through my presentations and seminars, I show businesswomen how to use the game of golf to build and deepen business relationships. I don't teach you how to hit the ball long or stress that you must shoot a low score—those aren't important in playing successful business golf. Instead, I provide the needed information to make you feel confident and comfortable in a business golf setting just as you would in a business meeting. I want you to, well, get *On Course for Business*, but also use the game to recreate, rejuvenate, and relax.

Selling Out or Wanting In?

During a presentation I was asked, "Are you saying that I have to play golf to succeed in business? I have to be one of the guys? It sounds like the times when women could only wear tailored masculine business suits." Let me be clear— you do *not* have to play business golf to succeed. You can succeed in many other ways that work for you. If playing business golf would compromise your integrity, your personality, or your beliefs about yourself, then you shouldn't play. If you took up the game only for the business benefits and don't enjoy playing, then you may want to stop.

I only ask that you keep an open mind about learning to play golf, or if you already play, to keep playing. Do your clients and prospects play golf? If you're in high-ticket sales for products or services, in a company in which your colleagues play golf, or in an industry where golf is often played as part of doing business, then perhaps you should consider learning how to play. Play not because you want to be one of the guys, but because you enjoy being out on the course and accomplishing productive work at the same time.

You might think playing golf with the boys is buying into the "good old boys' game." Actually, playing golf with men levels the playing field. Golf is a humbling game. The harder you try to play well or impress other players, the worse you will probably play. Everyone is an equal on the golf course, and titles and the hierarchy of the office are stripped away.

The game also has equalizers built into it. First, there is the handicap system that enables players of different abilities to play against one another. Unlike tennis, you or I could play against a top golf professional and have a chance of beating him or her because of the handicap system. (I tell you more about this in Chapter 3.)

The other equalizer is the different tees that players can use to hit their initial shots. Better players start a hole by hitting from what's called the *back* tee, which makes the hole longer for them. Women typically hit from the *forward* tees. The difference between the tees can be as much as 30 to 40 yards. The tees are designed so a man and a woman of similar playing ability will have their shots land in nearly the same area, even though the man has actually hit the ball farther.

Rather than feeling you're selling out and playing the game because you have to, it is my hope that you'll fall in love with the game as I have. For me, MasterCard's "Priceless" advertising campaign describes how I feel when I'm on the golf course as well as how I feel about the game of golf. You've probably seen some of the commercials. A father and his young son go to the baseball game. You see the cost of the tickets, the cost of the hot dogs, but the value of the time spent with each other? *Priceless*. Except for the costs to play golf, how do I value the beautiful surroundings of a lush green golf course, the feeling of satisfaction when I hit a shot just right, the joy of achieving my personal best score, or the pleasure of being with my playing partners? Like the value of close friends with whom I have shared my life, I can't put a dollar figure on the feeling.

What's Ahead for You

If you are considering learning to play business golf but are hesitant to do so, then Chapter 1 is a must read. I address the most common objections to playing golf. I call them the That's All False! Objections. I hope to overcome the TAFs by giving you what I call the FREEDOM benefits of playing golf, which are seven reasons why I believe golf is worth your time to learn and play. I also give you some thoughts by professional golf swing instructors on how you don't have to be an Olympic athlete to play golf well. And if looking foolish on the golf course is a concern, you'll learn how that's just "par for the course" and I'll show you how to overcome that worry.

I then introduce you to the game, its equipment, and its language. After reading chapters 2 and 3, you will have a basic understanding of the game, and you'll know your way around the golf course.

If you already play golf, but want to learn how to play successful business golf, then read chapters 4 through 6. You'll learn tips about the rules and proper protocol to make you an enjoyable playing partner regardless of the distance that you hit the golf ball. Contrary to what you may believe, most men enjoy playing golf with women. You just need a few secrets to make it a pleasant experience for all. I also show you how playing golf can reveal the personalities of your playing partners. You can then use that information in business settings to improve your workplace negotiations.

After you've learned how to manage your business golf game, I show you how you can expand your golf opportunities. In Chapter 7, I describe the different charity and corporate golf tournaments that you can play and the tournament formats that are beginner-friendly. After you've played more golf, you may want to host or organize a golf tournament for colleagues or your company. Chapter 8 includes strategies to consider so everyone has a great time. In Chapter 9, I offer suggestions for the men who read this book. Although I wrote this book primarily for women, it contains valuable information for men. In particular, Chapter 9 shows men how they can play golf with businesswomen, especially decision makers, and make sure those women have an enjoyable time. Perhaps, your husband, male friends, or colleagues might benefit from these tips on their next golf outing with a businesswoman.

After reading this book, you won't miss a bounce when the conversation turns to golf. You'll soon be able to share with prospects and clients your latest golf triumphs. Like Lisa, you may choose to play golf with colleagues to deepen your work relationships or gain new clients. Or, like the businesswomen you read about in this book, you may have tremendous business and personal successes as a result of playing golf.

A Final Note

For me golf isn't just a game or a way to enhance business relationships—it has become so much more. Sure, it's now my business. And I have enjoyed successes as a result of playing business golf—a national feature article in *Golf for Women* magazine about my business resulted from playing a round of business golf.

But the game is also a place where I can escape from business, gather with friends, get some exercise, and enjoy the beauty of the golf course. The game of golf can be as large a part of your life as you choose to make it. You'll learn how you can use golf to enhance your professional success and your personal life.

PART ONE

GOLF—THE BUSINESS TOOL AND THE BASICS OF THE GAME

CHAPTER 1

. . . .

Networking the Traditional Way— Golf's Strategic Advantage

On a summer weekday morning Linda joined her friend in a casual round of golf. She didn't expect to do any business. It was golf with a friend and two other women whom Linda didn't know. But the power of golf for networking was made evident—the round helped Linda land a six-figure sales position with a Southern California-based company and membership to a San Francisco Bay area country club.

In the middle of the round, Linda and her playing partners had a typical conversation on the golf course. They chatted about their lives, their families, and their careers. After playing a few holes, Linda mentioned that she was looking for a new position in the telecommunications industry. During lunch following the round, one of the women mentioned that her husband was looking for a senior person to manage a substantial account with SBC Communications. Linda expressed interest in pursuing the opportunity, and the woman offered to talk with her husband, who called Linda the next day. Linda flew to the company headquarters for a round of interviews and was offered the job that day! And as an added bonus, Linda's commute to work dropped to a mere 2 miles from her home.

That's the magic and power of playing golf! You never know whom you'll meet on the golf course. Linda parlayed her round into a six-figure contract.

With her increased income, she purchased a membership at a prestigious country club. And Linda now leverages that membership by inviting clients and prospects to play and doing more networking with members who are senior executives of San Francisco Bay area corporations.

Perhaps you're wondering how I had the tremendous good fortune to be featured in *Golf for Women*? I had entered as a single player in a golf tournament sponsored by an association for golf writers and golf-related media personalities. I was teamed with two freelance writers and a physical therapist who specializes in treating golfers.

One of the writers, Barry, had written feature articles for *Golf for Women* and *Golf Tips*, two popular golf magazines. Barry asked me a plethora of questions—from the type of presentations that I provide to organizations, to the reasons for my desire to educate women about how to use the game of golf for business, to my background as an attorney. Before we even finished the round of golf, he asked if he could pitch an article idea to the senior editor of *Golf for Women* that focused on me and my speaking business. You can imagine my response!

The article gave me added exposure and credibility in the world of golf. It resulted in features for other national publications, as well as an appearance in a television commercial for Liz Claiborne's golf clothing line, LizGolf. Besides the tremendous additional publicity, I received numerous inquiries about my business, which led to new clients, including the New York office of the largest investment banking firm in the country.

To receive such publicity, I would have had to pay thousands of dollars for a publicist. Instead, I invested only $40 for the tournament entry fee, and I also got to play a beautiful golf course. What's more, Barry and I have since become friends and professional colleagues.

Networking the Old Way

Where else could Linda and I have met individuals who changed our careers in such substantive ways? We could have met at a trade conference, association networking event, or some other forum where you can meet hundreds of people. Although you can learn information about a particular topic from event presenters, these venues have their limitations in building long-term business relationships.

Andrea, a business development director for a Silicon Valley Internet company, attends numerous conferences, meetings, and alumni events for her alma mater, Harvard School of Business. She knows a lot of people, but she feels unnatural at those formal events. She says that if someone *really* wants to know her better, he or she should play golf with her. "I'm much more in my comfort zone when I'm playing golf. I'm more natural," she says.

I certainly can relate to that feeling. It is rare at traditional networking events to have more than a few minutes to speak with someone. Other than the usual exchange of names, employers, and other superficial information, it's difficult to learn enough about each other to find out what you share in common.

In her book *Going to the Top* (Viking, New York, 2000, p. 68), Carol Gallagher found that these traditional networking events are often "a time-consuming waste of energy [since] the relationships formed are often too shallow to be meaningful or even helpful." Dr. Gallagher interviewed 200 women in Fortune 1000 companies who are within two steps of CEO. She reveals that the executive women developed their substantive professional relationships when working together on projects that test and reveal their character (rather than by simply exchanging social pleasantries). It was those relationships that propelled their careers.

Just as with Linda and me, you may develop those powerful relationships in just one round of golf. Playing golf with someone gives you the unique opportunity to spend four to five uninterrupted hours together. How else could you ask a client or prospect to spend so much time with you? During that time, you will learn more about a playing partner's personality than you ever could over lunch.

That's All False! Objections to Playing Golf

I have spoken around the globe about the advantages that women can enjoy by playing golf. Before explaining the benefits of golf, however, I want to share the three most common objections women have about learning and playing the game:

1. *Time.* "I don't have time to play. Golf takes too long to learn and to play."
2. *Athletic.* "I'm not athletic at all. I didn't play sports when I was young, so I doubt I'll be able to hit the golf ball."
3. *Foolish.* "I don't want to make a fool of myself out there. I'm not good enough. I'm a perfectionist, and I don't want to look silly in front of clients or colleagues."

You probably can relate to one, if not all, of these reasons. I call them the "That's All False!" Objections. Every time I hear one of these excuses, I say to myself, "That's All False!" Let's go through why I believe each one is false.

Time Is Ticking

Today we're all attached to our cell phones, pagers, PDAs, laptops, and e-mail and are on call 24/7. In addition to demands of work, many people also have responsibilities for spouses, children, and organizations. Before deciding that you lack the time to play golf, you should examine your thoughts about time and your life.

. . . .

If women were convinced that a day off or an hour of solitude was a reasonable ambition, they would find a way of attaining it. As it is, they feel so unjustified in their demand that they rarely make the attempt.

Anne Morrow Lindbergh

. . . .

Cheryl Richardson, author of *Take Time for Your Life* (Broadway Books, New York, 1999), shows people how to create a life they want and love. Her clients are often successful in their business and careers, but they crave more fulfilling lives outside their professional work. She sets forth seven strategies to overcome the obstacles that prevent you from living the life you want. Some of the strategies include taking care of yourself first; fueling yourself with a community of good friends; fun exercise and soul-nurturing activities (rather than adrenaline); building a soulful community of relationships that support, challenge, and encourage you to be your best; and honoring your spiritual well-being.

Thinking through her strategies, I can't help but believe that golf can be an integral part of helping you live the life you want. In fact, I have developed an acronym about the positive benefits of playing golf—FREEDOM. You'll soon learn the FREEDOM benefits of playing golf, which can help you succeed in your business or career. Just as important, however, golf can enhance your personal life through exercise and friendships on the golf course.

While learning about the FREEDOM benefits, consider how playing golf can replace other activities to fulfill your needs. For example, if you exercise at a gym, playing a round of golf can replace that workout. Later you'll learn how many calories you can burn while playing golf. Instead of an office meeting,

consider meeting a client at the driving range where you can get a bite to eat
and hit a bucket of balls or practice your putting. It will give you both a chance
to get some exercise and fresh air.

FREEDOM: Fabulous Fun

With our stressful lives, we could probably all benefit from having more fun.
Golf can provide that fun for you. Fortunately, we don't have the pressure of
the professionals who play for their livelihood. For us, playing golf should be
for the sheer fun of it, even when we are playing for business reasons.

· ·

*Golf combines two favorite American pastimes: taking long walks and hitting
things with a stick.*

P. J. O'Rourke

· ·

My clients tell me they have fabulous fun when they are playing golf. One
client, Mike, shared that hitting the golf ball reminds him of being a kid with
his buddies and hitting rocks with branches they found. Shawn talks about the
fun of hitting the golf ball well and hearing the ball "kerplunk" into the hole.
Denise likes spending time with colleagues and laughing with them about their
great shots and even their horrible shots.

I suspect most golfers are addicted to the feeling of hitting a shot just right.
It's that effortless feeling of swinging the club and hitting the ball right where
you're supposed to—on the sweet spot.

However, there are times that trying to hit that sweet spot can make F stand
for Frustration. I understand that feeling all too well. Your body doesn't seem
to move like you know it can. Or your swing is slightly off; as a result, the ball
just doesn't seem to go where you want. But if you can learn to temper that
frustration, where else can you mix play and work? It is a winning combination, regardless of how poorly you happen to be playing.

To help minimize my frustration, I recall a phrase I learned when I was
studying for the California bar exam: "Hit it and move on!" If I hit a bad shot,
I don't let myself fester over it and let it ruin my next shot, the next hole, or the
rest of the round. I tell myself, "Hit it and move on!" The shot is over and there
is nothing I can do to change it.

When you're starting to learn the golf swing, remember that you're moving
your body in a new way. It will likely feel awkward at first, but don't be afraid
to try something new. As you practice and swing the club more, your muscles

will get used to the new motions. As with learning anything new, the more time you can practice, the sooner you'll get the feel of the swing. If you haven't taken lessons from a golf swing instructor, it's worth doing so. Although friends and spouses mean well when giving you swing advice, it's best to learn from a professional golf instructor. (I give you suggestions about how to choose an instructor in Chapter 2.)

. . . .

The body is shaped, disciplined, honored, and, in time, trusted.
Martha Graham

. . . .

Don't let your frustration in learning the swing or how you hit the ball prevent you from having fun playing the game. The other benefits of playing far outweigh that fleeting temporary frustration.

FREEDOM: Rapport and Relationship Builder

Regardless of Donald Trump's personal life, I admire how he was able to survive his financial crisis in 1990 when the real estate market plummeted. To survive it, he wasn't locked in the conference room negotiating and renegotiating complicated contracts and loans. Instead he was out playing golf.

In his book, *The Art of the Comeback* (Times Book, New York, 1997), Trump lists playing golf as number one on his Top Ten Comeback Tips. He speaks highly about the benefits of golf, "I've found you get to know a person much better on the golf course than you can over lunch or dinner. You develop camaraderie. I made lots of money on the golf course—making contacts and deals." Playing golf was very profitable for him.

Here's why playing golf is such an effective rapport and relationship builder. The golf swing takes on average about 1.4 seconds. If your score is 100, you've swung the club for 140 seconds, or slightly more than 2 minutes. If you are playing with three others, then only about 10 minutes are spent actually hitting the ball. What are you doing the rest of the 4-hour round? Besides having fun and experiencing the many other benefits of playing, you are bonding and learning about one another's backgrounds, families, and career histories.

. . . .

If I were in school now, I'd learn [golf]; not learning was my biggest mistake.
Maybe I still will. Why? It's a game with quiet time where people can talk about
things. It's not like tennis, which I play and isn't helpful. Guys do a fair amount

of work on the golf course. Women need to be where decisions are being made, and like it or not, some are made on the golf course. It's not unusual to ask some-one, "Have you talked to so-and-so recently?" and he says, "I played golf with him Saturday." So I say, learn it and don't make it a negative. Make it part of the portfolio.

Ellen Hancock, former CEO, Exodus Communications

. . . .

It can be difficult to get in depth about such topics over lunch. You're interrupted by the wait staff or the restaurant is too noisy. But by sharing such information while on the golf course, you're building rapport with each other to create long-term, win-win relationships—business and social.

An added reason why golf can help build relationships is that—while you play with others—you're really competing only against yourself. You are trying to shoot your best personal score or hit shots as well as you can. You're not competing against your playing partners, unless you have agreed to a bet. Even with a bet, you don't try to make your client or prospect miss his or her shot.

Playing golf with others is very different from playing tennis, where you try to place the ball so your opponent can't return it. That creates a win-lose feeling. Instead, in golf, you'll always hear players (even opponents) praise one another's shots during a round. "Good shot!" and "Nice putt!" are heard often on the golf course. When playing to build business relationships, it is those shared positive feelings that are remembered and appreciated long after the round. And, if one of you should hit a hole in one, you will always have that special connection with each other!

The relationship building aspect of golf isn't limited to just business colleagues and clients. If you want to spend more time with your family, then consider making golf a family affair. Your spouse may benefit from playing golf in his career. It's a lifetime sport that both of you can enjoy for work, but also when you're traveling together. Your children can learn focus, patience, and how to handle challenges, as well as play a game that may help them professionally in the future. A single mother who plays golf for business purposes plays with her teenage son. She said, "It gives us a chance to spend time together doing something we both enjoy. And it's nice that we can compliment one another for our good shots."

You don't have to play eighteen holes to enjoy this benefit. If you are beginning to learn how to play, then consider playing nine holes only for business. It takes a couple of hours to play and you can still build rapport with your playing partners.

FREEDOM: Exercise for Your Body, Mind, and Spirit

If you're overworked and overwhelmed, that's when you most need to go outdoors, get some exercise, and reconnect with your spirit. Whether you play golf for business or pleasure, hitting the golf ball can give you that much needed time for yourself.

. . . .

Be active, be energetic, be enthusiastic and faithful, and you will accomplish your objective.

Ralph Waldo Emerson

. . . .

Playing Golf Burns Calories.   One stereotype about golfers is that they are overweight and ride around in golf carts all day. You might wonder what type of exercise is that? You're right—you won't get as much exercise if you ride in a cart.

However, if you walk you'll get plenty of exercise. The total distance of eighteen holes is at least 3 miles. If you carry your clubs or pull your clubs in a cart, you will probably walk 4 to 5 miles because you'll need to walk all over the course to get to your golf ball. And, if you play on a hilly course, you'll get even more of a workout.

If you need scientific proof, then consider the findings of a university's department of kinesiology. If you weigh 150 pounds, carry your bag, and play eighteen holes, you'll burn 1,080 calories. That's equivalent to running almost 7 miles! My clients love to hear this statistic, so they're guilt-free when they have dessert or a beer after a round of golf.

Table 1-1 shows the calories you'll burn by playing nine holes of golf (which takes about two hours) whether you ride a cart, carry your clubs, or use a pull cart. If you play eighteen holes, double the numbers to determine how many calories you've burned.

You can burn nearly as many calories playing golf and carrying your clubs as you would gardening. If you could do four hours of medium-impact aerobics, then you would burn only slightly more calories than if you played eighteen holes of golf. Still, you'll burn more than twice as many calories than if you went shopping.

Rather than burning your money by going shopping, go play golf, have fun, soak up some sunshine and exercise, and develop stronger relationships with clients, prospects, or friends and family. It certainly beats cleaning the house! And, to save time on the days you play golf, you can skip a visit to the gym without feeling guilty.

TABLE 1-1   Calorie Usage Comparison

Activity	Calories Burned in Two Hours
Golf (carry)	680
Golf (pull cart)	590
Golf (electric cart)	400
Aerobics (medium)	790
Gardening	690
Housework	360
Shopping	300

The added beauty of the game is you can play and burn calories into your old age. Many of the women I speak with say they wanted to learn golf because they were getting older and wanted a sport that wasn't so hard on their bodies as skiing, tennis, and running. I play at a country club where men and women in their 80s are playing golf. You would never know their ages by looking or talking to them. I will always remember when I asked a member how long she had been playing. When she replied thirty-five years, I stopped and said, "You've been playing golf longer than I've been on the planet. I'm only thirty-one." It was perplexing to hear, especially since she didn't look nearly her age of seventy-six as we walked up one of the many steep fairways on our hilly golf course.

Mental Gymnastics.   When I am very focused on a problem, I often don't know how to back off even though my mind is in an endless loop replaying the situation and not getting any closer to finding a solution. When I'm in this flummoxed state, I often leave the office to play nine holes or hit balls at the driving range. I have found that if I step away and give my mind a respite from that problem, then I can come back with a fresh perspective, and the answer often comes to me more easily and quickly.

In 1998, the *New York Times* reported on *Golf Digest* magazine's study on the correlation between the handicaps of the best CEOs and the success of their respective companies.* (You learn about handicaps in Chapter 3, but for now, in general, the lower the handicap the better the golfer.) From the study,

---

*"Duffers Need Not Apply," Adam Bryant, *New York Times*, May 31, 1998.

a pattern appears: "If a chief executive is a better-than-average golfer, he is also likely to deliver above-average returns to shareholders." Suggested reasons for this correlation include time on the golf course offers time to think big, strategic thoughts. Or perseverance and the ability to focus are also possible factors for the CEOs' success in the boardroom and on the golf course. Some of the noted CEOs with very low handicaps include Jack Welch formerly of General Electric and Scott McNealy of Sun Microsystems.

I don't want you to conclude that the opposite applies; that is, the higher your handicap, the less ability you have for strategic thoughts or that you don't have the other positive traits of successful CEOs. Obviously some of the CEOs have played golf since they were young children. Nevertheless, it is interesting to consider what makes a good golfer and how those qualities make a person an effective businessperson.

Try it! The next time you are faced with a stubborn problem, take some time to play golf. Then go back and see if your thinking is clearer and you are more creative. Rather than a waste of time, your golf excursion may give you a shortcut to finding your solution.

Exercise for Your Spirit.   In our fast-paced world, it is very easy to lose perspective on life. If you can't escape for a vacation, consider playing golf for two to four hours as a miniretreat. For me, a golf course is an oasis in the middle of a chaotic city.

At the golf course where I regularly play, I am blessed with panoramic views of the San Francisco skyline, the Golden Gate Bridge, and Mount Tamalpias in Marin County. It's a place where I can smell and step on freshly mowed grass, be in awe of the hawks hovering above, and watch the squirrels scurrying around.

During my interviews for this book, every woman I spoke with emphasized the importance of being able to get away from it all and how much they enjoy the beauty of golf courses. For example, Karen is the president of a resort and spa located in the San Francisco Bay area. She operates the largest Lincoln Log residence structure in the world, which houses bedrooms, conference rooms, and a spa. Although she can get free facials and massages down the hall from her office, when she wants to feel like she is on a week's vacation, she plays nine holes alone at nearby golf courses. She soaks in the silence, the surroundings, and the scenery of those courses.

FREEDOM: Examine the Personality of Your Playing Partners

You probably want to do business with people who have the level of trustworthiness, character, and integrity to which you hold yourself. It can take quite a while to discover who a person is when your time together is spent only in the office, over lunch, or at a networking function. We can all wear social masks, and those masks prevent us from seeing a person's character, temperament, integrity, and other important qualities.

. . . .

To find a woman's true character, play golf with her.
                                                    Adapted from P. G. Wodehouse

. . . .

Playing a round of golf can shorten this discovery process. While playing eighteen holes, you'll see, for example, whether a person cheats, how he or she handles challenges, if he or she has a sense of humor, or if the person is a team player. I tell you more about what you can learn about a person during a round of golf in Chapter 6.

One financial consultant in San Francisco takes prospective clients out for a round of golf to decide whether he wants to work with them and manage their portfolios. When one prospect threw his club into a tree after a missed shot, the financial consultant knew he didn't want him for a client.

The financial consultant and I share the same philosophy about clients: Not all clients are good clients. Some clients can be more demanding than the fees that they pay. Others are never satisfied with your work and have unreasonable expectations. I prefer to know this information before taking on such people as clients. By spending time during a round of golf before entering into a business relationship, you can avoid these types of negative relationships.

One word of caution: As you watch your playing partners and evaluate their personality, sense of humor, ability to handle challenges, and other characteristics, they may be watching you. In chapters 4 and 5, I show you how to handle different game situations so you present your professionalism on the golf course just as you do in the office.

FREEDOM: *Distinguish Yourself from the Rest*

Whether you are interviewing for a job, getting a promotion, or bidding on a project, it is helpful to differentiate yourself (of course, in a positive way) from the competition. Playing golf with someone distinguishes you from the rest of the pack.

One client, Jackie, entered an industry-sponsored golf tournament. She was teamed with three other players she did not know. After that round of golf, she has been able to call one teammate in particular for industry information and advice. They talk about their golf games and business. She believes the round of golf enabled them to get to know each other and helped establish her credibility as a business professional.

Another client, Peggy, a national account representative, credits playing in a corporate golf tournament for her promotion to vice president. Those making the promotion decision saw her at the tournament and saw her in action. She played with confidence and a sense that she belonged out on the course like anyone else. She knows if she hadn't played in the tournament, she'd have been just another name in the promotion game.

....

In the United States, 26.7 million people play golf, of which 21.7 million are men. A typical male golfer is just over forty years old, has a household income of $63,645 and plays twenty-two rounds per year.

....

Setting yourself apart from others is especially easy for women who play golf. It is presumed that men in business know how to play golf. But if a woman plays in a charity or corporate tournament, she will likely be one of only five to ten women out of a field of more than a hundred players. The women are going to be noticed! Don't worry. It's not your golf score—high or not—that will give you newfound popularity, since in most corporate golf outings the competition is a team format and your individual score is not kept.

Even off the course, you can distinguish yourself because you play golf. I use a day planner with a golf theme to show my love of the game. Or, you can decorate your office with golf paraphernalia—have a picture of you and your golf friends at your favorite golf course, or keep a putter in the corner so you can practice your stroke in the office. You can send note cards with a golf motif. You can also wear accessories with a golf theme, such as a lapel pin, scarf, or earrings to let others notice your interest in the game. Clients and colleagues will see that you like the game of golf. And since golfers love to talk about their golf games or the pro golf tournaments played over the weekend, you'll have plenty of topics for conversation.

FREEDOM: Opportunities Galore

Unlike most other sports, you don't need to find a partner to play a round of golf. You can go to a golf course or play in a tournament as a single player. The golf course staff will put you with three other players to create a foursome. This arrangement can lead to unforseen opportunities.

Denise, a senior account executive with a wireless equipment company, entered as a single player in her industry's tournament. She purposely signed up as a single to give herself an opportunity to meet new colleagues and prospects. Her method worked—she later signed a $1 million account.

Even if you don't land a new client, your round of golf can expand the network of people in your life. For example, Jackie didn't expect to find someone who has since become her mentor. You might find a referral to a great mechanic or a tax preparation wizard. One friend even met her husband thanks to playing as a single. I've created fabulous friendships with several players that I met initially on the golf course. The same goes for my business. Remember how I was featured in *Golf for Women* magazine?

I am always mindful of a saying: "Good luck is where preparation meets opportunity." By learning and making the time to play golf, you've done your preparation. You create an opportunity for yourself by going out to the golf course.

FREEDOM: Maximize Your Links on the Links

Whether it is to deepen relationships with existing clients or just to have fun with business colleagues, playing golf enables you to maximize the links you already have without the distractions of the office.

. . . .

According to the National Golf Foundation, 67 percent of business executives play golf.

. . . .

In her book *Going to the Top*, Dr. Gallagher emphasizes the value to senior executive women of creating alliances with executives in their company as well as those in other companies. Maintaining those long-term relationships requires a commitment of time in learning about the latest developments of your business and personal lives. A round at the golf course gives you the time that you ordinarily might not take to maintain those important relationships.

In Chapter 4, I talk about the type of golf rounds that you can create to maximize your links on the links.

Summary: FREEDOM Is Worth the Time

My hope is that the FREEDOM benefits of playing golf will be a reminder and a motivator for you to take the time to learn and play the game. What other activity can give you so many potential benefits for you to succeed in your professional life? By playing golf, you will work smarter and more effectively than if you simply sit at your desk. And golf gives you the freedom to take care of your personal life by exercising, getting fresh air, and being more creative.

Athleticism an Absolute?

The second That's All False! Objection to golf is about athleticism. Many women believe they can't play golf because they aren't athletic (or aren't athletic enough) and didn't play sports when they were young. I spoke to two of *Golf for Women*'s top fifty women golf instructors and a popular male teaching professional in the San Francisco Bay area to learn their thoughts on how athletic you need to be to learn the golf swing.

Each instructor emphasized that, rather than athleticism, a woman needs to believe she can learn the golf swing. Pia Nilsson, coach to Annika Sorenstam, today's top LPGA Tour player, suggests if women apply their overall confidence and positive self-esteem when they're learning the golf swing, they'll be able to learn much more quickly.

Another teaching professional agrees. "Any woman can learn the golf swing. She needs to make up her mind to learn one. Even if she was athletic, she needs to train and develop those muscles used for golf," says Winslow "Woody" Woodard of the Alameda, California, Chuck Corica Golf Complex.

The instructors also found most women don't really know if they're athletic. Dede Prongas Braun, Director of Instruction at Crystal Springs Golf Course on the San Francisco peninsula, discovered that many women, especially those over thirty-five, were discouraged from playing sports as a child. She says, "These women really have no idea if they're athletic or not. They've formed this opinion of themselves because they didn't play any sports. So, they're thrilled when they can pick up a golf club and are able to hit the ball well."

To play business golf, you need the ability to make consistent contact with the ball and, more important, to know how to be an enjoyable playing partner. Don't compare yourself to others who hit the ball longer or worry if your score is higher than someone else's. Instead, focus on how well you can play within your own game, since that is all you can control. You'll soon find the right golf instructor for you and learn the techniques and strategies to make you a playing partner anyone will want to have in their foursome.

Looking Foolish Is OK, Acting Foolish Is Not

The businesswomen I've met during my presentations are competent and successful in their professional lives. They are competitive in business, and don't want to play golf for business unless they can play well. Again, my response is

"That's All False!" Keep in mind that the goal is simply to learn the basic skills so you can hit the ball, enjoy the benefits of playing, and know how to play appropriately in business settings. When you learn proper golf protocol, you won't have the fear of making a golf faux pas prevent you from playing.

Some businesswomen who play golf admitted they used to worry that they weren't good enough players to play for business. They discovered, however, that most men in business golf outings weren't very good players either. Most women can't hit the ball as far as their male counterparts, but they can hit the ball straight and seldom are in any trouble.

I also spoke to businessmen in different industries about their impressions of women playing golf for business. They think positively of women who play golf and wish more women did so. Their advice to women who consider playing is that they learn the etiquette, rather than trying to hit the ball far. They don't care how well a person—man or woman—plays as long as he or she knows how to be an appropriate playing partner. In fact, they prefer to play with a less experienced player if he or she is fun to play with and knows how to play, rather than a better player who is obnoxious and unpleasant.

Remember that you are learning something new and you're bound to make mistakes. You may feel and look strange as you try to swing the club to hit the ball; it's part of the learning process. You weren't born with the ability to walk. You had to take small steps, fall, and regain your balance until you learned to walk without even thinking about it. The same applies to learning the golf swing. It is a new movement for your body and your muscles. With a little effort, you'll learn a golf swing and build muscle memory.

Looking Foolish Can Pay Off

Despite Corene's concerns of looking silly on the golf course, her first round of business golf was very profitable for her. In the mid-1980s, Corene was the youngest national account sales manager for the number one soft drink company in the country. Her client account portfolio was worth $400 million. She was in negotiations with a national discount store chain, a transaction worth $10 million annual revenue.

When negotiations stalled, Corene asked the distributor, whom she knew well and had worked with before, for suggestions on how she could get the deal moving with the head store buyer and the vice president of the store. He said the buyer and vice president were avid golfers, and he suggested that she invite them to play a round. She initially objected because she didn't know how to play. But the distributor assured her that he would tell her what to do and what not to do during the round. Despite her concerns, she had him set a date for a round of golf with the buyer and the vice president.

Corene had two weeks to take golf swing lessons at the local golf course. When the day arrived, she was able to hit the ball, but not very far and not very consistently. Of course, she was nervous and afraid of looking silly out there. But she also wanted her company to be the exclusive soft drink supplier for this store chain. Rather than being uptight about how she played, she realized that if she relaxed, had a good time, and even made fun of herself, then everyone might have a good time.

. . . .

The glory is not in never failing, but in rising each time you fail.
Chinese proverb

. . . .

Corene still laughs at how poorly she played. She recalls missing the ball many times in her attempts to hit it. On several holes she just picked up her ball after hitting it so many times. But her male playing partners also celebrated with her when she sank her putts. They joined in on the fun and weren't bothered by her poor play.

Corene says, "We just had a great time and laughed during the round. Sure the laughs were somewhat at my expense. But they weren't laughing at me as a business professional, but my inability to play golf. We were all having fun, and even laughed at some of the shots the guys made."

She knows she got the exclusive account because she was willing to look foolish. Corene said, "We didn't seal the deal on the golf course, but our negotiations after the round were more relaxed. Since we had such a good time, we talked about wanting to make the deal happen because we knew we could work well together." She added, "The buyer respected that I went out there even though I was a beginner. They knew if I could play with them, then I could also work with them."

You're in Good Company

If you think you're the only one out on the course trying to hit that little white golf ball, you don't need to worry. Noted trend analyst Faith Popcorn, in her latest book *EVEolution* (Hyperion, New York, 2000, p. 31), proclaims women are catching on to what men have known for years. She notes, "The fastest growing group of golfers is women. . . . Businesswomen are using the game as businessmen did before them—for networking, for entertaining clients, and for making business deals right on the links."

According to the National Golf Foundation, out of the nearly 27 million golfers in the United States, women account for about 6 million—more than half say they use the game as a business tool. And more than 1.2 million women started playing in 2000. The women playing aren't country club wives any longer, but are working women. Since 1990, the participation of working women in the game has grown by 26 percent, which is twice the rate of non-working women.

. . . .

According to the National Golf Foundation, the average woman golfer is forty-two years old and plays eighteen rounds per year.

. . . .

Of those working women who play golf, 40 percent hold managerial, professional or administrative positions. We learned from the *Golf Digest* survey reviewed in the *New York Times* that there is a correlation between low-handicap male golfer CEOs and the success of their companies.* A correlation also applies to women who golf and their incomes, which might be a motivator for you to learn how to play. The better the golfer, the higher her income—the mean income for women with handicaps of 10 or less was $146,900, whereas the median household income for an average female golfer is $68,265. Don't be discouraged if you don't become a 10 handicapper, however, since the national average handicap for a woman is 24. You learn in Chapter 3 what a handicap is, how to get one, and why you should do so.

Going to the Golf Course

Playing business golf offers a beautiful setting that is conducive to developing and deepening business relationships. You'll have the time to learn information and characteristics about each other that you might otherwise never have known. I hope the FREEDOM benefits have persuaded you that playing golf is worth your time.

The fear that you must be athletic to play golf should be more manageable now given the feedback from two of the top fifty women golf instructors. Although you may look foolish sometimes while playing golf, if you're willing to share in some self-deprecating humor, playing can have its rewards.

If you've decided playing golf isn't right for you, or that one of the "That's All False!" Objections is still true for you, I appreciate you taking the time to explore whether you want to make an investment in learning and playing golf. I wish you much success in your professional career and personal life, but do

---

*"Duffers Need Not Apply," Adam Bryant, *New York Times*, May 31, 1998.

also consider that maybe you should at least learn the language of golf so that you can join in the Monday morning conversations about the weekend's pro golf tournaments. Or, if you know a colleague, client, or friend that would benefit from this book, then pass it on.

However, if you're eager to learn how to play and are anxious to enjoy the advantages of doing so, then I look forward to taking you on a journey into the world of playing business golf. I explain the basics of the game first so you'll feel comfortable with the language, the customs, and your surroundings. I show you the finer points of playing business golf, how to create successful business golf rounds, and how you can play with anyone, regardless of your handicap.

Staying on Course

_____ If you have objections to playing golf, besides the "That's All False!" Objections, think of benefits to offset your concerns.

_____ Use the FREEDOM benefits to remind yourself that playing golf is worth an investment of your time.

_____ If you think of yourself as unathletic, forget that limiting belief once you begin to hit the golf ball consistently. With a commitment to quality instruction and practice, you can learn to play consistently and respectably.

_____ You may feel foolish trying to hit the ball, but remember that it's more important to learn how to handle yourself on the golf course like an experienced golfer.

_____ Use golf as a diagnostic business tool to evaluate prospects, colleagues, and clients—and yourself!

CHAPTER 2

Golf 101—A Primer

Imagine that you are traveling overseas for the first time. If you don't consult a travel guide, you won't know the customs, the culture, or what to see. If you're adventurous, this may be perfect, but most of us would prefer to have basic information about the country before going. Knowing some native phrases and customs helps us appreciate and enjoy the experience.

Women who want to learn to play golf venture to the golf course but often have an unpleasant first experience. They're unfamiliar with a golf course and don't understand what they're seeing and hearing. Worse still is going unprepared onto a golf course to play. If they're playing with strangers, they'll likely encounter dirty looks and hostile verbal barbs from other players without even knowing what they're doing wrong. Disheartened and discouraged, many never return to the golf course.

To prevent you from having such an experience, I am going to take you on a virtual tour of a golf course. I start with a visit to a golf course. Then I discuss how to find a golf swing instructor who is best for you, the various types of golf lessons, and what you can expect to learn. I also cover the basics on equipment so you'll be properly outfitted for your journey. Throughout you'll learn the language of golf.

The Game of Golf

This game has a simple premise: to hit the golf ball from a designated starting area (called the *tee* or *teeing area*) into a designated hole in the fewest strokes possible. You count all your strokes, even those that don't actually hit the ball! Golf also has a set of predefined rules.

. . . .

In 1754, the Rules of Golf comprised thirteen articles. Today, the United States Golf Association (USGA) and the Royal and Ancient Golf Club of Saint Andrews oversee the thirty-four Rules of Golf.

. . . .

In some situations, you may also have to add *penalty strokes* to your score for violating a rule of golf. For example, let's say that you took five strokes to get the ball into the hole, but that you also violated a rule of golf with a corresponding one-stroke penalty. Your actual score for the hole would be a six.

A round of golf is normally eighteen holes played in a specific order. Many people prefer to play only nine holes.

. . . .

In the United States, 40 percent of all rounds played are nine holes only—women played over 60 percent of these rounds.

. . . .

Your score for the round is the total number of strokes over the eighteen holes. The lower your score, the better you played.

Golf at the professional level is very competitive, and each player is playing against the field for prize money and a trophy. In recreational golf, however, the game isn't usually competitive, although occasionally small bets are wagered to "make the round interesting." When I play, it's usually me against the golf course and myself on that particular day. This personal challenge to improve your lowest score is why golf can bring out the worst in people, so it's important to be aware of how you react to your scores and to learn not to take golf too seriously. Golf is one of the few sports where there's no one else to blame for how you play other than yourself.

Golf Courses—Your Playground

The golf course is where the action takes place. On days that you are playing business golf, think of the course as your office for a few hours. The golf course is where you can learn a golf swing, practice, and play.

Types of Courses

In general, there are three types of golf courses: public, private, and semiprivate.

. . . .

According to the National Golf Foundation, the United States has 17,108 golf courses, of which 12,335 are public. Five states have the most golf courses: Florida (1,261), California (1,007), Michigan (971), Texas (906), and New York (886).

. . . .

Public Golf Courses

As the name suggests, a public golf course is open to everyone. Many are owned and managed by the city. Other golf courses are run by golf management companies, such as American Golf Corporation, ClubCorp, and Arnold Palmer Golf Management Company. Sometimes they don't own the golf course land, but they manage the operation, from the pro shop to food service to course maintenance.

More golf courses than ever before are being built, primarily because of the recent rise in golf's popularity. This increase is due to many factors, such as the aging baby-boomer population looking for a lifetime sport, and Tiger Woods's making the game front-page news. The game is no longer for the old and wealthy members of exclusive country clubs. More public "daily fee" golf courses have been built in the last decade of the twentieth century than ever before, which expands the opportunities to play for more people.

You may hear a golf course described as an *executive golf course*. One woman asked me if this course was open to only executives. Actually, an executive course is a great place for beginners. Most courses have only nine holes. Each hole is shorter, and, overall, the course is flatter than most courses. With such a layout, beginners can gain confidence and practice playing on a golf course before going out onto more challenging courses.

Private Golf Courses or Country Clubs

Private golf courses are open only to members, who have purchased the right to use the facilities, and guests of the members. The initiation fee to purchase this right can be a one-time fee of several thousand dollars to several hundred thousand dollars, depending on the golf course. After paying the initiation fee, members pay a monthly fee to play golf; they may also be required to spend a minimum amount for food and beverages. A country club typically offers additional amenities for its members, such as a fine dining room, an exercise room, tennis courts, and a swimming pool.

· ·

If you are considering joining a country club, ask about any restrictions on when women can play.

· ·

You might assume private golf courses are better than public ones simply because they are private. Private courses are usually maintained better than public courses, but some of the most beautiful and famous golf courses are public. For example, Pebble Beach Golf Links in Monterey, California, is a public golf course. It costs substantially more to play than most public golf courses, and it is difficult to get a tee time to play. Cost aside, everyone is welcome to play at Pebble Beach.

You may also hear some courses referred to as *resort courses*. These courses are typically part of a hotel. They have the feel and amenities of a private golf course, but are open to hotel guests and the public.

Without a member's invitation, you can only play a private course if you enter a tournament that is open to the public. Therefore, receiving an invitation to play at a private country club by a member is an honor. Because of the exclusivity of a private club, you have an opportunity to play a course you might not otherwise have.

To add to the confusion, some public golf courses may be called XYZ Golf Club, but they are open to the public. If you're not sure whether a course is private or public, call the golf course and ask.

Semiprivate Golf Courses

A semiprivate golf course has some members as does a private club, but it also provides access to the public to play, albeit sometimes at less than prime times. Prime tee times are usually early mornings during the week and on weekends. At some semiprivate clubs, only members are eligible to reserve those tee times, while the public has midmorning and later times.

Practice Facilities

Improving your golf game takes practice, which isn't the same as playing on the golf course. Basically, there are four parts to your golf game: Your *long game* (which is a full swing), your *short game* (pitching and chipping near the green), putting, and hitting out of bunkers or sand traps on the golf course.

· ·

Most golfers also refer to the "mental game"—a golfer's ability to focus on hitting the golf ball without reacting adversely to any negative or challenging experiences, situations, or comments.

· ·

To play golf for business, you don't need to be able to hit the ball far, but you should be able to hit the ball consistently. You learn how to make consistent ball contact with the golf club in your swing lessons. Distance comes as you play more.

Most golf courses, whether public or private, have facilities to practice different parts of your game. I describe each type of facility and the shots that you'll be practicing.

Driving Range

At a driving range, you'll see *hitting stations* or stalls from which each player can hit balls. For your safety, never walk beyond the area where you hit the ball, even if you hit a very short shot and can quickly reach the ball. It's not worth the risk of being hit by an errant golf ball from another golfer.

Players on the range hit what are called *range balls*. These golf balls are specifically for use at the driving range. You shouldn't use a range ball on the golf course. Range balls have distinctive marking, such as two solid lines or a red stripe. After you've located a hitting stall, you can buy a bucket of range balls from the golf course staff or from a machine that dispenses the balls.

Nicer courses or private clubs have hitting areas on natural grass so you have a golf course feel to your practice session. But most driving ranges have artificial grass mats in the hitting areas. If you're left-handed, you'll likely have to move the golf ball tray and the flexible rubber tee that you may use to the left side. If a course doesn't have a driving range, they often have hitting areas where you hit into a net to warm up.

You can practice your *long game shots* by aiming at different targets, which are marked with flagsticks that have different colored flags. The flagsticks are placed at various distances, such as 150, 200, and 250 yards. You can also practice 75 and 100 yard *approach shots*, which are shots from the fairway to the putting green. Most driving ranges have a sign that tells you how far each target is located so you know how far you can hit a ball with a particular golf club.

The driving range can be an intimidating place for a beginner because you may have a player next to you hitting the ball 200 yards or more. Don't compare yourself to that player. You are new to the game, and each player has his or her own pace in learning the golf swing. Instead, focus on what you're practicing and how well you're hitting the ball.

Practice Green

Putting is almost 50 percent of a golf score. To score well, it's important to practice this part of your game. Putting is the easiest part of the game for beginners to master. You can practice your putting at home or in your office. Strength isn't required to be a good putter but the ability to *read the green* and have a good touch with your putter are needed. Reading the green is being able to visualize how the ball will travel to the hole. If you are on a sloping green, the ball won't roll straight to the hole. It will curve or break to the right or to the left, depending on the slope as it rolls to the hole. Likewise, an uphill putt will roll slower than a downhill putt. At a driving range or a golf course, you'll find a practice putting green with several holes on the green.

. . . .

When golfers say they'll meet you at the "putting green" of a golf course, they are usually referring to the practice putting green at a golf course.

. . . .

Putting greens have what's called a *speed*. A green that is considered "fast" is a green that, when you stroke the ball, it will go farther than if the green were "slow." You want to practice your putting before beginning play on a course to warm up. Practice your putting from different distances to the holes. You also want to get a feel for the speed of the greens, especially if you're playing a course you've never played.

Chipping and Pitching

When your ball is less than 90 to 100 yards from the green, you can either chip or pitch your ball toward the hole. These two shots are referred to as your *short game*. You're hitting a *chip shot* or *chipping the ball* when you use a short swing to get the ball to fly low to the green and then roll toward the hole. Or, you may hit a *pitch shot* and you're *pitching the ball*, which is using a short swing again, but the ball flies higher than a chip shot and then bounces toward the hole.

Short game shots require finesse to get a feel for how far you need to swing the club to get the ball to travel the distance you want. You can practice your chipping and pitching at areas specifically set up to do so. At my golf course, for example, they have a small green with three flags to practice those shots.

Bunkers

Besides an area to practice your pitching and chipping, you may find a bunker to practice. Bunkers are located on holes of a golf course where the grass has been dug out and filled with sand. Many golfers refer to them as *sand traps*. Bunkers are designed to make a hole more challenging by forcing you to avoid hitting your ball into them.

Stand-Alone Driving Ranges

Because of the popularity of golf, you can find driving ranges that are not part of a golf course. For example, in San Francisco, the Mission Bay Driving Range offers a lighted, double-decked driving range where you can practice all year round even during the evenings. It also has a practice putting green. For a high-tech, multitiered driving range, the Golf Club at Chelsea Piers in New York has heated stations and an automatic tee system, so you don't have to bend down and place your ball on the tee. Although you can't play golf at most of these driving ranges, you can take swing lessons and practice your putting.

· ·

In Japan, most golfers never play on a golf course because of the expense. They go only to driving ranges, where they may have two-hour waits or need to make a reservation.

· ·

Other Facilities at a Golf Course

Besides the practice facilities, you'll find other facilities to make your visit to a golf course an enjoyable day:

- *Pro shop.* You call the pro shop to make tee times—your reservations for when you want to play on a particular day. When you arrive at the golf course at least 20 minutes before your scheduled tee time, check in with the pro shop staff to tell them you have arrived for your tee time. In the pro shop, you pay for your *green fee* to play nine or eighteen holes. It is also where you ask to rent a golf cart, and pay your cart rental fee. You can buy golf balls, sun block, gloves, clubs, and other golf equipment and clothing in the pro shop.

- *Women's and men's locker room.* Locker room may be a fancy term for a simple rest room, or it may include amenities such as lockers, showers, and a card room for club members.
- *Restaurant and/or bar.* This is commonly referred to as the "nineteenth hole" because it's where players go to talk about the round or chat about business. Most restaurants at golf courses offer both sit-down service and counters for faster service. Today, many of these restaurants have a country club atmosphere.

. . . .

In a Robert Half International survey (February 2001), executives said their most successful business meetings outside the office were conducted over a meal. The second most popular place was a golf course. Trade shows were third. Playing a round of golf and having a meal in the nineteenth hole are a winning combination!

. . . .

- *Clubhouse.* This is the main building that usually houses the pro shop, locker rooms, and the restaurant and/or bar.
- *Snack bar.* If an eighteen-hole golf course is not laid out so you're near the restaurant after you've played your first nine holes, then there will likely be a snack bar. If you're playing eighteen holes, you shouldn't stop at the snack bar and eat. Instead you should take along your food and eat while you continue playing.
- *Refreshment carts.* Many eighteen-hole courses have carts equipped as a snack bar. These carts are driven around the course so you can pick up snacks and drinks during your round.
- *Water coolers.* Many courses have water containers with disposable cups located throughout the course, especially if you are playing golf in a hot climate.
- *Golf course rest rooms.* Most courses also provide rest rooms and/or portable bathrooms on the course.

People Who Work at Golf Courses

The men and women who work at a golf course usually love the game, and most are professionally trained and certified members of the Professional Golfers' Association (PGA) or the Ladies Professional Golf Association (LPGA).

. . . .

The PGA is an organization to promote the game of golf to everyone. It provides education and certification to its male and female members. The LPGA is a similar organization for its women golf professionals.

. . . .

Individuals you'll probably meet at a golf course include:

- *Head professional.* This person is usually a member of the PGA and/or the LPGA. He or she is in charge of managing golf lessons and the teaching staff. He or she may also be in charge of managing the pro shop, including buying merchandise. (Just to clarify, the golf professionals we see on television, such as Tiger Woods on the PGA Tour and Annika Sorenstram on the LPGA Tour are often called *touring pros.* Most head professionals weren't touring pros, but are members of the PGA and/or the LPGA.)

. . . .

The USGA, the PGA Tour, and the LPGA Tour conduct their respective golf tournaments, which you can see in person or watch on television.

. . . .

- *Director of instruction.* This person is usually a member of the PGA and/or the LPGA and provides lessons and clinics on the golf swing.
- *Assistant professionals.* These individuals are apprenticing and attempting to qualify to become a member of the PGA or the LPGA. They may also provide lessons to students.
- *Starters.* Starters are the pro shop staff who organize and manage the flow of people playing on the golf course. Before high tech hit golf courses, you would call the pro shop and reserve a tee time. Today rather than speaking to a person to reserve a tee time, you may use an automated system that takes your tee time reservation and confirms it with e-mail. Starters also check in golfers when they arrive at the pro shop for their tee times. At some courses there may also be a starter at the first tee. Often the starters in the pro shop and the starter on the first tee coordinate players and their tee times via walkie-talkie.
- *Bag boys or bag girls.* They work for the golf course and help you remove your golf clubs from your car. If you're riding, tell them your name and tee time and they'll put your clubs on the golf cart. They're usually located near the clubhouse at what's called the *bag drop.* When you enter the parking lot of a golf course, look for the bag drop before you park

your car. A word of caution: If you're playing at a public golf course that doesn't have bag boys or girls at the bag drop, it may not be safe to leave your bag unattended. But if you've been invited to play at a private golf course or a resort course, or you're playing in a golf tournament, then you should have no problem leaving your clubs with the bag boy or girl.

- *Marshals or ambassadors.* They're usually volunteers who drive around the golf course to try to keep the flow of the players moving and to enforce golf course rules. Their golf carts often have a special flag or sign so you'll notice who they are. If you're playing too slow relative to the foursome in front of you, a marshal or ambassador may give you a warning to speed up your play. At some courses, if you fail to catch up to the group ahead, the marshal can ask you to leave the course without a refund of your green and cart fees. It's important to learn how to play what's called *ready golf*, which I describe in Chapter 3.

- *Golf course superintendent and greenkeepers.* The superintendent is in charge of keeping the golf course lush and free of weeds and insects. The greenkeepers maintain the golf course. As you start to play more and at different courses, you'll begin to appreciate courses that are well maintained—from paved cart paths, weed-free fairways, fluffy sand in the bunkers, to smooth pristine putting greens.

Golf Lessons

Some women have attended my presentations and shared how discouraged they feel about learning to play golf. They've had unpleasant encounters with golf instructors or friends that have deflated their enthusiasm and confidence about playing. For example, one woman said that she was excited about hearing the FREEDOM benefits of playing, but a golf instructor told her after a series of lessons that she could never learn how to hit the ball. Another woman said she played golf with her then-husband and father-in-law, and after tips and advice on every hole, she left after eight holes discouraged and in tears, vowing never to play again.

. . . .

If you are having trouble understanding and learning from your [golf] teacher, it is not your fault. Find one who will guide you positively, simply, and as an individual.

Harvey Penick, legendary golf instructor

. . . .

Unfortunately these women didn't go to a golf instructor who was an effective teacher. Friends and family members just aren't qualified to teach the golf swing. Just as with learning to drive a car, a spouse should never teach his or her counterpart to play golf.

Your experience with a golf teaching professional is vital in determining whether you'll take up the game and enjoy playing. It's therefore important that you choose a golf instructor you enjoy talking with and learning from.

Let's look at where you can get lessons, from whom, and the type of lessons that may work best for you.

Selecting a Swing Instructor

Finding a good swing instructor is like looking for a good attorney, doctor, or mechanic. Instead of calling a local golf course and signing up for a lesson, spend some time getting a few referrals. Ask friends, colleagues, and other golfers to recommend an instructor whom they like. Find out what they like about a particular instructor—is it his or her teaching style, personality, or communication skills?

You may be more comfortable learning the golf swing from a woman instructor. Some women feel a female instructor is more sensitive about the physiology of a woman's body and understands the female body's build and the limitations of female upper body strength. Other women say they don't think male instructors know how to communicate well with women students. For example, one male instructor told a woman student that swinging a golf club is like throwing a football. Since she had never thrown a football, she couldn't relate to what he was saying.

Before choosing an instructor, you should spend a few minutes interviewing the candidate. Some factors to consider are:

- Does the instructor usually teach beginners or more experienced golfers? Someone who teaches mostly experienced golfers may not be as patient with a newcomer learning the basics. Or, he or she may use concepts that are unfamiliar to you since you're a beginner.
- How does the instructor teach beginners? Does he or she have one swing that he or she tries to make you learn, or does he or she work with your body's natural swing and correct major flaws in your swing?
- How many students does the instructor teach every week? If you go into a golf shop, you may meet someone who says he or she can teach you a golf swing. You want to find an instructor who teaches regularly, has PGA or LPGA golf-swing training, and is experienced in teaching.

- What percentage of the instructor's students are women?
- Do you feel comfortable talking with him or her? Do you understand his or her responses? Is the instructor willing to spend time talking with you?
- Is his or her teaching style very technical? For example, some instructors use terms such as, "ninety degree angles" or "pound per square foot on your right side." If your mind shuts down when you hear that kind of terminology, then that instructor isn't right for you.
- Does he or she teach young children or seniors who are beginners? If so, this can give you a sense of his or her patience level.
- Is video equipment used? If you learn better by seeing how something should be done, then it may help you to see your golf swing on video. You will be able to see what you're doing correctly and know what you have to improve on.

Group or Private Lessons

Because golf has become so popular, you can take lessons at your local community college, city recreation center, driving ranges, and, of course, golf courses. The local college or recreation center will probably offer only group lessons. If you prefer one-on-one instruction, however, driving ranges and golf courses are a better choice for you.

In a typical group lesson, you're one of six to ten or more students. Each lesson lasts forty-five minutes to an hour, and you sign up for a number of sessions in advance. In contrast, a private lesson is a session with a golf instructor for thirty minutes to an hour. You can sign up with an instructor for a single session or multiple sessions.

You'll have a different learning experience if you're in group lessons rather than private lessons. An advantage of group lessons is you're committed to a series of lessons at a given day, time, and place. You can put it in your calendar in advance and know you will learn the basics of a golf swing after four to six weeks. In addition, group lessons are usually less expensive than private lessons. Group lessons are also longer than private lessons, so you have more time on the driving range to integrate the lesson. With group lessons, you are also already starting to use golf to develop relationships, whether as practice and playing partners or for social or business purposes.

A disadvantage of group lessons is that you are one of many students, so you will not get the complete attention of the instructor. Check the size of the group, since you'll probably want as small a group as possible. The instructor will speak to the entire group, and then check with each student for a brief period. Still, some women prefer a group setting; they find private lessons intimidating because the instructor focuses only on them.

If you decide to take group lessons from a local college or recreation center, check to see if the instructor also teaches at a nearby driving range or golf course. Since you've already learned this person's approach to the golf swing, you may want to have the option of taking individual lessons to continue working on your swing.

What You'll Learn

I won't try to teach you the golf swing in this venue, but I do want to familiarize you with what you'll probably learn in your lessons. The instructor should have you warm up before each lesson. He or she will teach you stretches for your arms, legs, and back so that you won't hurt yourself and give you some balls to hit to warm up. It's important that you arrive at least fifteen minutes before a lesson to warm up and to leave the office and traffic behind. After you've stretched, the instructor will cover the basics of a golf swing, which include:

- Holding the club properly. You'll learn how to grip the club. Most teaching professionals say a proper grip is the foundation to having a good golf swing. There are several different ways you can place your hands on the club. A good instructor will show you all the ways and help you choose which is most comfortable and works for you. This is the grip you'll use for every club except the putter.
- Addressing the ball. This refers to learning the *stance*, which is where to place the ball between your feet and a proper distance from your body and putting the bottom of the club (the sole) on the ground behind the ball.

   The challenge in learning your stance is the terminology. You suddenly don't have a left and right foot. Instead you have a "front" and "back" foot. Let's assume you are a right-handed golfer, so you stand on the left side of the ball when you face the target. Your front foot is your left foot, which is closer to the target. Your back foot is your right foot, which is away from the target. The instructor may say, "Place the ball back in your stance." This means move your feet so the ball is closer to your back foot. If the instructor says, "Place the ball forward in your stance," then move your feet so the ball is closer to your front foot. As for the distance of the ball from your body, you'll learn there is a place that is neither too close nor too far.

So far, your lesson is focused on your "set up," that is, getting you in position to hit the ball. If you don't have a proper set up, then you'll have a harder time making good contact with the golf ball.

The next topic the instructor will cover is:

- Swinging the club. You will learn the "take away," which is taking the club back by turning at your waist, and the "follow through," which is the downward motion of the golf club as you hit the ball toward the target. Your instructor may demonstrate what a proper golf swing looks like and/or physically move you, so you can feel the swing.

As you get a feel for the mechanics of a golf swing, your instructor may use the terms *timing* or *tempo*. These terms describe how your golf swing and lower body are moving in relation to each other. Your timing may be off because you are swinging the club too fast or too slow in comparison to your leg and hip movement. Tempo is a term to describe the overall speed and rhythm of a golf swing. To see golf swings with good tempo, watch the golf professionals in a weekend tournament. I'm always amazed at how little effort it appears for the professionals to hit the ball so far. They aren't throwing their bodies uncontrollably to hit the ball. Tiger Woods has one of the most aggressive swings, but it is a smooth, controlled, and fluid swing,

When your aim, set up, and swinging of the club come together for you, you'll feel that satisfaction of hitting a golf ball in the sweet spot.

. . . .

Most right-handed golfers unknowingly aim too far right. Use a twig, leaf, or spot on the grass on your target line immediately in front of your ball rather than the target farther away.

. . . .

It's an exhilarating feeling to hit the ball and watch it fly in the air. Again, don't be discouraged if your shots don't go as far as those of others on the driving range. You're just learning, and it takes practice. And don't feel embarrassed about your shots. Everyone is focused on his or her own swings rather than looking at you.

After you've learned the basic golf swing, your instructor may cover:

- Using each of the clubs. You'll learn about the different golf clubs and when to use them. For your lessons, your instructor will usually provide you with what's called a 7-iron. It is a relatively short club, so it is easier for you to control the club. After you can consistently hit the 7-iron, your instructor may have you hit with the longer clubs, including the clubs called *woods*, even though there is not a sliver of wood used to make them. I describe clubs later in this chapter.

- Chipping and pitching. These swings are shorter than your full swing. You'll use them when your ball is close to the putting green. I referred to these earlier as your short game.
- Putting. You'll move to the practice putting green to learn how to grip the putter, take your stance, and stroke the ball. This is where you hear the kerplunk of the golf ball as it goes into the hole.
- Bunker shots. You'll learn how to hit out of bunkers, or sand traps, with the sand wedge, which is designed specifically to help you hit the ball out of bunkers.

Tips for Getting the Most Out of Your Lessons

Some tips to ensure that you and your swing instructor work well together are:

- Develop a realistic goal with your instructor about the progress you want to achieve by the end of each lesson.
- Record times and dates in your calendar for lessons and practice sessions in advance, and schedule around your commitment to learning to play golf.
- Arrive at least fifteen minutes early to warm up and get mentally prepared for your lesson.
- Set goals with your instructor on what to practice between lessons. When you go to the driving range, focus on those goals. Be specific about what part of your game or swing you want to work on when you're practicing.
- If you're uncomfortable with an instructor touching you, let him or her know in advance.
- Don't ask the instructor for feedback on every shot. As you learn the golf swing, you will begin to feel and see the results of a good swing. If your instructor sees you consistently repeating a mistake, he or she will tell you what you're doing wrong.
- Don't get overwhelmed by the minute technical details of a golf swing. Each of us has our own golf swing. The instructor will help you find yours and refine it. Your swing may not look like anyone else's, but if you swing the club and can hit the ball straight, that's all that matters.
- If you don't understand what your instructor has said, ask for clarification. It's part of his or her job.

- If you're having difficulty with your instructor for any reason, speak to him or her about it immediately. Don't wait until the lessons are over. If you're still having difficulty, change to another instructor.

. . . .

If you think you can, you can. And, if you think you can't, you're right.
                                                                Mary Kay Ash

. . . .

Practice, Practice, Practice

The proper golf grip, stance, and swing usually feel pretty awkward at first. If you're not comfortable right away, stick with it! Remember, you're learning something new, and your body needs time to learn this unfamiliar motion.

To get the most out of your lessons, try to practice at least once or twice between each lesson. If you can't go to the driving range, at least rehearse at home the golf swing movement to build muscle memory. To build hand–eye coordination, you need to hit some golf balls. Go to the driving range and ask the staff to borrow or rent a 7-iron and a putter. You need to buy a bucket of range balls from either the staff or a ball-dispensing machine. When you're first learning, start with a small bucket of twenty-five to forty golf balls. Before you swing the club, warm up and do some stretches. Your practice sessions can be as short as thirty to forty-five minutes. It's not the length of time you practice that is important, but that you're practicing at all.

Be specific about the shots you're trying to make. Make it fun and aim at the closest flagstick for a few shots. Then aim for a flagstick farther away. Take your time in setting up and feel your golf swing as you practice. Don't worry about the shots that aren't so good. When you hit a shot that you like, try to remember the feel of that golf swing, so you can repeat it.

. . . .

Harvey Penick suggests a practice routine at the driving range: Stretch. Always aiming at a target, use your wedge to hit five full shots. Use your 7-iron to hit five full shots. Use your 3-wood to hit five full shots. Use your 7-iron again to hit five full shots. Afterwards, practice your putting and short game.

. . . .

As soon as you start to tire, stop hitting balls. If you continue to hit balls when you're fatigued, you'll pick up bad swing techniques to compensate for your tiredness. Take a break or go to the practice putting green.

Some golf courses have *shag bags*, which hold fifty or more golf balls and have a mechanism that you push on the balls to collect them. You can take a few balls or a shag bag to the practice putting green, and practice your putting.

Warm up with short putts, say, about 2 feet, to build your confidence as you sink several balls into a hole. Then as you sink those putts, add another foot or two, and so on. Try a few uphill and downhill putts and putts that break to the right and to the left. Again as you practice your putting, get a feel for the shots and how far back you take the putter to have the ball travel a particular distance. You can also practice your short game, if it's safe to do so. Aim for a hole, then chip balls from the *fringe*, the taller grass around the putting green surface, toward the hole.

Many golfers primarily practice their full golf swings rather than the short shots that require finesse and touch such as pitching and putting. Hitting these short shots well can lower your score tremendously! If you have an excellent short game, you'll score well even though your full swing shots aren't as long as you would like. I know this from experience. I play with women who often are older than I am, so I usually can hit the ball farther than they can. But when it comes to their short games and reading the greens, they're very accurate and often score better than I do.

Golf Schools

If you prefer to immerse yourself in the game during an intensive one day clinic or three-day weekend, you can attend one of the hundreds of golf schools located virtually around the world. You can find a national golf school or others that are associated with golf courses and resorts. Check the Internet and advertisements in golf magazines for a school and location that appeals to you. Some schools are for beginners, whereas others focus on more experienced players who want to fine-tune their golf swing and game.

Golf schools can be a fun way to learn the game and the golf swing, especially if you attend with friends. You'll be with a group of three to ten students. Before signing up, you'll want to ask some questions:

- What's the school's philosophy regarding the golf swing? Are they teaching *their* swing or working to develop *your* swing? If you're learning their swing, do they have instructors near your home so you can continue to learn that swing?

- Total cost of the program—lessons, accommodations, meals, transportation to and from the airport?
- What is the schedule each day? How much time do you have on your own?
- What is the student–teacher ratio? You want a low student to teacher ratio of three to five students per instructor.
- Will you receive a videotape analysis of your golf swing?
- What playing privileges or restrictions for playing the golf course are in place?

You'll be given lots of information on swing techniques, so bring a notebook or a microcassette recorder to make notes during a break. You'll also want to refer to these tips after the school is finished. If you're not used to hitting a lot of balls, take short breaks. Remember, bad habits creep in when you're fatigued and continue to hit balls.

Try to have a few practice sessions soon after you've returned home to integrate what you've learned. The more you practice, the sooner your muscles will be able to soak in all of the information.

Even after attending the school, you may want to work with a local swing instructor to help you with certain aspects of your swing.

Equipment

When you're ready to get on the golf course regularly, you'll have to invest in some equipment: golf clubs, shoes, clothes, balls, and other miscellaneous items. You'll want to have your own set of clubs as you begin to play more. You need some time to feel comfortable with the look and weight of each club. Most golf courses also require that each player has his or her own set of clubs to prevent slowing down the pace of play. In the following section, I explain what clubs make a set, where to buy your equipment, and some money-saving buying tips.

What's in Your Bag?

Clubs are given descriptive names according to the design of the golf club. Each golf club has three basic components:

- The *grip* is typically made of rubber or other synthetic material to simulate the leather grips of the past.

- The *shaft* is made from steel or graphite.
- The *clubhead* is graphite, steel, or some metal composite. It is the part of the club that makes contact with the golf ball.

Each club is numbered to distinguish it from the other clubs. Here's a general rule to remember: The lower the number of the club, the lower the trajectory or ball flight and the farther the ball will travel.

. . . .

The lower the number of the club, the farther the ball will travel, and the harder the club is to hit well.

. . . .

The higher the number of the club, the higher the ball's trajectory or ball flight and the shorter the distance the ball will travel. Think of your clubs as tools to choose from depending on the distance that you want the ball to travel. One client asked if she should swing the club harder to make the ball go farther. You don't vary your swing or how hard you hit the ball. Instead, you change the club you use. For an average woman golfer, the difference that the ball travels between each club is about 10 yards. So if you can hit about 100 yards with your 7-iron, then you should hit about 90 yards with your 8-iron.

Language of Golf Clubs

You'll hear several words used when golf clubs are talked about. Here's a list of the most common terms, so you'll be familiar with them when you're taking lessons, playing, or shopping for clubs:

- *Club face.* The grooved side of the clubhead used to hit the ball.
- *Sweet spot.* The center of the club face and where you want to hit the ball. Each club makes a distinctive sound when you hit the ball in the sweet spot.

. . . .

The sweet spot is where is the ball comes off the club face absolutely straight without spinning to the right or left. Although golfers want to hit the ball in the sweet spot, doing so is the challenge of the game.

. . . .

- *Toe and heel.* If you visualize the head of the club as a foot, you'll see where the toe and heel are. The toe is the tip of the club face that is farthest from the shaft. The heel is the part of the club face closest to the shaft.

- *Sole.* The bottom of the clubhead.
- *Hosel.* The part of the clubhead that holds the shaft.
- *Flex.* Each shaft is made with a certain degree of flexibility. In general, the faster a player's swing speed, the stiffer a shaft the player needs. Shaft flexibility ranges from *stiff* to *regular, senior,* and *ladies,* the most flexible shaft.
- *Loft.* The angle of a club face. This might also be called *degree of loft.* The steeper the loft, the higher *up* a ball will fly, but the less *far* it will travel.
- *Lie-angle.* The angle of the shaft as it goes into the clubhead.
- *"Hit a club."* This is golf talk for how far you can hit a ball with a particular golf club. For example, when a woman says, "I can hit my 5-iron 130 yards," she means the ball will travel 130 yards when she uses her 5-iron to hit it. She's not hitting her golf club with something that makes it travel 130 yards.

A full set of clubs typically includes the following:

- Two or three woods (a driver and a 3- or 5-wood)
- Seven or eight irons (usually numbered 3 through 9)
- A pitching wedge
- A sand wedge
- A putter

Woods

Woods are the golf clubs with heads that look like a solid piece of metal shaped like a D. As a young girl, my father's clubs in our garage had heads made out of wood. Today, the name is a misnomer. Woods may be sold in sets of three, but are usually sold individually.

The most common woods are numbered 1, 3, and 5. The 1-wood is also referred to as the *driver*; it's used to hit the ball as far as possible. Most players use the driver only on the tee. For many, the driver is the hardest club to hit. If you're a beginner, I recommend that you not use or even buy a driver. I used to hit a driver, and I discovered that I wasn't able to make consistent contact with the ball and couldn't hit it straight very often. So I took the club out of my bag and now use my 3-wood off the tee, which I can hit much more accurately and confidently.

A 3-wood is easier to hit than a driver for two reasons. First, the loft of a 3-wood's club face is steeper than a driver, which makes the ball fly higher than when hit by a driver. Second, the shaft of a 3-wood is shorter than the shaft of a driver. In general shorter clubs are easier to control during the swing than longer clubs.

A 5-wood is even easier to hit than a 3-wood. With a 5-wood, the ball will go higher into the air than with a 3-wood, but the ball will not travel as far. Some club manufacturers, such as Callaway Clubs, Cobra, Titleist, and Taylor Made, also make 7- and 9-woods. The theory is it is easier to hit a wood than it is to hit an iron the same distance. You may also hear the term fairway woods, which refers to any wood that is not the driver.

Irons

Irons are the golf clubs with heads that look like triangles at one end. Unless you get your clubs custom-made, you usually buy a *set* of irons. There are different types of clubheads for irons. Club manufacturing is a high-tech science and manufacturers have designed clubs to be more forgiving. So if you hit the ball with the toe or the heel of the club, rather than the sweet spot, the ball will still travel straight and far. The type you should look for are often referred to as *cavity back*—hollowed out in the back of the clubhead—or *oversized* clubs that have larger club heads so there is a bigger sweet spot. The clubs you want to avoid are called *blades* or *forged clubs*, which are much more difficult to hit accurately. A set of irons typically includes clubs numbered 3 through 9 and a pitching wedge. If you lean each iron against the wall next to one another numerically, you'll see the differences in length and loft of the clubs. The 3-iron has the longest shaft and the loft is the least steep, so the ball will fly low to the ground and far. Some manufacturers of women's clubs have taken out the 3-iron and replaced it with a sand wedge because the 3-iron is more difficult to hit than the 4-iron.

You're probably most familiar with the 7-iron since you likely used that club in your lessons. If you're able to hit the ball with the 7-iron well, then continue using it at the driving range. If you're having trouble hitting it, then try an 8- or 9-iron to build confidence in your swing. As you start to improve, you can then try to hit some balls with the 6-iron or 5-iron.

Wedges

There are two basic types of wedges—the pitching wedge and the sand wedge. Both wedges are used to hit the ball high so that it lands softly on the green. The sand wedge is used to hit the ball out of bunkers. You'll be able to tell which club is the sand wedge because it has a flange on the back of the clubhead to prevent it from digging into the sand. A pitching wedge will usually have stamped on the sole either a P, a W, or a PW, whereas a sand wedge usually has an S or SW on the sole.

Putter

The putter is designed for rolling the ball on the green instead of hitting it into the air. Putters have different clubheads as well. Some have a blade; others look like the head of a wood. Choosing a putter is very personal, so try different ones in stores and try other people's putters to see which style you like.

Buying Equipment

. . . .

Women spend about $6 billion on golf merchandise and playing fees annually. In 1999, golfers spent $22.2 billion on equipment and fees.

. . . .

I've reviewed the different types of golf clubs and when you'll use each. How should you decide which golf clubs to buy? I don't want you to get frustrated because you think you'll never learn the golf swing when your difficulty is caused by the clubs you're using. If you're using the wrong clubs, you won't make good contact because the club is too long or too short, or the shaft is too stiff or flexible. It's like trying to wear size 10 shoes when you're only a size 7. Here are a few tips to be an informed buyer:

- Talk with your golf swing instructor when you're ready to invest in golf clubs. When you're starting, you can use a partial set of clubs that is easier for you to hit and make good ball contact. For example, a set can include: a 3- or 5-wood, 5-, 7-, and 9-irons, a pitching wedge, a sand wedge, and a putter. As you start to play and then want to make a greater commitment to the game, your instructor (or a knowledgeable salesperson) can help you choose golf clubs that fit you and your golf swing.
- Consider your budget. To buy woods, irons, a sand wedge, and a putter, your investment can be several hundred dollars to several thousand dollars. Graphite-shafted clubs are more expensive than steel-shafted clubs, but they're lighter to swing and easier for most women to carry. Clubs fitted specifically for you can be custom-made, although they can be more expensive. Look for "demo days" at courses and driving ranges. You'll be able to try different clubs. You don't have to buy your woods and irons from the same manufacturer; you can even choose different manufacturers for each wood as long as you like each club.

- Consider brands such as Nancy Lopez Golf and Lange Clubs that make clubs only for women.
- You might start with used clubs that fit you. You can find used clubs for sale in some golf shops or used club stores, from notices on the bulletin boards at golf courses, or on the Internet. Be sure to check the grips of used clubs. If they're slick or too big or too small, you will want to have new grips put on them.
- Golf clubs have something called "feel," which is how the club feels when you swing it and hit the ball. This feel is a very personal choice, so keep looking until you find clubs with a feel that you like.
- You should like the looks of the clubs and the sound a club makes when it hits the ball. Golf is a mental game. If your last thought before you swing the club is "This club is ugly!" you probably won't hit the ball well. Or, if you don't like the sound of the sweet spot, you may unconsciously not often hit it there.
- You should choose the clubs you want. Don't choose your clubs simply because your favorite golf professional, husband, client, or friend raves about them or because of pressure from a salesperson. Do ask your friends or playing partners if you can hit their clubs on the driving range, so you can get a feel for the clubs.
- Don't worry about hitting men's or senior men's clubs, rather than ladies' clubs. Fewer manufacturers are using these terms to distinguish the different shaft lengths and flexibility of the clubs. I am almost 5'8" and have a faster swing speed, which means I swing the club faster than the average woman, so I don't use ladies' clubs. They would be too short and too flexible for me.
- Don't choose a club because of the color of the shaft. At one time club manufacturers marketed clubs for women by painting pink the shafts of men's clubs. Today club makers know women players are sophisticated business professionals who don't buy things simply because they're pink.
- Use headcovers for the woods. Most woods come with headcovers that protect the heads from dents and nicks. Headcovers look like long socks that you pull over the wood; they are marked with the number of the wood on them.
- Don't try to keep up with the latest golf club technology. Like buying a high-tech gadget, the club that you buy today will be outdated in several months. The manufacturer will always have the newest and the latest. If you hit the ball well with the clubs you have, stick with them.

....

Equipment Buying Tips

- *Buy what you want—don't let your spouse, friends, or salespeople decide for you.*
- *Make sure the clubs fit you properly—ask advice from your golf swing instructor.*
- *Buy clubs that you like the looks of.*
- *Buy clubs that feel good to you.*
- *Make sure you like the sound the clubs make when you hit the ball well.*
- *Buy what you can afford—consider used clubs, if necessary.*

....

Where to Buy Clubs and Equipment

Besides golf courses, you can buy golf clubs and equipment at a variety of other places:

- Retail stores that specialize in golf equipment and may also sell used equipment
- Sporting goods superstores
- Mail-order golf catalogs
- The Internet
- Custom golf club builders

When you're looking for golf clubs, ask the store or company about its exchange and lending policy. When you buy a club at some stores, you can use it for thirty days. If you don't like it, you want to be able to exchange it for another club. Or, a store may allow you to take a club to a driving range or a golf course for a few hours to try before you decide whether you want it. This gives you a chance to see the ball's flight in the air and to get a feel for the club. The salesperson might put some masking tape on the clubhead to protect it.

If you don't receive adequate attention or product knowledge from sales staff at a store, don't take it personally. Unfortunately, the salespeople in golf shops, as in many retail establishments today, may not be well trained, and many have not thought of women golfers as customers in the past. More golf shops, mail-order catalogs, and Web sites cater to the woman golfer as this target market has grown. So, if you don't get the service you like in a store, find another local store or try one of the women-only golf stores or Web sites.

Choosing a Golf Bag

When you've purchased some clubs, you'll need a golf bag to hold them and other accessories. Here are a few factors to consider when choosing your golf bag:

- Do you plan to walk and carry your bag? If so, you'll play the way golf is played in its homeland of Scotland. I have some suggestions to save your back and shoulders. First, choose a smaller bag made out of lightweight, durable material. You don't want to load yourself down with a heavy bag. Buy a bag with a stand so you don't have to lay it on wet grass, and you don't have to bend down to pick it up. Also, choose a bag with backpack or X straps, or you can buy the straps separately. Rather than having to alternate shoulders, your bag is carried evenly on both shoulders and lies across your back.

- Do you plan to ride a golf cart or walk and pull your bag? If so, then you'll need a bag with the pockets facing out for easy access.

- If you have clubs with graphite shafts, get a bag with dividers to prevent the shafts from getting scratched. In the future you may want to sell your clubs or trade them in, so you want to keep them in good shape.

Pull Carts

You may prefer to walk most of the time when you play and not carry your golf bag. If so, then you might want to invest in a pull cart, which, like cars, come in basic models as well as those that are fully loaded. The basic models will typically have beverage and scorecard holders. You'll either push or pull these basic models. The fancier models are painted in bright colors and have battery-operated motors. You can even get remote-controlled carts! The deluxe motorized carts have a seat on one side, so you can take a seat and rest.

How to decide which pull cart is right for you?

- Budget. Pull carts can cost as little as $50 or as much as $500 plus.

- Size. Most pull carts fold down and become compact. At some golf courses (mostly private clubs), you can pay to store your pull cart. If you can't leave your pull cart at the golf course, then you want to make sure you can get it into your car or SUV easily.

Shoes

When you're taking lessons and starting to play on the golf course, you can wear tennis shoes. Eventually, you'll want a pair of comfortable golf shoes for traction. A good pair of golf shoes will prevent your feet from slipping while you're walking on slopes or when you're taking a swing.

Women's golf shoes have become very fashionable, with styles that include all-leather shoes from Italy, wing-tips, and tennis shoe-style golf shoes.

Here are a few buying tips:

- Buy comfortable shoes. Even if you're riding a cart, you'll be walking and standing quite a bit, so you want happy feet.
- Buy waterproof shoes. They're slightly more expensive than water-resistant shoes and worth the investment. Trust me on this—wet socks and feet aren't a pleasant feeling! Even during the summer, the golf course can be wet from morning dew or irrigation. To reduce the cost, buy shoes with a one-year waterproof warranty, rather than a two- or three-year warranty.
- Buy shoe styles that you enjoy wearing. Again, golf is a mental game. You don't want to be focused on the ugly or dirty shoes that you're wearing or how bad your feet hurt before you hit the ball.
- Make sure your shoes have proper spikes. Most courses now require soft plastic spikes, known as *soft spikes*, rather than the traditional metal spikes. Why? Because soft spikes are gentler on the putting greens. If your new shoes don't come with soft spikes, make sure that you purchase a set of soft spikes to change when necessary.
- To help dry and shape your shoes, use cedar shoe trees.

Golf Gloves

Gloves prevent blisters and help you hold the club properly. If you're right-handed, you'll need a glove for your left hand. The glove should fit as tight as a drum in the palm area and be not too wide or too long in the fingers. Many women choose not to wear gloves. Some don't feel it helps them grip the club, and others don't like having one hand tanned and the other not. If you have large hands, try a man's glove to find one that fits you properly.

Some buying tips for gloves:

- Consider your budget. Leather gloves are expensive, and you have to be careful that they don't dry out. You can buy cheaper synthetic leather gloves, which don't breathe as well as leather and can get hot.

- If you have long fingernails, one glove manufacturer makes a glove with slits at the fingertips.
- Consider your need for winter gloves. These come in pairs as do golf mittens for cooler days when you still want to play.

Golf Balls

There is a vast array of golf balls and brands. All golf clubs and balls must meet certain specifications set by the USGA, the body that governs the rules of the game and the handicap system and that conducts national championship tournaments.

You'll find plenty of golf balls and brands to choose from in a golf shop. Ball manufacturing is a science unto itself. The cover, the dimple pattern, and the core are all studied and tested. Manufacturers want to make golf balls that fly as far as possible and yet feel good when you hit them.

. . . .

Why are there dimples on a golf ball? The dimples are what cause the ball to rise, which is why you should clean the ball before you tee off. It is also a good idea to clean the ball before you putt, so dirt doesn't affect the roll of your ball.

. . . .

I suggest you buy what's called a two-piece ball. The two-piece ball has a hard inner core and a cover made out of Surlyn, a durable plastic, so it won't cut easily. Because of the price, I would stay away from the Balata ball, which is a soft-covered ball that low-handicap players use because they like the feel and are able to control it but the ball is easily damaged.

Balls are rated according to their compression, which affects how the ball feels when you hit it. Golf balls come in 80-, 90-, or 100-compression, with 80-compression having the softest feel while 100-compression has the hardest feel. I suggest you use 80- or 90-compression.

You can purchase a box of a dozen golf balls, or you can buy a *sleeve* of three balls. As you improve your swing, experiment with different brands and types of balls to find a ball that you like—buy a sleeve, rather than a dozen. Stay away from X-ed out balls. Ball manufacturers test each ball to make sure it is made according to their specifications. When a ball doesn't meet the specs, the manufacturer's logo is X-ed out on the golf balls. If you're playing a business golf round, use white golf balls for a professional image—avoid pink, yellow, or orange golf balls.

. . . .

In a business golf round, use white golf balls and don't use X-ed out balls.

. . . .

Other Accessories for Your Bag

I've attended many golf industry tradeshows, and I'm always amazed—and often amused—at all of the items golfers can purchase. You may find items at golf stores that you might like to buy, but consider whether they'll make you look like a beginner or are gadgets that you'll only use once.

Here's a list of items you should carry in your golf bag:

- At least four to six golf balls.
- Tees. Carry a handful in your bag and in your pocket while you're playing. Most are wooden, but plastic tees that are biodegradable are also available.
- Ball markers. You'll need to mark your ball when you're on the putting green. Ball markers come in dime- or quarter-size plastic and metal styles. Carry two in your pocket while you're playing. On your golf glove, you'll see a pea-sized button that snaps off. You can use that button as a ball marker also.
- Ball mark repair tool. The ball can leave an indentation when it lands on the green. You use this tool, which has two prongs, to fix the ball mark.
- Golf towel. Use a towel specifically made so you can hook it onto your golf bag. Carry one even when it's not raining to clean your clubs and balls.
- Sun protection. Sunblock, sunglasses, lipstick or lip balm are recommended.
- Golf umbrella. Your golf bag has straps to hold the umbrella. Don't use a folding, personal-size umbrella on the course, because you'll look out of place.
- A small zippered bag. Keep your jewelry, car keys, money, and so forth in a bag so you can easily find them after the round.
- Snacks and water. Keep your energy up while you're playing.
- Scorecard and pencils. Besides using the card to keep score, you'll use it to learn the layout of the golf course and the distances of each hole.
- Permanent ink marker. Make a distinguishing mark on your golf ball so you will be able to identify it.
- An easy-to-understand rule book. In Appendix A, I cover the basic rules. Carry a rule book in your bag so you can determine how to apply a rule.

Golf Clothing

Most golf courses, especially private country clubs, have some sort of dress code for men and women. It's always a safe bet that you can wear a polo shirt and khakis at most courses. And I'm pleased that women no longer have to wear full-length skirts and blouses buttoned to the neck like the women golfers who preceded us.

If you've been invited to play at a private club, call the pro shop prior to the round and ask what clothing is appropriate. Most private clubs, and many public courses, prohibit blue or any other color denim jeans, shorts that are more than five inches above the knee, tank tops, and tee shirts. If you're not properly dressed, you won't be allowed to play. If this happens, not only will you be embarrassed, you'll also embarrass the person who invited you to play at his or her country club.

Here are some buying tips for clothing:

- Consider your budget. You can buy designer-labeled golf clothing or less expensive department store clothes that are appropriate for golf. If you're playing business golf, you want to look professional on the course as well.
- Make sure the clothes are comfortable and give you the freedom to bend, turn, and twist easily.
- Make sure pants and shorts have deep pockets. You'll be carrying balls, tees, and other accessories in your pockets. If the pockets are too shallow, these items may fall out as you're riding in the cart.
- Prepare to dress in layers. Consider purchasing sweaters, vests, and a wind shirt, which is a lightweight, thin pullover jacket.
- Purchase hats and visors. You'll want to shade your eyes and protect your face from the sun.
- Consider purchasing a rain suit. Charity tournaments are seldom canceled due to poor weather. A good rain suit will help you stay relatively dry and thus still enjoy the round. (However, if there is lightning, leave your golf cart and clubs and seek protection near several trees, not just a single tree.)

You're Ready to Hit the Course

I've covered quite a bit in this chapter as I introduced you to a golf course and who the staff is to help you. You've learned how to find a golf swing profes-sional so you can hit the ball consistently. You also know about the different equipment you'll be using during your round, from golf clubs to clothes, and some money-saving tips on what to buy.

In Chapter 3, I take you, your newfound golf swing, and your equipment to a virtual golf hole and golf course, so you know how all of this comes together. Get ready to tee up!

Staying On Course

_____ Ask friends, colleagues, and clients for referrals to golf swing instructors or golf schools.

_____ Interview several instructors or golf schools before committing to lessons.

_____ Invite others to take lessons with you—build business and personal relationships even while learning the golf swing.

_____ Schedule your golf lessons in your calendar or PDA. Remember that learning golf is a commitment—it requires discipline, patience, and, most of all, having fun!

_____ Practice, practice, practice. Schedule your practice sessions. Mark your calendar or PDA for at least one practice session between lessons. You can also practice putting and the golf swing motion in your office or home.

_____ Keep your clubs and shoes in the car so you can have an impromptu practice session. You'll be able to wind down and relax, rather than sit in traffic.

_____ Combine your practice sessions with business meetings as an incentive to practice and as a time maximizer.

_____ Shop for golf equipment that is right for you. Your golf swing instructor should be able to give you some guidance in equipment selection. Visit golf stores and golf Web sites. If you receive bad service, take your business elsewhere. Don't let it discourage you from playing.

_____ Start a database of those who are golfers in your business circles. Take notes on their skill level, whether they're members of a country club, and how often they play. As you start talking about the game, you'll discover others who also play.

_____ Look for cues when visiting clients and prospects. Do they have golf souvenirs, pictures, or trophies in their offices?

CHAPTER 3

Knowing the Lay
of the Land

By now I hope that you've taken lessons from a golf swing teaching professional and have purchased, borrowed, or rented everything you need from
clubs to clothes. Before you step on to the golf course to play, however, it's important to know the layout of a golf hole and a golf course, as well as the etiquette and basic rules of the game.

Earlier I said that while women are the fastest growing population of new
golfers, they're also the fastest to drop the game. I think it's because they never
feel at home on the golf course and, as a result, they don't enjoy playing. Your
first time on a golf course can be an overwhelming and stressful experience.

You'll undoubtedly have many questions—what am I seeing, what am I
supposed to do when the other player is hitting, who hits first, and so on. It's
an intimidating experience and unfortunately can be a horrible one if done
without preparation. By knowing in advance what to expect and what to do,
your initial experience can be a pleasant one, regardless of your score.

You also need to know the basics so you can be respectful of the game, its
traditions, and other players. A complaint many golfers have about golf today
is slow play. A foursome should play eighteen holes in only four hours and fifteen minutes to four hours and thirty minutes. Taking five to six hours to play
makes for a very long day, especially if you're walking. In the United States,
we're very fortunate to be able to play golf without having to show any type of
qualification. In Sweden, before you can set foot on a golf course to play, you
must receive a Green Card by demonstrating to a course's assistant golf professional that you can hit the ball, can play at a courteous pace, and that you
know golf's basic rules.

. . . .

In Germany, you need a Platzreife before you can play on any golf course—public or private. To get this license to play, you need to pass a playing test and a written test of fifteen questions on both etiquette and the rules of the game.

. . . .

In this chapter, I cover how to get a tee time, your reservation at a golf course. Then, to get you acclimated to a golf course, I point out the features of a golf hole. To help you become a good playing partner, you'll play a hole of virtual golf so you can learn the etiquette and the basic rules. I also give you some tips on how to manage your golf cart.

After I've played a hole with you, you'll be on your way to becoming a more comfortable and confident golfer. At that point, you'll want to keep score, learn the scoring terms, and get a handicap. Having a handicap is a rite of passage for golfers. If you're at a traditional networking event and golf is talked about, you'll likely be asked if you have a handicap. By responding that you have one or are in the process of getting one, others will know you're a committed golfer, regardless of your handicap. You also want a handicap so you can play in tournaments that require players to have a handicap—you don't want to be left out of an event where so much great business networking can take place.

Tee Times

A tee time is like an airline reservation. You have to make a reservation in advance, check in early, tell the starter you're there, and get to the first tee on time or you lose your place.

Getting Tee Times

To get a tee time at a public course, you'll probably have to call several days in advance, especially if you want a prime tee time on Saturday or Sunday morning. When the golf season is in full swing, you'll probably have to call at least one week in advance. Some courses allow you to make a tee time as far as a month in advance.

Many golf courses have strict policies about making tee times. In addition, making tee times for the weekend can be very challenging because avid golfers will call in as soon as the pro shop opens for reservations and snag the good tee times. (This often is as early as 5:30 or 6 A.M.!) Check your local course's policy on making tee times. Part of the draw for a private country club membership is that it's usually much easier to reserve a tee time.

When you call to make a tee time, be prepared to tell the person:

- The day you want to play
- The approximate time you want to play
- How many will be in your group

Tee times are usually given in seven or eight minute increments. You may be required to provide a credit card number to reserve a tee time. If this is the case, be sure to ask how far in advance you are allowed to cancel without being charged for the round. As with airlines and restaurants, last-minute cancellations and no-shows are frowned on and you may be charged a cancellation fee, especially at popular courses.

How Tee Times Flow

Try to arrive at the course at least thirty minutes before your tee time. When you arrive, tell a member of the pro shop staff that you're there. He or she may ask if your entire party has arrived. Some courses will have you pay your nine- or eighteen-hole green fee (your cost to play) and your cart rental fee at this time, or some will have you come back and check in. Regardless, you will always pay for your round before you play.

· ·

According to the National Golf Foundation, the median cost of a weekend round of golf at an eighteen-hole municipal golf course in the United States is $36 including cart and green fee.

· ·

If the course uses a separate check-in process, the pro shop staff (the starter) will call you using a public address system. He or she will say something like, "Jones foursome, check in." Usually, you'll be able to hear this call in the restaurant, outside near the pro shop, at the driving range, and the practice putting green. But check with the staff to make sure you're in a location where you can hear this announcement.

When you hear your last name, go back into the pro shop and pay your green and cart fees, if you haven't already done so. You will probably be asked again if your entire group is there, and the staff will let you know how many groups are ahead of you at this point.

Golf courses use a system to inform players how many groups are ahead of them. If you're "third up," that means there are two groups ahead of you, so you have about twenty minutes to practice and warm up. If you're "second up" or "in the hole," there is one group ahead of you. The group ahead of you should be on the tee and ready to go next, and you and your group should be near the first tee, preparing to tee off. When it is your time to tee off, you'll hear your name called: "Jones foursome on the tee" or "Jones on the first tee." When you hear your foursome called, you should move immediately to the first tee. If there are only two in your group, then you'll hear one of the last names of the twosome you're playing with, or the last names of two single players.

Some courses have a separate starter in addition to the pro shop personnel. You pay in the pro shop, and they give you a receipt to give to the starter, who is near the first tee. The starter will tell you who you're playing with if you don't have a foursome, local rules, if any, and will let you know when you can hit safely.

Like flying standby on major airlines, you can also play golf as a single to enjoy the Opportunities Galore benefit of FREEDOM. Simply go to the golf course alone and ask the starter to put you with the next group that has an opening. Your wait may be as little as minutes or as long as an hour or more. If you're an early riser, you can play the second nine holes (numbers 10 through 18, called the *back nine*) first. Most eighteen-hole golf courses let players play the second nine holes in the early morning. These tee times are first-come, first-play. You can play the back nine holes because the reserved tee-time golfers are playing the *front nine* holes. This option, however, is only available for a couple of hours until players who began on the first hole reach the second nine holes.

Tee Time Challenges

When I speak to groups, I invite attendees who already play golf to bring up challenges they've experienced at the golf course. Many women comment about the less than stellar service they receive from golf course staff. This seems to be particularly true when women try to get on the golf course as singles. I hear stories about being ignored by the staff or even being physically pushed aside by other players. Many of these horror stories come from women who appear to be self-confident and assertive.

I recommend that you put aside thoughts about discrimination. It's far more effective to regard this situation as another facet of the foreign world of golf. With the right information and a little practice, you'll know how to handle these encounters prior to teeing off. Here are some tips:

- Don't wait for starters to ask, "May I help you?" They expect you to come to them and tell them what you want.
- Don't expect an orderly line with men and women waiting to speak to the starters. Say that you're next to be served when it is your turn.
- If you don't have a tee time and want to play as a single, check in with the pro shop staff, and ask what the expected wait is for you to tee off. If the staff estimates it will be about forty minutes, then check back with staff after twenty minutes or so. Be assertive about getting a tee time.
- At the golf course you'll likely play regularly, get to know the pro shop staff and starters by name, and tell them yours. Be friendly and talk pleasantly with the starter unless he or she is very busy at that particular moment. Remember Karen, the owner of the resort inn and spa, who says playing nine holes alone is like a week's vacation for her. She has gotten to know the starters at different public golf courses so she can have a tee time to herself. It is a rare privilege to be able to get a tee time alone on a public golf course.
- If you're playing with men you know, don't let them check you in. Go with them to check in, at minimum. This way you'll learn the procedure and can become a familiar face to the staff.
- If you're not going to keep a tee time, call to cancel. Again, try to exchange names and chat it up! If one or more in your group cancels, call ahead and inform the pro shop so they can add players to make a foursome. Having more players on the course increases the golf course's revenue. Informing the staff of changes is common courtesy, similar to informing someone who is running a meeting that a person will be unable to attend.
- After your round, go into the pro shop, and find a good reason to speak with the staff (don't make a complaint). Maybe you need a new ball marker. Or, you can ask about lessons. You may want to comment on how nice the course is being maintained. Think of this as rapport-building, just as you do in the business world!

Layout of a Hole and a Golf Course

A typical golf course has eighteen holes with each hole having its own unique design and features. You can also find golf courses with only nine holes. Regardless of size, golf course design is a blending of art and science. A golf course architect's goal is to carve from a parcel of land a course that is aesthetically pleasing as well as a challenge to play.

. . . .

Why is a game of golf referred to as a round? In the early days of golf, all courses were built in a circular design with the first hole starting and the last hole finishing at the clubhouse.

. . . .

Each golf hole has certain features and may have some additional challenges called *hazards*. Let's take a look at a typical golf hole.

Tees

At the beginning of each golf hole, there can be three to six tees or areas where you can begin to play the hole. Every separate tee area is designated by two markers, such as large-colored balls or wooden blocks. The different tees are available for players of varying abilities, since the holes become longer the farther the tees are from the hole. Let's say there are four sets of tees on a hole. Very good amateur players or professionals hit from the back tees, which are also called the *tips*. Average players hit from the middle-back tees. Women typically play from the middle-forward tees. Seniors, juniors, or beginners can hit from the forward tees.

Notice that I didn't refer to gender to specify the different tees. In the past, for example, women's tees always referred to the red tees where women would hit. Just as with golf club manufacturing, however, course designers are eliminating those gender references. Why? I believe course designers prefer that players play the tees that are appropriate to their handicap and skill level, rather than according to gender reference to the tees.

How do you know which tees to use? Today many golf courses have scorecards printed with suggested tees according to your handicap level. This is another good reason to get a handicap. If the scorecard doesn't tell you, then start from the forward tees if you're a beginner. Or, if you play a course often and know the total length of nine or eighteen holes that you play, then on a new course choose the tees with a similar length. You can always ask the pro shop staff for their recommendation.

Regardless of which tees you decide to play, you must play from the same tees the entire round. Unfortunately, some players think they are better than they actually are and play from tees that are too challenging for them. By doing so, they slow down the pace of play for everyone behind them.

At the tees you'll also find ball washers to clean your golf ball before teeing off, a brush to clean your shoes, and a placard to give you the length for the hole, and sometimes a short description of the hole with a picture.

Fairway and Rough

When teeing off, aim for the *fairway,* which is the low-cut grass that runs from the tee to the hole. You want your ball to land in the fairway because it is easier to hit the ball from the low grass. It can be more difficult to hit the ball as accurately or as long if it lands in the *rough,* which is the slightly taller grass that runs along the fairway. The rough is on both sides of the fairway and surrounds the putting green.

In the fairways, you will likely find distance markers. These markers give you the distance in yards to the middle of the green. They can be plaques on sprinkler heads, dwarf trees, painted rocks, or plastic colored plates in the fairways. Remember when I discussed hitting balls at the driving range so you know how far you can hit each golf club? By knowing the distance to the middle of the green, you can decide which golf club to use.

. . . .

If you know the distance you can hit with each club, trust your golf swing and the club to hit the ball the distance you need to.

. . . .

At some courses, you can also buy yardage books that give precise distances to the green from bunkers, from the middle of the fairway, and from other locations on a hole. I remember how I felt when I saw a scorecard for the first time—overwhelmed by all of the numbers. I feel the same way about yardage books. Although I want to know the approximate yardage to the hole, I don't need to know the exact yardage. If you find the books helpful, then certainly use them.

By the way, never spend too much time debating distances or deciding which club to use. When you're over the ball and about to hit, you should be certain about your club choice so you can swing confidently.

Some holes have a sharp curve in them. On these holes, if you are standing at the tee, you may not be able to see the green because the fairway curves either left or right. These holes are referred to either as "dogleg left" or "dogleg right" holes because the layout looks like a dog's leg.

Putting Green

The putting green, also known as the green, is your target; it has the flagstick or pin in the hole. The green has the shortest grass where you use your putter to roll the ball to the hole. The flagstick will have a colored flag that designates its location on the green.

At the green, you'll see a collar about the width of 1 to 3 feet of slightly taller grass than the putting green surface, but not as tall as the rough. That grass is referred to by several names: the *fringe,* the *collar,* or the *apron.*

Not all putting greens are flat—if they were, the game would be a lot easier but also a lot less challenging. A ball will curve because of the slope of the green. The curve is called the *break.* So when you "read the greens," you're able to visualize the break and compensate your aim. When a golfer says, "The green breaks left to right 3 inches," she's saying that the ball will start left and then curve to the right about 3 inches.

If a green is too wet or under repair, the greenskeeper may make a temporary green in the fairway. There will likely be a local rule because of the hole's condition that allows you to take only two putts maximum for scoring. And when you have a temporary green, always remember to adjust your distance when playing shots from the fairway since the hole is now shorter than its official length.

Par

Every hole is designated by *par,* which is the number of strokes a very good golfer needs to hit the ball from the tee into the hole. Par for a hole is determined by the gender of the player and the length in yards of the hole (Table 3-1). Par 3 means that a player will take one stroke from the tee to hit the ball onto the putting green, and then the player is presumed to take two putts to sink the ball into the hole. Par 4 means the player will need two strokes to reach the green, and then will take two putts. And, for a par 5, a player will take three strokes to reach the green and will take two putts. Since gender is a factor in determining par, it is possible for women to play a par 5 hole, but for men playing the same hole it is a par 4.

TABLE 3-1   Distances Defining Par

Par	Men	Women
3	Up to 250 yards	Up to 210 yards
4	251 to 470 yards	211 to 400 yards
5	More than 470 yards	401 to 575 yards

For beginning golfers, you might create your own personal par. On a par 4 hole, for example, your personal par may be a 5 or a 6, depending on your skill level and handicap. By having a personal par, you have a more realistic goal to shoot for, rather than feeling discouraged because you didn't score par.

If you're watching a professional golf tournament on television, you may see a statistic for *greens in regulation*. For every hole, it's presumed a player will need two putts to hit the ball into the hole. With a par 4 hole, a player is on the green in regulation if her ball is on the green after two strokes. A player is on the green in regulation with a par 3 hole when the ball is on the green after the first stroke, and, for a par 5 hole the ball is on the green after three strokes. The higher percentage or number of greens in regulation that a player hits, the better for the player.

At a typical golf course with eighteen holes, you'll play ten par 4 holes, and four each of par 3s and par 5s.

Hazards of a Hole

Hazards on a golf course are designed to add challenge and beauty to a golf course. The golf course designer, for example, may have built the hole next to an existing creek, or added a bunker on the fairway to force golfers to make different shots than they ordinarily would.

One hazard is the *bunker,* which is filled with sand. Another is a *water hazard,* such as a lake or a pond. A golf course will use yellow stakes or yellow lines painted on the grass to indicate a water hazard. Another type of hazard is a *lateral water hazard,* where a stream, creek, or environmentally protected area parallels the hole. It's marked with red stakes or red painted lines. Different rules apply for the two different types of water hazards, so it's important to understand which is which.

Playing a Hole Together

In this section, we play a virtual hole of golf. My goal is to provide most of the information that I would give if we played together in person. As we play the hole, I give you instruction on the basic rules and etiquette. I also provide information about the differences between the official USGA rules of golf—which you'd follow in tournament play and in most rounds of business golf—and casual play customs.

The Joy of Rules

I've talked about how golf can be a revealer of someone's integrity. One reason this is true is because golf is one of the few sports where you call a penalty on yourself. Although there are only thirty-four official rules of golf, most golfers think there are more because of the many subsections and definitions. Reading the rules of golf is where my legal training has come in handy. In fact, I believe attorneys probably wrote the official rules, and if you ever have trouble sleeping, read the rules book. I cover the rules you should know or at least be familiar with in Appendix A. There are books on the market that give you the rules in easy-to-understand language. I recommend you buy one, read it, and keep it in your golf bag for reference.

Before we begin playing, I want to give you the basics on penalties for breaking rules. The penalty for violating a rule depends on the format you're playing: stroke play or match play. Stroke (or medal) play is the most common format. Players count each stroke and the player with the lowest score (less his or her handicap) is the winner. If you violate a rule while playing stroke play, you add one or two strokes to the strokes you had on that hole. In match play, each hole has a winner. The winner of the game is the golfer who scores the lowest on the most matches (holes). If you're playing in a match play competition and you violate a rule, you lose the hole in most cases.

Most people play stroke play. Here are some general rules to follow when playing stroke play:

- A bad shot, such as losing your ball or hitting into a water hazard, is at least a one-shot penalty. You add one stroke to the number of strokes you took to play the hole. In some instances, such as a lost ball or a ball out of bounds, the penalty is stroke and distance because you have to hit the ball from where you just hit it, rather than where the ball is lost or went out of bounds.
- If you violate a rule you should've known, such as exceeding the maximum of fourteen clubs in your bag or hitting another player's golf ball, you must add two strokes to your score for that hole.

Again, the rules of golf can be confusing, even to long-time golfers. Over time you will become familiar with the rules that apply most frequently during a round. If you're ever not quite certain what to do, rather than risk the appearance of cheating by guessing the applicable rule, simply ask one of your playing partners. Always remember to keep in mind the need to play in a timely fashion.

Preparing to Tee Off

Let's imagine we have a tee time for 3 P.M., and we're going to play a hole on a course together as a twosome. Here is a list of things we should consider before we even arrive at the golf course:

- Are we properly dressed to play at the golf course, especially if it's a private country club?
- Do we have all of our clubs and everything else we might want or need in our golf bag? By the way, there is a certain way to arrange the clubs in the golf bag for easier access. The bag is usually divided into three sections: a section closest to the strap, a middle section, and a section farthest from the strap. You should put your woods in the section closest to the strap, then your irons go in the middle section, and your putter, sand wedge, and your pitching wedge should be in the section farthest from the strap.
- Do we want to hit some practice balls and/or practice our putting before teeing off? If so, then we should arrive at least thirty to forty-five minutes before our tee time.

Arriving at the Golf Course

When we arrive at the golf course, there are several things we have to do before we can begin playing. We need to decide whether we want to use the bag drop and leave our clubs with an attendant. If we leave our clubs with the attendant, then we should give a tip of a dollar or two.

If we're playing a public golf course, we can change into our golf shoes at the car. At a private country club, though, it is more appropriate to change our shoes in the locker room. We can leave our street shoes in the locker room, rather than carrying them or taking them back to the car.

We then go into the pro shop and tell the starter our names and tee time. The starter may offer us an earlier tee time, but we decide we'd rather take some time to practice. We pay for a small bucket of balls and our green fees. We've decided to get some exercise, so we don't need a cart. We also each pick up a scorecard so we know the yardage and layout of the holes.

At the driving range, we do some stretching and warm-up exercises before hitting balls. We start with the pitching wedge so we can take short easy swings and work our way up the irons and then the 5-wood. We make sure to save some time to practice our putting so we can get a feel for the speed of the greens at the course.

Five to ten minutes before our tee time, we head to the first tee. As we head to the tee, we hear the starter announce our twosome and the name of another twosome. We've been paired to make a foursome. The starter also says we're second up.

On the First Tee

We walk to the first tee where there is another starter. We show him our receipt, tell him our names, and he points out our playing partners. We introduce ourselves by our first names and shake one another's hands. (Since I'm focusing on working with you, I write our playing partners' names, John and David, on my scorecard, although they'll be keeping their own scores.) We each have our golf bag with no more than fourteen clubs. As right-handed golfers wearing gloves on our left hands, we each have in our right pocket an extra ball, several tees and ball markers, and a ball mark repair tool—it's easier to reach into our pockets without a glove on.

I ask our playing partners which tees they will play from. They're playing from the middle-back white tees, and we'll play from the forward red tees. You and I exchange information about the type of ball each of us is using. The rules require you to hit your ball throughout the hole, and it must be the same ball. You tell me, "I'm hitting a number three and four Titleist." As it happens, I have the same type and numbered balls, so I make a distinguishing mark on mine with a permanent marker.

While we're waiting to tee off, our playing partners determine who will tee off first. For golfers adhering to the traditional *honors system*, the golfer with the highest handicap plays first. Then the second highest handicap golfer hits his or her ball, until the lowest handicap golfer tees off. Today, unless playing in an official tournament, most golfers, like the twosome we are playing with, use a more casual system. John tosses a tee in the air. The tee points to David, so he gets to hit first, and John hits second.

The foursome ahead of us is now far enough away for us to tee off safely, so the starter tells us to go ahead. Our playing partners are playing from the white tees, so they hit first. We stand off to their side where it's safe and where we won't distract them. As soon as either player is ready to hit, we stop chatting and are careful not to make any noise. We don't want to distract other players as they are getting ready to hit the ball. The worst offense is pulling the Velcro of our golf glove or the zipper on our golf bag.

. . . .

A player is ready to hit when he or she has stopped taking practice swings and is standing over the ball in the address position—this is when you should be quiet.

. . . .

They both hit good drives into the middle of the fairway, so we say, "Nice shot!" It's now our turn, and we walk to the forward tees.

Ready Golf

Since this is your first time on a golf course, it's a good time to describe the basis for *ready golf*. A round of eighteen holes for a foursome should take a maximum of four and one-half hours. However, since so many players are either inconsiderate or don't know how to play ready golf and keep up the pace, rounds can take much longer.

The trouble with longer rounds is that the game loses its flow. Golfers have to wait between each shot, which can make players lose their momentum and focus. Since many golfers don't play as well under these conditions, it's not as much fun. Golf courses do what they can to prevent slow play. Golfers can help keep the flow of the round going by playing what's called ready golf. The goal of ready golf is to keep one safe shot behind the group in front of us—not simply to keep ahead of the group behind us.

. . . .

If you become frustrated with players in front playing slowly, it may affect your swing and, therefore, your score. Unfortunately many of the players at my club don't play ready golf or seem to care about their pace of play. Rather than lose my tempo and temper, I take a few practice swings while I'm waiting. I also don't watch the group ahead, but instead I take in the beauty of the golf course and the views, as well as enjoy my conversations with playing partners. Try these tactics next time you're faced with slow play!

. . . .

Teeing Off

Now that you know the premise for ready golf, let's tee off. Where do you tee your ball? Imagine a line between the two red markers. You can't tee your ball ahead of that line closer to the hole. Now, also imagine lines the length of two golf clubs behind each of the red markers, and between the two lines. You can tee the ball anywhere within this imaginary rectangular area. To keep it simple, I suggest that you tee the ball about 6 inches to 1 foot behind and between the markers. You must tee the ball anywhere within that rectangular area, but your feet can be outside of that rectangular area.

You ask me which club you should use? I explain that according to the official rules, if you ask for advice and if I tell you my opinion, we'd *each* be penalized two strokes. This is an easy rule to break, so here are some examples of what you should *not* ask:

- "What club should I hit?"
- "What club did you use?" (If you must know this, you can look in my bag.)

In contrast, you may ask and I may tell you about information available to all players, such as:

- "Where is the closest distance marker to my ball?"
- "What does the distance marker give as the distance?"
- "What is the rule of golf for this situation?"
- "How long is the hole?"

Understand, though, that in casual rounds this information is often shared, with no penalties assessed. The camaraderie of playing together usually overrides the technical rules.

This rule also applies to asking for, receiving, and giving swing advice. If you're a beginner, you've probably had strangers offer you tips on your swing during the round. They mean well, but you may be confused or frustrated by getting tips while you're playing. Discourage advice-giving with a simple, "Thank you," or you might say, "Thanks. I work with a golf swing professional, and I don't change my swing until I talk with her."

You should follow the USGA rules when you're playing in tournaments and during business golf rounds. However, as I've mentioned, the customs for recreational play are much more lax. You'll hear most people ask each other about club use and distance from the hole. In ready golf, players will often help each other with distances so they don't waste time looking for and walking to distance markers. If I see a ball near a distance marker, I tell the player the distance according to the distance marker.

When is it safe for you to hit your ball? You can hit when you're confident that your best shot will not hit or land too close to any player on the fairway. Say you're on the tee. Here's an easy way to tee the ball. You're right-handed, so with your palm facing the sky, put a tee in between your index and third finger, then clutch the ball on top of the tee. To put the tee in the ground push down on the ball until about half the ball (or slightly less) is above the top of your 3- or 5-wood. If you're using an iron to tee off, then tee the ball so it's slightly off the ground.

After teeing the ball, step back from it and take no more than one or two practice swings (as part of keeping the pace, avoid taking more than two practice swings). While I wait for you to hit, I'm careful not to make any noise. I am ready to hit when you're done; my glove is on, my 3-wood is in my hand with the headcover off, and I have a ball and a tee in my hand.

While you're hitting, I'm standing where you can see me so you don't have to worry about hitting me in your back swing. I'm also standing far enough away so you can freely swing your club, but I'm not in front of you. I'm holding still because a movement or making any noise may distract your concentration.

After you hit, I watch where your ball lands. This saves time searching for your ball. In addition, it's often difficult for beginners to focus on swinging correctly *and* watching where the ball goes. You should feel free to ask your playing partners to help watch your ball for you.

After you hit the ball, pick up your tee and stand away from the teeing area. If your tee is broken, throw the pieces away. You hit a good shot and your ball flew pretty far, so I say, "Nice hit!" If you had a great shot and your ball is in danger of hitting the foursome in front, both of us would yell, "FORE!" loud enough for the group to hear. It's good practice for all playing partners to yell fore in case the person hitting the ball doesn't realize how far it has gone.

. . . .

Most golf historians think fore originated in the sixteenth century with the British army. The soldiers in the back would yell before they fired "Beware before" to the soldiers in the front to warn them to lie down as cannonballs flew overhead. Cannonballs then are golf balls today.

. . . .

By the way, if you should hear "fore" don't look around because as you're turning around, the ball could be headed at you. Instead, crouch down and make yourself as small a target as possible. Protect the back of your head with your hands.

Now it's my turn. I tee up my ball and then tee off. I prefer not to take a practice swing. You watch to see where my ball lands, just in case I lose sight of it. I took a divot, which is a Scottish term for a piece of turf. So, I pick up the divot and stomp it back in place (like fitting a puzzle piece). If I couldn't find the divot, and the golf course provided grass seed mixture on the tee, I'd sprinkle the mixture over the bare ground. (Look for a small bin of sand and grass seed mixture near the tee box.) We want to leave the course in as good as, if not slightly better, condition than we found it.

We need to review some golf terms that could describe the drives or the shots that we had off the tee.

- *Whiff.* When a player takes a full swing and misses the ball. This counts as a stroke. But if the player is wiggling and waggling the club to get comfortable, and knocks the ball off the tee accidentally, that doesn't count as a stroke.
- *Mulligan.* A "do over." It is customary for the other players to offer you a mulligan but you shouldn't ask to take one. Mulligans are usually offered only on the tee during a casual round, or during a tournament when they are sold to raise money for a charity. If you decide to take a mulligan, you hit another ball. If this second ball is worse than your first ball, you don't get to hit the first ball. Mulligans are not recognized in the official rules of golf. If you're playing with traditional, by-the-book players, they won't offer you a mulligan or take one if it's offered.

Golfers also use certain terms to describe the ball's flight while in the air. These are listed here as they apply to right-handed golfers. You'd reverse them for left-handed golfers.

- *Fade.* The ball starts straight, but at the end it "leaks" or curves slightly toward the right.
- *Slice or banana slice.* The ball makes a hard turn to the right.
- *Draw.* The ball starts straight and at the end curves slightly toward the left.
- *Hook or duck hook.* The ball takes a hard turn to the left.

Golf professionals and accomplished players can hit these different shots when they need to do so. For the average player, the preference is to hit the ball as straight as possible. However, you'll soon discover there is no such thing as a perfect golf shot. At this point, all you want to do is hit the ball and get it into the hole in as few strokes as possible. You don't need to get fancy.

Also, over time you'll probably notice that you tend to hit the same type of shots, such as a fade. This information is important to know for two reasons: you can take this tendency into account when aiming a shot, and you can inform your swing professional of this and ask for advice on how to hit straighter shots.

In the Fairway

After you and I hit our balls, we each put the headcover back on our wood, put the club back in the bag, and then immediately walk down the fairway toward our balls. As we walk, we start talking to get to know each other. Our playing partners may join in on our conversation, or they may carry on their own conversation.

Since I watched where your ball and my ball landed, I know the first ball we come to is yours. To make sure, however, look for your ball's brand and number. If you can't see that information, you can tell me that you need to lift the ball to identify it. You do so by placing a tee to mark the location of the ball, lift it, and look at it. (If you had to clean the ball to identify it, you can clean only enough to identify it, and not the entire ball.)

Now that we have identified your ball, we see that it has landed near an old divot, a patch of bare ground where grass used to be. You know it will be harder to hit out of that divot, so you ask me if the ball can be moved. Unfortunately, it can't. According to the rules of golf, you can't touch your ball unless you're hitting it with your club. You have to hit the ball where it has landed. You should know, however, that many casual golfers *bump* their balls a few inches with their clubs to give themselves an easier shot. Under the official rules and for many golf purists, bumping the ball is considered cheating.

One exception to having to hit the ball where it lands is referred to as "Winter Rules," which is not an official USGA rule but is usually invoked by a course as a local rule if there has been a lot of rain and the course is very wet and muddy. When "Winter Rules" are in effect, you can mark the location of your ball with a tee, pick it up, clean it, and then place the ball 6 inches to one-club length from its original location as long as it's no closer to the hole. How far you can move the ball varies from course to course. At my course, we are allowed to move the ball only 6 inches and no closer to the hole.

As with describing golf shots, golfers use terms to describe how the ball has landed in the grass. They refer to how the ball is sitting on the grass as the *lie*. The official rules require that golfers play the ball *down* or *as it lies*. You're supposed to hit the ball where it has landed. A golfer may say, "I have a good lie," which means she thinks the ball will be easy to hit because it is sitting on a tuft of grass. If she says, "I have a bad lie," that means the ball will be harder to hit. For example, the ball could be surrounded by tall grass or in a divot. The ball could also be in *deep rough*, which is long, thick grass.

Now back to playing. Under the honors system, the person farthest from the hole plays first. In ready golf, however, the idea is to relax these general guidelines and the player who is ready to hit safely is the next to play. This speeds up the game, and is ideal for all involved as long as all players know who is hitting at a particular time—you never want two players swinging at the same time.

We've confirmed this first ball is your ball. So you remove your bag from your shoulder, and I remind you to be careful where you put your bag. You don't want to accidentally hit the ball with your bag or club because you will be penalized one stroke. If you take a swing and your ball hits your bag, you'll be penalized two strokes because you shouldn't have placed your bag where your ball could hit it.

You take a swing, and you've hit another nice shot. You've made a divot, so you replace the chunk of grass in the bare spot and stomp on it so the grass can regrow.

. . . .

If you hit your ball onto the fairway of another hole, the players on that hole have the right of way to hit their balls before you do. Wait until they have hit their balls past your ball, then you can hit the ball back onto the fairway of the hole you're playing. For your safety, stand to the side of the fairway and watch those players' shots.

. . . .

The next ball on the fairway belongs to David. He and John have walked up the side of the fairway toward David's ball, ahead of us. They made sure to watch you hit, just in case you hit toward them. This is ready golf—they advanced as far as they could safely. Some golfers are bothered when players walk too far ahead of them, so watch to see how far in front of you they walk so you get a sense of their comfort level.

Before David hits his shot, he can remove *loose impediments* such as branches, twigs, and rocks as long as he doesn't cause his ball to move and because his ball is not in a hazard. David hits a nice shot, and we continue walking.

While we're walking to my ball, I give you a few additional ready golf tips about saving time:

- Begin to decide which club you're going to hit next while you're walking to your ball. Look for the distance markers in the fairway. You will get used to estimating how far your ball is from a distance marker. You can also take steps about a yard long from a distance marker to calculate how far you have to the center of the green. Decide quickly, and remember that your first club selection is usually best.

· ·

On every kind of golf shot, you must make up your mind exactly what it is you want to do. Do not have the slightest doubt. As a friend of mine says of the way he lives his life, "I may be wrong, but I am never in doubt."

Harvey Penick

· ·

- If a playing partner hits his ball into the trees or tall rough, help him look for it. If no one can find the ball after looking for a while, encourage the golfer to hit another ball. Official rules give a player five minutes to look for a ball, but you should spend only two to three minutes so you don't hold up your foursome.

We're on a par 4 hole. Our partners and I have all hit twice and our balls are on or next to the green. You've hit twice and still have a way to go to reach the green. You ask if you're playing too slow. Because you're a beginner, you can expect that there will be some golf holes where you take more shots than the rest of us. The thing to do is to pick up your ball from the fairway and drop it near the green. This ready golf tactic prevents you from slowing down the foursome, and it avoids your feeling rushed or frustrated with how you're playing.

Of course, picking up is not permissible under the rules of golf, but to keep the pace of play, other golfers prefer you to pick up. If you're keeping score so you can get a handicap, count at least one or two strokes for the distance that you picked up.

· ·

Let's say our group is falling behind and the group behind us is only a threesome, so they're playing each hole faster than we are and have to wait on each shot. We don't like the pressure, so we let them play through. Or they may ask if they can play through, which some courses require you to allow when your foursome is slow.

Here's how playing through works: We are about to play a par 3 hole. If a player from the group behind is close enough and without disturbing another golfer about to hit, one of us can shout, "We're going to let you play through!" He or she will probably say, "Thanks. That's great!" and let his or her playing partners know. While the threesome is finishing the hole we just played, we should hit our balls on the par 3 hole.

After hitting, we walk to our balls. Any player who has a ball on the green should mark his or her ball. Then, each of us should stand to the side of the green as far as possible and wave the players to tee off. We should watch the players hit because this is somewhat dangerous. The threesome then plays the hole. As a courtesy to us for letting them play through, they pick up their pace in playing the hole. After they're done, we finish playing the hole. Now the threesome is ahead of us.

. . . .

As we walk toward the green, I explain that the color of the flag helps you determine the distance to the hole. At my golf course, a red flag means the hole is closer to the front of the green. A white flag shows the hole is in the middle of the putting green, and a blue flag means it is farther toward the back of the green. Other courses may have a chart to show you *pin placement*, areas where they have placed the flagstick on the greens for that day. If you're not sure how a golf course is designating the flagstick's location, ask the starter or someone in the pro shop.

It is important to know the approximate location of the hole so you can choose the proper club to hit the ball onto the green. If the flag is red, I might use *less club* because the hole is playing short. Less club means I use a club that hits less far than the one I might usually use. Let's say I'm at the 100-yard marker and the flag is red. Rather than using my 9-iron to hit 100 yards, I'll use my pitching wedge because I know that the hole is less than 100 yards with a red flag. The hole is playing short since the hole is closer to the front of the green.

If the flag is blue, then I might want to use *more club* because the hole is playing long. In this case, I'll use my 8-iron to hit because the hole is playing longer than 100 yards with the blue flag. With markers in the fairway and a given colored flag, you'll be able to calculate the distance to the hole and choose the appropriate club to use.

There are other factors that affect distance such as wind and if the course is wet. Strong head wind or tailwinds may require you to hit one more or one less club for the estimated yardage distance. If the green is above or below the fairway, you may also take one less club for the approximate distance.

Again, having said all this, you shouldn't spend an inordinate amount of time judging distance and selecting a club, especially if you are a beginner. As you play more, you'll begin to have an intuitive sense about which club to use. If you're debating between two clubs, pick the club you feel most comfortable swinging—and hit that club.

Putting Green

As we walk to the green, I tell you the next tee is over to the right, so we put our golf bags on that side of the green to save time when we finish the hole. (This is ready golf. If we didn't know where the next tee was, we'd watch or ask our partners.) We place our bags in the rough—never place your golf bag (including the stand) or pull cart on the green.

John's ball is farthest from the hole. The ball is not quite on the green, but on the fringe—the slightly taller grass surrounding the green. Generally, if a ball is off the green, that player hits first. There are some exceptions that more experienced players may point out as the situations arise. But for now, the player who is off the green hits first.

Your ball lies between the player chipping onto the green and the hole, so you should ask John if he wants you to mark your ball (I describe how to do so below). He says, "Yes, please," so be careful and try as best you can not to step on any part of the green that John's ball may travel when rolling to the hole.

Putting Green Etiquette

When we're on the green, each of us should be looking for our ball mark to repair. We insert the ball mark repair tool on the edges of the mark and twist the grass up. Then we use our putter to tap the grass down. Since we should leave a golf course in as good condition if not better than we found it, we can fix another ball mark if time permits and the repair won't disturb anyone's putting.

As you walk to your ball, you want to avoid stepping on another player's *putting line,* the area of the green that the player wants to putt the ball. You also don't want to cast your shadow over another player's putting line. In your own putting line, you may fix old ball marks and pick up twigs, sand, or grass, but under the rules you can't repair spike marks, which is why you don't want to step on someone's putting line. This rule was designed to prevent a player from repairing a series of spike marks that could affect the roll of his putt. You also don't want to stand in the peripheral vision of a player who is about to putt or stand too close to the hole.

Tending the Flagstick

David's ball is closest to the hole. John asks, "Do you want it tended?" He is asking if David wants him to hold the flagstick and be ready to take it out if the ball might go in the hole. David says he doesn't need the flagstick tended and John can remove the flagstick.

· ·

The player whose ball is closest to the hole should remove the flagstick. When removing the flagstick, lay it on the green, rather than dropping it onto the green. Place the flagstick off to the side where no ball can roll into it.

· ·

To tend the flagstick, you hold the flag against the pin (so it's not blowing in the wind and disturbing the player) and pull the flagstick slightly out of the hole. As soon as the player strokes the ball, you pull the flagstick away so the ball doesn't hit it. If the ball hits the flagstick, the golfer who is putting is penalized two strokes. Causing this to happen is not a good way to make friends on the golf course!

Let's say David's ball is on the fringe. Since his ball is not on the green, he has a choice of either having someone pull out the flagstick or tend it. If any part of the ball is on the putting green surface, however, the ball is on the green, and David must have the flagstick removed or have it tended.

Marking Your Ball

John putts and his ball rolls up very close to the pin, but not in the hole. David says, "Good lag," praising him for putting the ball very close to the hole. John walks to his ball and avoids stepping on any of our putting lines. He marks the ball with a marker he has in his pocket. To mark his ball, John lines up the ball and the hole, and he pushes the marker into the green directly behind the ball, but he's careful not to move the ball. After marking his ball, John then picks up the ball and cleans it. Since all of our balls are now on the green, and he is the closest ball to the hole, he pulls the flagstick and puts it off to the side of the green.

John's marker, however, is in my putting line. We're playing a casual round of ready golf, rather than playing strictly by who has honors and having the farthest away putt first. So to save time, I suggest that John putt, which he does. If we were in competition, I could have asked him to span, or move, his marker to the right or left, out of my direct putting line.

Spanning Your Marker and Cleaning Your Ball

Let's say I ask John to span his marker. To do so, he'd put the heel of the putter at his marker and point the toe of his putter at a stationary object, such as a tree or rock. He would then place his marker at the toe of his putter. Now I can putt without worrying that his marker might deflect my ball. After I putt, as a courtesy, I remind John to respan his marker—he points his putter toe at the same stationary object and places his marker at the heel of his putter. His marker should be at the original location before he spanned his marker.

Now it's your turn to putt. You've marked your ball, then cleaned some mud off it with a towel. If you had forgotten your towel at your bag, you could rub the ball with your hands or rub it in the rough, but you can't rub the ball on the putting green; that would be a penalty.

. . . .

Golf courses use pesticides and fertilizers, so use a towel to clean your ball before putting.

. . . .

You make an excellent putt and your ball rolls into the hole and makes that great kerplunk sound! I say, "Great putt!" as you get your ball out of the hole. By the way, don't use the head of your putter to get the ball out as you might damage the hole.

I then bend down to read the break of the green for my 6-foot putt. I hit the ball and say, "I *pushed* it." That means I hit further to the right than I wanted to and missed the putt. I could have *pulled* it, so the ball would veer to the left. To finish the hole, I tap the ball into the hole.

Gimmes

David is about to putt. He putts the ball close, and John says, "It's a *gimme*." Because David's putt is so close to the hole, within the length of his putter grip, he can pick up his ball and not putt again. It's not an official USGA rule, but John is assuming he would make that short putt. The gimme still counts as a stroke.

If you've been offered a gimme, say, "Thank you," and pick up your ball. If you try to putt it and miss, you lose the gimme and have to count all of your putts until you get the ball into the hole. Some players let you practice your putting and still give you the gimme, since it's a good idea to practice your short putts.

The player who finishes or putts out first should replace the flagstick in the hole when everyone is finished putting. The grass around the cup is referred to as the *lip*. Be careful when replacing the flagstick not to damage the lip — simply place the flagstick straight into the hole.

Bunker Play

We played that hole pretty well. None of us got into trouble by hitting the ball into a bunker. Let's say, though, that I hit my ball into a bunker near the green. There are some bunker etiquette and rules information that you should know.

I enter the bunker where it is easiest to walk in, and I'm careful not to step on the edge of the grass, the *lip* of the bunker. I pick up the closest rake that is either in the bunker or lying outside of it and place it out of my way so I can take a swing. Because I can be inaccurate when I hit out of bunkers, I make sure the rest of you watch for my ball, so I say, "Heads up!"

Under the rules of golf, I am not allowed to put the sole of my sand wedge on the sand or *ground* my club when I'm hitting out of the bunker. I have to hold the clubhead above the sand before I take my swing to hit out of the bunker. When none of you are putting, I rake the sand where the ball landed and where I hit. I also walk backwards, retracing my footprints, and raking over them. Then, I replace the rake in the bunker with the rake's teeth in the sand and the handle pointing toward me. That way a ball won't get trapped between the rake and the lip of the bunker. Again, I am leaving the course in as good condition as I found it. If there are footprints left by another player that are close to mine, I rake those as well.

Managing Your Golf Cart

Even though you may enjoy walking and carrying or pulling your clubs, on occasion you may play in a corporate or charity golf tournament where you must use a golf cart. You may be using a basic golf cart or a high-tech version with a global positioning system with a screen for layout of the hole and distances to the green.

Here are some tips on how to use a cart, so you won't disturb other players:

- If you're sharing the cart, decide who is going to drive. Whoever is driving the cart should strap his or her bag on the cart behind him or her. If this is a round of business golf that you're hosting, you should drive the cart.
- Most courses that allow you to take carts onto the course require use of the *90 Degree Rule* or the *H-System* when driving onto the fairway. Drive the cart on the cart path until you reach the first ball, then turn 90 degrees, or at a right angle, into the fairway to the ball. After you hit the ball, drive the cart back to the cart path, and drive on the path until you reach the ball ahead. If it's a short distance to the ball ahead, you can drive on the rough. The purpose of this rule is to prevent carts driving on the fairway unnecessarily, since they can damage the grass.
- Obey the cart signs near the putting green. Most courses do not want you to drive your cart closer than 30 yards or so to the putting green and the bunkers.
- Some golf courses are "Cart Paths Only," which means you never drive your cart anywhere except on the cart path. This means that you will do

much more walking to and from your ball. To keep the pace of play, always take several clubs with you when walking to your ball, including the club you think you need, one club more, and one club less. Just remember to pick up your extra clubs after you hit.

- Don't drive the cart or release the brake when someone in your foursome is getting ready to hit. If you're driving up to the tee or green of another hole where someone is about to hit, stop the cart as well.
- To keep up the pace, and when it's safe, you can drop your cart partner off at his or her ball, and then drive to your ball.
- Maneuvering a golf cart up the hole requires communication between you and your cart partner. For example, when you've taken the clubs you want out of your bag, you can say, "Okay. I have my clubs." Or if you're going to walk to your ball while your cart partner is hitting, tell your partner, "I'll walk to my ball," or "You've got the cart." You want to prevent both of you walking ahead and leaving the cart behind.
- If your ball is off the green, and your cart partner is on the green, take the clubs that you'll need, such as your pitching wedge, sand wedge, and your putter, to hit your ball. You can tell your cart partner that you have your clubs, and he or she can then drive to the green while you're getting ready to hit.
- If you're the passenger and your foursome needs to speed up your pace of play, you don't need to replace your clubs in your bag—hold them inside the cart until you get to the next ball.
- At the green, park the cart where the golf course has marked or where you can easily walk to the putting green. You should always park on the side of the hole nearest to the next hole to save time.
- If you're the only person riding in your foursome, when possible, abide by the 90-degree rule and drive slow enough to talk with the players who are walking.

We just played a hole together and you learned the etiquette and some rules from tee to green. You also know bunker etiquette and how to manage a golf cart. As you start to play more, all of this will become second nature. Until then, you can review this section before you play to remind yourself of the basic etiquette and rules. You've also learned some of the language of the game, so you'll be able to keep up with the golf talk on Monday mornings.

When the round is finished, it is traditional to shake hands and thank each playing partner for the game. To be considerate of the players behind you, do this after all of you have left the green.

· ·

Top Ten Etiquette Tips

 1. *Be quiet and still when others are hitting their balls.*
 2. *Play ready golf—select your club quickly and take no more than one or two practice swings.*
 3. *Replace divots or fill divots with grass and seed mixture.*
 4. *Keep the pace—stay within one safe shot of the group ahead.*
 5. *Be a courteous cart driver and manage the cart with your partner.*
 6. *Beware of others' putting lines.*
 7. *Repair your ball mark and, if time permits, one other ball mark.*
 8. *Tend, remove, and replace the flagstick when appropriate.*
 9. *After hitting your ball out of the bunker, rake the sand and place the rake face down.*
10. *After all players have putted out, leave the green promptly to mark your scores.*

· ·

Keeping Score

As you start to play regularly, you'll want to keep track of how you're improving by keeping score and getting a handicap. Golf has unique terms to describe your score. The scorecard also gives you lots of information about each golf hole and the golf course. If you've never played a course before, I suggest you take a few minutes to review its scorecard before you play.

Most scorecards contain this information:

- The yardage, par, and handicaps for each hole from each tee
- Course and slope ratings for the course
- Local rules applying only to the particular golf course
- A layout of the golf course showing the location and shapes of each hole. Scorecards for private country clubs may not have the course layout because it's presumed members are familiar with the course.

In this section, I cover handicaps for each hole, course rating, and slope rating in the Handicaps section.

Yardage

Let's look at a sample scorecard (Figure 3-1). At this course, the scorecard shows men play from the back tees, whereas women play from the forward

Back 73.1/137						H O L E	Shawn		Jane		Forward 73.7/128		
Men's Course Rating/Slope											Women's Course Rating/Slope		
Back Tees	Par	Hcp									Hcp	Par	Fwd Tees
366	4	9				1	5		5		4	4	336
544	5	7				2	9		6		2	5	511
391	4	3				3	5		5		10	4	365
164	3	13				4	4		4		16	3	147
320	4	15				5	5		6		8	4	301
189	3	1				6	4		5		12	3	157
370	4	11				7	5		6		14	4	346
162	3	17				8	3		5		18	3	137
390	4	5				9	7		7		6	5	380
2896	34					Out	47		49			35	2680
Initials											Initials		
338	4	14				10	5		5		5	4	304
365	4	4				11	5		5		13	4	338
146	3	18				12	4		4		15	3	131
517	5	8				13	9		7		1	5	489
343	4	16				14	5		4		9	4	308
337	4	10				15	6		5		11	4	314
166	3	12				16	3		3		17	3	129
399	4	6				17	5		4		7	4	365
401	4	2				18	7		9		3	5	378
3012	35					In	49		46			36	2756
5908	69					Tot	96		95			71	5436
Handicap							28		23		Handicap		
Net Score							68		72		Net Score		
Adjust							94		94		Adjust		

Scorer   Attest   Date

FIGURE 3-1   Sample scorecard.

tees. There are more tees on the course, and men and women can play from any tee, but let's keep it simple. Men refer to the information on the left side of the scorecard, and women use the right side.

The scorecard gives the length of each hole for each set of tees, the length of both front and back nine holes, the total length of the entire eighteen holes, and par for each hole.

On hole number one, the length of the hole from each tee is as follows:

- From the back tees, the hole is 366 yards
- From the forward tees, the hole is 336 yards

If you're playing from the forward tees, and your male playing partner is hitting from the back tees, you have a 30-yard advantage on this hole.

Scoring

To score each hole, you count every stroke, whiff, and add any penalty strokes that you might have. Here are common scoring terms:

- *Bogey.* Score is one stroke more than or over par
- *Double bogey.* Score is two strokes over par
- *Birdie.* Score is one stroke less than or under par
- *Eagle.* Score is two strokes under par
- *Snowman.* A euphemism for a score of eight

If you watch a professional golf tournament on television, a player's score-card is often shown with his or her score on each hole. Symbols are used to highlight scores. For example, a triangle is used to show that the player shot a birdie on that particular hole. If the player had a bogey, then the score is inside a square. If the player shot par, then the score is inside a circle.

So, if I shot a five on hole number one, I would write a five with a square around it. If you made a three on the hole, then you shot a birdie! As cruel as that may sound to nongolfers, you played the hole very well! You would write a three inside a triangle to show you had a birdie.

Hole in One

Let's say you're playing a par 3 hole, and you sink the ball into the hole on your first shot. Congratulations! Any guesses as to the odds of hitting a hole in one? Some say 1 in 12,600. A hole in one requires skill and an abundance of luck, which is why when you make one you're supposed to buy drinks for everyone in the clubhouse. It's a time to celebrate your good fortune and share it with all, especially when you know people who have played for twenty years and have never had one.

I was fortunate to have a hole in one at my club—the first time ever a woman had one on that hole. I will never forget finding the ball in the hole and later celebrating with my playing partner and other players in the clubhouse. I was thrilled to buy everyone a drink!

Handicaps

I have mentioned how the handicap system allows players of different abilities to play against one another. This system sets golf apart from other sports. Again, it's more important that you're an enjoyable playing partner rather than a low scorer. Nevertheless, a golfer with a course handicap of 26 is considered a *better* golfer than a 34 handicapper by eight strokes.

Take a look at the sample handicap card shown as Figure 3-2. The Handicap Index is calculated using the best ten of your previous twenty scores when you play an eighteen-hole course. If Jane's course, Sunny Brook Golf Club, has a course rating of 69, then she's expected to shoot 96 on average.

Name	**Jane Smith**				
	XYZ Golf Association				
Club	**Sunny Brook Golf Club**				
Club#	**5**			USGA	
Effective Date	**07/01/01**			HCP INDEX	
Scores Posted	**22**			**21.2**	
SCORE	HISTORY	MOST	RECENT	FIRST*	IF USED
1	104	102*	97*	99A	104
6	107	94*	100*	97*	98*
11	109	105	96*	104	103*
16	104	101*	105	103*	107

Figure 3-2   Sample handicap card.

. . . .

A player's handicap reflects his or her potential because it is based on the best ten scores of the player's last twenty rounds. A player is expected to play to his or her handicap or better only about 25 percent of the time. Example: A 20-handicap on a par 72 course will likely score 92 or less at most once out of four rounds.

Source: USGA

. . . .

Let's say Jane has a 23 handicap and is playing at her home course against Shawn, who has a 28 handicap. Both Jane and Shawn are playing from the forward tees. Jane must give Shawn five strokes. Under the stroke play format, Shawn subtracts five strokes from her score. Let's say both played very well—Jane shot a 95 and Shawn a 96. Jane shot a lower gross score than Shawn. But Shawn's net score is 68 (the difference of 96 and 28) and Jane's net score is 72 (the difference of 95 and 23), so Shawn won by four strokes.

If you look at the sample scorecard, you'll see the column entitled "Handicap." Each hole has been rated for difficulty in comparison to the other holes. The hardest hole on the golf course is rated number one, which is the thirteenth hole for women and the sixth hole for men, while the easiest hole is rated number eighteen, which is the eighth hole for women and the twelfth hole for men.

Let's say Jane and Shawn are playing a match play tournament where they are competing hole by hole, rather than the net scores. Shawn gets five strokes, but on which holes does she get the benefit of the handicap strokes? She gets the strokes on the five most difficult holes, which are holes numbered thirteen, two, eighteen, one, and ten, respectively. If Jane and Shawn both shoot a five on hole thirteen, Shawn wins that hole because she has a handicap stroke, also known as a *pop* on that hole. If she received two handicap strokes, then she'd have a *double pop*.

That's the beauty of the handicap system. A lesser player, according to handicaps, can beat a better player on a given day. You want a handicap to pass this rite of passage as a golfer, and so you can track your progress and enter tournaments. Tournament organizers often have *flights* or *flight* a tournament, so players of similar ability are competing against one another. They determine the flights based on handicaps.

. . . .

According to the National Golf Foundation, less than 20 percent of all golfers maintain a handicap. Get a handicap to set yourself apart from the rest.

. . . .

Getting a Handicap

To get a handicap, you need to:

- Play ten rounds of golf and keep a scorecard for each round. In most states, you can post nine-hole scores also, so check with your local golf course. Otherwise, you must play eighteen holes.
- Join a golf club for a nominal fee at the golf course you'll likely play the most, your home club. Or, you can join an independent golf association, such as a company-sponsored club or a women's club.
- After you have ten scorecards, submit the cards or scores to the club. You will be issued a Golf Handicap and Information Network (GHIN) number. Your GHIN number is your identification for handicap purposes.

Posting Your Scores

After each round of golf (nine or eighteen holes), you need to *post* your score by entering your GHIN number and score into the computer at the golf course specifically for handicaps (or send your scorecards to your club).

· ·

If you played thirteen out of eighteen holes (or seven out of nine holes), then you should still post your score. For the holes that you didn't play, score par plus the number of strokes that you receive for your handicap. Example: The fourteenth hole is a par 4 and you get one stroke on that hole, then give yourself a five for that hole.

· ·

Each month you will be issued a new sticker that updates your latest twenty scores, and your handicap index is calculated on the best ten scores.

You may have played some holes during a round that are worse than how you usually play. If that is the case, you need to apply the Equitable Stroke Control system and *adjust* your score by posting the maximum score shown in Table 3-2 for any hole according to your handicap for that course.

Equitable Stroke Control prevents having one or two holes change a player's handicap substantially. Let's look back at the sample scorecard (Figure 3-1) and Shawn's round of golf. Shawn's handicap is 28. According to Equitable Stroke Control, Shawn can only have a maximum score of eight. Since Shawn had nine on both holes two and thirteen, she must adjust her score. To do so, she subtracts two strokes from her total score, one stroke for each hole she had a score of nine.

TABLE 3-2   Maximum Score on a Hole

Handicap	Maximum Score
Up to 9	Double bogey
10–19	7
20–29	8
30–39	9
40 and above	10

On the sample scorecard, Shawn's total score is 96. Her adjusted score is 94, which is the score she would post for handicap purposes. If Shawn were playing in a tournament, her total score of 96 would be used for the competition.

Here's a ready golf tip: If Shawn is playing in a casual round, she could have picked up her ball after the seventh stroke, since the maximum score she can take is eight. Besides saving time, picking up is wise to lessen her frustration about her score.

Handicap Index

Prior to using the handicap index, players with the same handicap were considered to have equal playing abilities. So if Michele and Ann each had a handicap of 20, neither would give the other strokes. But, let's say Michele plays on a much more difficult home golf course than Ann—Michele's course is longer and has more hazards than Ann's course. In actuality, Michele is a better player than Ann, but the handicaps didn't reflect this difference.

To compensate for the difference, the USGA created the handicap index and the course slope rating system. On the sample handicap card in Figure 3-2, 21.2 is listed under USGA Hcp Index. Don't worry about how the USGA calculated the index. Depending on the difficulty of the golf course you're playing, your handicap may go up or down.

The slope rating system ranks each golf course according to difficulty. Slopes for golf courses range between 55 and 155. A course with a slope of 100 is considered a relatively easy golf course, whereas a course with a slope of 135 is considered more difficult. The average slope rating for a course is 113.

To find your handicap at a course with a given slope, you need your handicap index and the slope rating of the course. You can find the slope rating on most scorecards. On the sample scorecard (Figure 3-1), the slope for women playing from the forward tee is 125. If your index is 21.2, then according to the handicap conversion listing shown as Figure 3-3, your handicap at this course is 23. In the "Slope Rating of 125" column, find your handicap index. The number to the left is the handicap you'll use on this course.

Play to This Course Handicap	Slope Rating of 125	Play to This Course Handicap	Slope Rating of 125
+4	+3.5 to +3.2	21	18.6 to 19.4
+3	+3.1 to +2.3	22	19.5 to 20.3
+2	+2.2 to +1.4	23	20.4 to 21.2
+1	+1.3 to +.5	24	21.3 to 22.1
0	+.4 to .4	25	22.2 to 23.0
1	0.5 to 1.3	26	23.1 to 23.9
2	1.4 to 2.2	27	24.0 to 24.8
3	2.3 to 3.1	28	24.9 to 25.7
4	3.2 to 4.0	29	25.8 to 26.6
5	4.1 to 4.9	30	26.7 to 27.5
6	5.0 to 5.8	31	27.6 to 28.4
7	5.9 to 6.7	32	28.5 to 29.3
8	6.8 to 7.6	33	29.4 to 30.2
9	7.7 to 8.5	34	30.3 to 31.1
10	8.6 to 9.4	35	31.2 to 32.0
11	9.5 to 10.3	36	32.1 to 32.9
12	10.4 to 11.2	37	33.0 to 33.8
13	11.3 to 12.2	38	33.9 to 34.8
14	12.3 to 13.1	39	34.9 to 35.7
15	13.2 to 14.0	40	35.8 to 36.6
16	14.1 to 14.9	41	36.7 to 37.5
17	15.0 to 15.8	42	37.6 to 38.4
18	15.9 to 16.7	43	38.5 to 39.3
19	16.8 to 17.6	44	39.4 to 40.2
20	17.7 to 18.5	45	40.3 to 40.4

FIGURE 3-3   Handicap conversion example.

When you play a new course, it's a good idea to bring your handicap card, so you know your handicap index and can find your handicap at that course. You'll likely find the slope conversion chart in the pro shop or women's locker room.

By the way, other golfers will ask, "What's your handicap?" Although you might be a beginner, you can respond so they know you've studied the game. Rather than simply saying, "My handicap is 24," answer with "At my home course, my handicap is 24," or "My handicap index is 21.2." You'll have more to talk about as they realize you know the difference between a handicap and a handicap index and they'll likely want to know where your home course is.

Course Rating

Most scorecards will also include the course rating for men and women playing from particular tees. The course rating tells you the difficulty of a golf course factoring in the gender of the player. On the sample scorecard, the course rating for women playing from the forward tees is 72.1 and par is 71, so a scratch woman golfer (a very good player with a zero handicap) will on average score or shoot par on seventeen holes and have a bogey on a hole. Using the slope rating and the course rating, you can compare a course you haven't played with your home club to determine if the new course is easier or more difficult.

You also use the course rating if you are competing against a man. For example, the course rating for men off the back tees is 68.8 and par is 69. According to the course rating, the course is more difficult for women to play than for men. Therefore, a woman playing against a man would receive three strokes (the difference of 72.1 and 68.8 is 3.3), in addition to any difference in their handicaps.

For example, let's say I'm playing against Bob. My handicap is 14 and Bob's handicap is 9. He gives me five strokes because of the difference in our handicaps. He gives me an additional three strokes because of the difference in the course ratings from the tees that we're each playing from. So, Bob gives me a total of eight strokes—one pop on each of the eight hardest holes according to the ranking on the scorecard.

You're Ready to Play

You now have all the information you need to go on the course. You might not play well during your first few rounds, and you may even be nervous. The evening before your tee time try to review playing a virtual hole so you can get the feel of playing with others. If you can initially play with more experienced golfers and friends who can help you integrate what you've learned about the etiquette and the rules of golf, you'll be ahead of most golfers, including men, who start playing this game. Don't get discouraged! Remember, your goal is to be able to hit the ball consistently and to be an enjoyable playing partner for your business golf rounds. You're on your way!

Staying On Course

_____ Research public golf courses and driving ranges near your home and office. Look especially for par-3 and executive courses, which are more suitable for beginners.

_____ When you can make consistent contact with the ball, invite experienced playing partners to your inaugural nine holes of golf. Tell them that you're a beginner, have reviewed the etiquette and rules of golf, and want their feedback on how you can be an enjoyable playing partner.

_____ Before your first round of golf, review the virtual hole of golf we played together for etiquette tips and the basic rules of golf in Appendix A.

_____ Schedule a tee time for your inaugural round of golf. Request a tee time when the course is not as crowded. Make sure you always keep up the pace and play ready golf!

_____ Solicit feedback and suggestions from your playing partners on how to play with proper etiquette and with knowledge of the rules of golf. Watch how other players handle themselves on the course.

_____ Join a golf club at work or a local golf course. You'll expand your network of colleagues and friends as you begin to play more.

_____ Play five rounds of golf and apply for a GHIN number.

_____ When you've built your stamina, play your first round of eighteen holes of golf.

_____ Post ten rounds of golf to get a handicap. Remember, having an accurate handicap allows you to play in tournaments, and it's a yardstick for you to measure your progress—like a sales quota.

PART TWO

Taking It to the Links—Payoffs of Playing BizGolf

CHAPTER 4

....

Ins and Outs
of Playing
Business Golf

How do you know when you're ready to play business golf? How good of a golfer should you be before you play a round of business golf? After all, you don't want your business golf with clients or colleagues to create a poor impression because you lack experience in playing golf appropriately. That would produce the *opposite* result of what you're trying to accomplish with business golf—building stronger business relationships.

In this chapter, I give you some guidelines so you can determine when you're ready to play a round of business golf. I suggest ways you can start enjoying the benefits of playing business golf without playing eighteen holes. I also share how some women use a round of golf to further their business success and objectives. Finally, I give you suggestions on how to host a successful business golf round as well as how to play as a guest.

When Are You Ready for Business Golf?

You don't have to break 100 or be able to hit the ball 150 yards before you can play business golf. While these accomplishments may be personal goals, they are arbitrary numbers. Instead, you'll know you're ready to play business golf when you can hit the ball consistently, regardless of the distance, and are comfortable with the etiquette and rules.

If you've taken golf lessons from a golf teaching professional and are spending time practicing at the driving range and playing on a course, your ability to hit the ball far and consistently should be improving. Remember, your playing partners won't recall how far you hit the ball, your score, or how well you did or didn't play. If you kept up with the pace of the group, were courteous toward the other players, and were fun to play with, you'll always be welcome in a foursome.

....

The best part of golf is that if you observe the etiquette, you can always find a game.
Harvey Penick

....

The pace of a round is very important. If you've been playing recreational rounds of golf, you have probably started to sense the rhythm and tempo that occur within a foursome. I refer to the rhythm and tempo as the "dance of etiquette," which is most important around the tees and greens because players are closest to one another in these locations and thus can more easily distract one another. The more you play, the more you'll have that confident feeling of knowing when it's your turn to hit, where you should stand when others are swinging or putting, when and how you should mark your ball, whether you should offer to tend the flagstick, and other tactics to keep your foursome playing smoothly and quickly. This is like dancing in another way: often most of these things happen without talking about them; you and your playing partners simply know what to do next.

By having played more, you've also probably seen how other players have applied the rules of golf in different instances such as when a ball is lost, out of bounds, or in a water hazard. Although you don't need to be an expert at the rules, it's helpful to have some basic familiarity with them. Remember, you can always ask your playing partners what the rules permit. Rather than incorrectly guessing the applicable rule and risking the appearance of cheating, your playing partners will be glad to help in those situations.

If you've started to feel comfortable playing casual rounds of golf, you're ready to start playing business golf.

Business Golf Isn't Always Eighteen Holes

Many beginners mistakenly believe to enjoy the benefits of playing business golf, they must be able to play eighteen holes. Alternatives to playing eighteen holes, however, can be just as effective in using golf to build and deepen business relationships.

Playing Nine Holes Is Business Golf

When you're new to the game, playing eighteen holes can be tiring, especially if you're walking and carrying your clubs. There's also the time factor: playing eighteen holes can take an entire day.

Playing nine holes is quicker and less tiring than a full round. I suggest you build stamina and endurance by playing several rounds of nine holes on an executive course to start. After playing nine-hole rounds, when you feel ready try to play eighteen holes one day. If you usually walk and carry your clubs, walk the front nine holes, then ride a cart for the back nine holes. Most golf courses will allow this—you simply pay for the nine-hole cart rental fee when paying your green fee and you'll be given a cart key.

Initially, try to play with those who have been encouraging you to play business golf. Many of my clients have at least one boss, colleague, client, or good friend who has been encouraging them to play golf for business. If you're fortunate to have such a golf mentor, then invite him or her for your first golf outing. This can be a less intimidating way for you to begin playing business golf. It's also a great way to thank that person for encouraging you to play, as well as, of course, a venue for you to talk about careers and business.

Even if you're only playing nine holes, you can also invite a client or colleague to join you for a short round of business golf. One client, Kirsten, is a financial consultant, and she had a client for whom she was managing a $400,000 portfolio. A novice at business golf, Kirsten and I worked together so she came to understand golf's terminology, scoring, and etiquette. Kirsten knew the client played golf and invited her to play nine holes at an executive golf course.

After their day of golf, Kirsten noticed over time that her client shared more details of her life. Within a few months, the client asked Kirsten to manage all of her assets: $3 million worth. Although they only played nine holes, the short round paved the way to an enhanced personal and business relationship; Kirsten had a tremendously successful business golf round.

Michelle, the president of a construction company specializing in commercial buildings, also played a successful business golf round of nine holes with a woman prospect. The prospect was an asset manager for a Fortune 500 company. Her responsibilities included hiring construction contractors for the company's substantial real estate holdings. In their first conversation, each woman admitted that she was a beginner golfer.

Michelle suggested that they meet to play nine holes. As Michelle describes it, "We were horrible! We could kick the ball farther than we could hit it. She said we just had a great time laughing at how lousy each of us played." Playing poorly didn't stop the asset manager from giving Michelle several construction projects thereafter. Michelle knows it's the old adage: You do business with people you know. Thanks to having a good time playing nine holes together and getting to know each other, they developed a mutually profitable business relationship, even though neither one's golf game was particularly sterling.

Business Golf Can Be a Practice Session

Another alternative to playing eighteen holes is to have a business golf practice session. Ask a client or prospect if he or she would like to meet at the driving range, so you can hit a bucket of balls, practice pitching and bunker shots, and/or practice putting, which makes for an ideal short meeting of an hour or so.

Some golfers don't particularly like to practice. To help you both focus on your golf shots and to have fun practicing together, you can create some minicompetitions:

- When hitting balls, have one person select a flag. Then, each of you hits to see who lands the ball closest to the designated flag.
- Imagine that you are playing a hole that you're both familiar with, then begin with the drive, hit your approach iron, and then pitch shot.
- At the chipping green, you each take three balls, pick a designated cup or flag, and then see who can come closest with each chip.
- On the putting green, count the total number of putts when playing a set series of holes.

Putting is a particularly fun practice session because it doesn't require all of your clubs or too much physical exertion (since you both probably have to return to the office afterward!). When scheduling a putting meeting, meet at a course with a great putting green—one that's large, has two tiers, and is well kept. On such a putting green, it's great fun—and a real relationship builder—to try long and short putts. I recently putted on a practice green north of San Francisco that permitted 30- or 40-foot putts—with about 20 feet of break!

The real advantage of a practice meeting is that this quick outing can be done at any time of day. You can jumpstart your day with fresh air and some exercise by practicing your golf game, then talk business over breakfast. Or, it can be a refreshing break from the office in the middle of the day—golf and a delicious lunch at a nearby high-end public golf course restaurant. Or, your session can be a relaxing end-of-day activity, with some light business conversation later over refreshments and appetizers.

Shawn is a sales trainer and consultant, and an experienced business golfer. She uses this method of mixing golf practice and business with clients and prospects. She says, "If I know a person is a golfer, and we have some business to discuss, I'll suggest that we meet at the driving range and have a bite to eat. We both need the golf practice, and it's a relatively short meeting. We do some business and have a good time together." It can be fun to meet at a grill of a local upscale golf course. You can discuss golf and business in a relaxed environment and maybe browse in the pro shop afterward.

Reasons for Playing a Business Golf Round

. . . .

Most golfers prepare for disaster. A good golfer prepares for success.

Bob Toski

. . . .

In addition to playing golf to strengthen relationships, here are some examples of how some women use a round of golf to further their business success:

- *Thank-you round.* Denise, an account representative, sells wireless equipment and services enabling merchants to accept credit cards without requiring a telephone line. After signing a contract, she provides ongoing training and support services to her client's staff. Soon after a contract is finalized, she invites her client to a round of golf as a thank you for doing business with her. She's doesn't do any selling during the round. Instead, Denise uses the round to reinforce a comfort level and to let her client know that she is available to troubleshoot problems with the equipment or services.
- *Networking round.* Marilyn is a public relations specialist. Previously she worked with two senior management executives in different companies. The senior vice president in one company wanted to leave. The other was looking for an executive to fill a newly created position, but was not able

to actively look for candidates. Marilyn had a gut feeling that the two executives would like each other and work well together, so she invited both to a round of golf. Within a couple of months, the senior vice president went to work for the other senior executive, and both are grateful to Marilyn for her insight and initiative in getting them to meet on the golf course. Marilyn also benefited by receiving 20 percent to 25 percent additional business, since both executives needed her public relations expertise for their divisions.

- *Brainstorming/problem-solving round.* Linda is on the board of a university in the Silicon Valley. She and another board member often meet to play golf and discuss marketing and fund raising ideas for the university. She said it's a good way for both of them to get away from the distractions of the office and be creative in a relaxed setting.

- *Presenting a contract round.* Marsha is a sales representative for a company that provides to government entities credit card acceptance services for payment of taxes and fees. She often invites government officials to a round of golf at her country club (although the officials are ethically required to pay their own fees). Before she presents a contract and reviews the terms with them, they play a round of golf. As one government official said after an enjoyable round, "This is the way I like to do business. I've had a chance to get to know you better and now we can review the technical details of how we can work together."

- *Introduction round.* Meriby is the founder of a business incubator. Her clients are startup, growing young companies who often need venture capital, strategic partners, and/or providers of legal, accounting, and related services. In some instances, Meriby will target a specific company as a potential strategic partner for a client company. If she doesn't know anyone at the company, she'll call the human resources department, identify who she is, and ask who at the company is an avid golfer because she would like to invite him or her to play with her at a local charity golf tournament. Meriby is often referred to CFOs, CEOs, or directors of marketing—the exact individuals she needs to speak with about a possible alliance with one of her clients. While playing, Meriby doesn't blatantly sell to the executives, but she does learn about their companies and introduces her services and her clients' needs to the executives when appropriate.

As you start to play business golf, I'm sure you'll find your own reasons for playing a business golf round. Let's look at what steps you can take to extend an invitation and host a successful round of golf.

Hosting a Business Golf Round

Business golf is a strategic tool. Like an important business meeting, plan and prepare accordingly by considering participants, location, logistics, and goal of your business golf round.

Whom Should You Invite

Is there a client, prospect, referral source, or colleague you want to develop a stronger business relationship with? You'll probably say yes. In fact, you probably have many, and one of the advantages of business golf is that you can host up to three other people. You should carefully consider the mix of who you invite for a particular round. Is there a colleague in your company that will work closely with this client?

When deciding whom to invite for a round, consider the personalities, golf experiences, and common business interests of your prospective guests. Don't forget, you can have a business golf round as a twosome, or you may decide to create a foursome. If you're inviting more than one guest, give some basic information about each guest to the others so they'll have some familiarity with their backgrounds when they meet.

Another good option is to look for a local civic or charity fund-raising tournament and put together a foursome. (I discuss more about these tournaments in Chapter 7.) These events are usually played in a team format, rather than a competition using individual scores. Therefore, it's a good team-building exercise and great for players of all levels. Since these tournaments are often played at private country clubs, you also have an opportunity to play at a very nice venue. The entry fees may also be considered a full or partial charitable deduction if not a business expense. Normally these events include tee prizes and lunch and/or dinner, so it could be an all-day event.

Tell Them They're Your Guests

If you plan to host the round, let your guests know when you invite them by specifically stating something to this effect: "I'd like to have you as my guest for a round of golf." In almost every instance when you are inviting someone else for a round, you should be the one paying.

There are several exceptions, of course. Some government and other organizations, such as certain media, forbid employees from accepting gifts from a business acquaintance. If you have any questions about your guests' ability to accept a free round of golf, simply ask them. Be careful when playing with these guests—even buying a sleeve of three golf balls or a new golf glove might be a technical violation of the company's or governmental agency's no-gifts policy.

Let Guests Know Your Playing Ability

Unfortunately, there are still some experienced golfers who do not enjoy playing with beginners. Most are afraid that beginners will disrupt their games. To combat this, tell your invitees about your playing abilities. Be honest but forthright. If the guest doesn't want to play with someone of lesser ability, he or she can decline graciously. Don't apologize for being a beginner; instead simply say, "I would enjoy playing a round of golf to learn more about you and your business. I'm still improving my game, but I know how to play ready golf, and I keep up the pace. Regardless of how I play, I know we'll have a good time." Knowing that you can play with proper etiquette and that you understand the concept of ready golf, most golfers will likely accept your invitation.

Choose a Golf Course

You want to choose a golf course that your partners will likely enjoy and one that is not too difficult for them to play. It's useful to get a sense of your guest's playing ability—ask what his or her handicap or average score is so you'll know what to expect. Or, ask your guests if they have a favorite local golf course. If you think that you can handle the level of difficulty (ask for the slope rating and whether there are a lot of hilly lies, which are more challenging for beginners), then play your round at that course. Otherwise, choose a local upscale public course with a country club feel that you're familiar with. Also, ask beforehand if your guests prefer to walk and carry or use a cart, so that you can be prepared to rent a golf cart.

Of course, if you're a member or have playing privileges at a private country club, by all means extend an invitation to play that course. Your guests will feel fortunate to have an opportunity to play at an exclusive course. You should also tactfully let your guests know the dress code of your club and the spike requirements. For example, when inviting a guest to my club, I add, "You probably know this, but tee shirts, jeans, and shorts 5 inches above the knee aren't allowed. And you can wear either metal or soft spikes." You want to avoid any embarrassment for your guests (or yourself) at your club.

There is something else to take into consideration when choosing a golf course—your budget. Green fees at courses can vary significantly. Call ahead to find out exactly how much the round will cost, including carts.

Select a Tee Time

You want to make sure you and your playing partners have time for the nineteenth hole conversation, and none of you is feeling rushed to leave after your round of golf. Ask what is the best time for your guests to play. Discuss whether you want to practice at the driving range before playing. Also clarify if you want to have breakfast or lunch before playing, and/or drinks or dinner after the round. An afternoon tee time often works best, since all of you can work during the morning, play eighteen holes, and then finish in the early evening. During daylight savings time, you can tee off as late as 2 P.M. or 3 P.M. and still finish eighteen holes. Two other advantages of late-afternoon/early-evening tee times is that many courses offer reduced off-peak green fees, called *twilight rates*, and the weather is usually cooler and more enjoyable. (Playing golf during the heat of the day can be a very draining experience, even when riding a cart.)

If you and your client are beginners, a late morning or afternoon tee time is the best time to play. You won't be as rushed by experienced players who tee off in the mornings, especially if you're playing on the weekends.

Confirm Your Tee Time

With everyone's hectic schedules, extend an invitation to play a round of golf at least two to three weeks in advance. Suggest a couple of days and times that work for you and your guests. After reserving the tee time, immediately let your guests know the date and time. The day before your outing, call the golf course to confirm the tee time and the number of players in your group. A few days prior to the date, you should confirm with your guests:

- The date and time that you're going to meet (at least thirty minutes before your tee time) and your tee time.
- The name of the golf course (include a general description of the course's location, such as the main road or nearest major intersection, to avoid any confusion as to which course).
- The meeting place at the golf course, such as the pro shop, restaurant, practice putting green, and so on.

If you know your guests have never played the golf course, one nice touch is to send a confirmation note stating how you look forward to playing and include the course's scorecard. Your guests will appreciate having the phone number of the golf course, as well as a chance to become familiar with the course. Or you can send an e-mail with a link to the golf course's Web site. Many golf courses, including private clubs, have Web sites with directions to the course, and a virtual tour of the golf course and the facilities.

You should also have and discuss with your guests a contingency plan in case of rain. If it's a possibility, suggest that you still meet at the given tee time for a meal at the golf course. If you're not discussing confidential information, you can at least talk about business away from the office and in a more relaxed atmosphere.

Conversation During the Round

Playing golf for business gives you a venue for building relationships with clients and other business associates. You'll notice whether a client wants to discuss business, or if he or she would rather focus on enjoying the round of golf. Don't bring up a contract issue when he or she is deciding which club to use to hit the ball 175 yards over the water.

As a general rule, I recommend that you not raise business topics while you're on the golf course. Most clients or prospects will know why they've been invited to play and will likely initiate a business conversation at some point during the round. Even if the client begins to discuss with great specificity his or her business matters, try to keep the conversation light and wait until the nineteenth hole or your next office meeting to get into the details.

Why not plow ahead with business on the course? You and your playing partners are on the course to enjoy playing and learning more about each other. While your round is a business-related activity and some business discussions may arise, the reason for playing is to have a good time and build rapport with each other. If you must talk business during a round of golf, try to do so during the middle of the round—between holes six and thirteen. Thus, you can begin and end the round on a relationship-building note. In addition, you can talk business on the tee as you wait for the group in front of you or at the turn when you buy snacks or water.

. . . .

There are two basic rules that should never be broken. Be subtle. And don't, for God's sake, try to do business with anyone who's having a bad game.
William Davis

. . . .

There are, of course, some situations when business will be discussed more frequently on the course. If you and your client have chosen a round of golf to solve a problem, then it's appropriate that you talk about the matter during the round. Or if you've set up a networking round, tell your playing partners that you thought they would enjoy meeting one another and that you wanted to introduce them. Still, even in these instances, business conversation should be kept to a minimum. Some background information and general information can be shared, but leave the details and specifics for the nineteenth hole.

Prepare Yourself Before the Outing

A couple of weeks before your business golf round, include in your schedule and complete two or three practice sessions at the driving range and putting green, especially if you haven't played in a while.

. . . .

If you're on the road a lot, keep a few clubs in your car. Rather than being stuck in traffic and stressed, stop at a driving range and practice.

. . . .

You can also practice putting in your home or office. Why practice if you *know* how to play? You want to be able to hit the ball and feel confident of your playing abilities, and confidence comes with practice. Since golf etiquette and knowledge of the basic rules are also important, review the "Playing a Hole Together" section in Chapter 3, the etiquette of business golf later in this chapter, and Appendix A on the basic rules.

The Day of Your Golf Outing

Besides the preround preparation, there are steps you should take to ensure your playing partners have a great time on the course.

Arrive Early

Plan to arrive at the golf course at least a half hour before the planned time to meet your guests. You want to take care of the logistics of checking in and paying green and cart rental fees before your guests arrive. If you and your guests want to hit balls at the driving range before playing, then also buy range balls. If it's a warm day, buy bottled water for your guests. Linda, the telecommunications consultant, goes a step further. If she knows her guests enjoy cigars, she brings each a good cigar. She ordinarily doesn't enjoy being around cigar smoke, but since she's outdoors with them, she can endure the smoke. Also bring extra cash for paying bets, buying refreshments and snacks at the turn (between the front and back nine holes) or from the beverage cart, at the nine-teenth hole, or for other miscellaneous things.

Consider Golf Cart Arrangements

If you and your guests are using golf carts during your round, consider who should share a cart with whom. If you're playing with only one guest, then you should drive the cart and have your golf bag strapped on the cart behind you. If you have two or three guests, consider whom you want to spend more time with, and share the cart with that person. Or, put the two people that you want to get to know each other in one cart.

If you've invited a colleague from your company to join you with two client representatives or prospects, then you shouldn't share the cart with your colleague. Your purpose for the round is to court the client representatives or prospects, not your colleague. Another option is to for you and your colleague to each drive a cart and switch cart partners after nine holes.

Greet Your Guests

At the agreed time and place, meet your guests and suggest a warm up. If your guests are late, then consider whether you want to ask the starter for a slightly later tee time. Or, if you're in a group and one player is late, ask if the golf course staff can drive the player to your group on the course when he or she arrives. (I hope you won't have to face this situation, since it can be stressful for you and your other guests as you wait for a player to arrive minutes before your tee time. It also can throw off the tempo of the players.)

After greeting your guests, if you have time to hit balls, then head to the driving range. Place about fifteen to twenty range balls in the ball tray at each of your guests' hitting stalls, and keep some balls for yourself. If your guests don't have a warm up or stretching routine, go ahead with your routine anyway. You want to make sure you're comfortable and you don't want to hurt yourself. After practicing at the driving range, and if time permits, then you and your guests may want to practice at the putting green.

At the First Tee

Five to ten minutes before your tee time, invite your guests to the first tee. Give each guest a scorecard so he or she can keep his or her own score and also so that each player will know the yardage and layout of the course. If your company has logoed items such as tees, ball markers, or sleeves of balls, give these to your guests at the first tee. (I have my BizGolf Dynamics' logo on quarter-sized ball markers that I give to clients during a consultation on the course. It's a nice souvenir of our outing that will have repeat impressions.)

At the first tee, discuss which tees you and your guests want to play from. If you're playing with men, and there are four sets of tees, they'll likely choose the back or middle-back tees. They'll also expect you to play from the middle-forward or forward tees because you are a woman. I have had only one gentleman offer to join me on the middle-forward tees, rather than play from the tees men would typically play from. He explained that he hadn't played much recently, and it would be good practice for him. It left an impression on me that he would play from the so-called women's tees, without feeling he was somehow lessening his masculinity.

For more experienced female golfers who can hit the ball nearly as far as most male playing partners, hit from the back tees with your male guests. Most women, even very solid golfers, are surprised to hear this suggestion because they feel they're giving up the advantage of the forward tees. It's true that the women are giving up the distance that they would gain by playing the forward tees. But, the goal of business golf isn't to beat your playing partners or to shoot your lowest score—and it's definitely not to outdrive your sensitive male playing partners. Instead, your goal is to build rapport and strengthen the relationship with your playing partners.

By playing from the same tees as your male playing partners, you're always in the conversation. When you play from the forward tees, however, you may miss parts of the conversation as you walk to the tees and when your group waits for you to hit. The foursome also moves more smoothly off the tee when everyone begins from approximately the same area, rather than having to stop at the forward tee for you to hit. The other advantage of playing from the back tees is that you are sending a message of your confidence and desire to get to know the gentlemen.

Wait for the men to choose which tees they are going to play from, then say, "I want to get to know all of you better, and rather than stopping at the forward tees, I'll play from the same tees as you. I'll pick up if I'm holding us up." If they have decided to play from the back tees, then say you'll play from the middle-back tees—so you're at least closer to the group than if you played the forward tees. They'll likely be surprised and impressed with your confidence.

This technique is best used at a golf course where the different tees are not too far apart. At my course, for example, the difference in length between the middle-back and middle-forward tees is only 10 to 20 yards or less at many holes. So the disparity between our drives is not as great. Before trying this in a business golf round, practice playing from the back tees during recreational rounds to get comfortable with it. Like anything new, it will feel awkward at first. And don't get discouraged if you don't score as well when playing from the back tees—your goal for the business golf round is not to play your best golf ever, and a higher score is to be expected given the additional length.

When your playing partners can safely hit their drives, invite your guests to tee off first regardless of handicaps or honors.

During the Round and Nineteenth Hole Tips

As host, you should offer to buy refreshments and snacks at the snack bar or from the beverage cart. Your guests will probably offer to pay for these goodies as a way to reciprocate for being invited to play. If they seem insistent on doing so, let them pay, but make sure you pay for the nineteenth hole festivities.

Later in this chapter, I discuss more etiquette issues that specifically apply when you're playing business golf rounds.

Accepting a Business Golf Invitation

If you've been invited to play in a business golf round, here are some things you can do to graciously accept the invitation.

Clarify the Invitation

An uncomfortable situation can be avoided if you clarify if you are his or her guest. For example, if a client mentions he's playing at the expensive XYZ Golf Club on a given day and asks if you would like to join him, is he intending to pay your green and cart fees? Or is he asking if you would like to play with him, but you are expected to pay your own way? To determine whether you are his guest, ask, "How much are the green fees at XYZ Golf Club?" If he tells you the amount, then assume you will be paying your green fees. But if he intends to have you as a guest, he'll probably say, "Don't worry about it. You're my guest." Knowing this in advance can spare both of you a sticky situation at the beginning of the round.

Let Your Host Know Your Playing Ability

Your host may be creating a foursome and may want to have players of similar playing abilities. To avoid any confusion at the first tee because you are a beginner, let your host know that you're relatively new to the game. Again, without being apologetic, you can say, "Thank you for the invitation. Just so you know, I'm a beginner, but I know how to play ready golf and to keep up the pace. And, I'm sure we'll have a good time playing together." If you have a handicap index and a handicap at your home course, you can share that as well. Or, let him or her know that you're in the process of getting a handicap, and your average score. Again most experienced players don't mind playing with beginners if they know you won't disturb their game.

Confirm Your Tee Time

If your host doesn't confirm with you a few days before your outing, then you should do so. You want to avoid any possible misunderstanding about which golf course you're playing, the date and time, and where you are meeting. Make sure you arrive at least thirty minutes before your agreed meeting time.

Preparing for the Round

If it is possible and practical to do so, play a practice round at the golf course you've been invited to play. That way, you'll be more confident during your golf outing because you'll have a feel for the course and its difficulty. You can also decide whether you can play from the tees your male playing partners will likely play from.

Of course, if the golf course is a private country club, you probably won't be able to play a practice round because you are required to play with a member. You should still call the pro shop of the country club and ask the staff about the dress code (typically, no jeans, tee shirts, and shorts more than 5 inches above the knee are allowed), and spike requirements. You should also ask whether ladies can play on the day you and the member have agreed on.

Many country clubs still have restrictions on days and times when men or women can play. For example, at my golf club, women are not allowed to play during certain hours on Wednesdays—it's considered men's day. Likewise, men are not allowed to play on ladies' day between 7:30 A.M. and 11:00 A.M. on Thursdays. To avoid a potentially embarrassing situation because you aren't allowed to play, make sure you call the pro shop and confirm that you can do so on your planned day and time. Your host may have simply overlooked that you may not be able to play because of the gender restriction.

One advantage of not having played a course before is that it gives you the opportunity to engage your partner in dialogue about the course, creating a "we're-a-team" feel. Don't overdo this, however. I've seen people stand on a tee for several minutes studying the hole from every angle, and then hit a weak pop up 50 yards in front of the tee. Learn about the hole while playing ready golf.

Country Club Etiquette

While on the subject of playing golf at a country club, here are some additional etiquette tips that specifically apply in a country club setting:

- Carry your golf shoes in a shoe bag, and change into them in the women's locker room rather than in the parking lot. You can leave your street shoes in the locker room, and change back into them after your round. If the other players are doing the same, you can take your golf shoes and clubs back to your car before the nineteenth hole. Or, you can leave your shoes with your clubs near the pro shop. Make sure you clean your golf shoes with the shoe brushes mounted near the entrances before you enter the clubhouse or pro shop. Some clubs prohibit wearing golf shoes in the clubhouse.
- Use the bag drop when you arrive at the golf course. Tip the bag boy or bag girl a couple of dollars. Mention the name of the member that you're playing with and your tee time.
- If you arrive before the member who invited you, let the pro shop staff know that you are meeting the member as his or her guest and you have a tee time.
- In the clubhouse, beware of men-only areas, such as bars, card rooms, or cigar rooms. Check with the pro shop staff to learn if there are any such areas at the club.
- Most country clubs do not accept credit cards for food and beverages. Members typically charge items to their accounts and pay at the end of the month. Bring extra cash to pay for refreshments and snacks.
- Some country clubs prohibit the use of cell phones in the clubhouse. If you need to make a few brief phone calls before starting the nineteenth hole festivities, preferably while your host is doing the same, ask where you may use your cell phone.
- Make favorable comments about the condition or layout of the golf course, as well as the quality of service or food. Your member-host will appreciate that you've noticed.

. . . .

Anyone who criticizes a golf course is like a person invited to a house for dinner who, on leaving, tells the host that the food was lousy.

Gary Player, Senior PGA Tour Player

. . . .

During the Round

Besides following the basic etiquette of playing golf, here are some suggestions to ensure that you and your partners have a pleasant experience playing your round of business golf. These etiquette tips are appropriate for all rounds of golf, but are especially true when playing with business associates.

. . . .

In a USA Today *survey, 92.4 percent of golfers responded that they are very aware of golf etiquette; 76.4 percent responded that golf etiquette is very important to them.*

Source: USA Today, October 15, 1999

. . . .

Appear Professional

How you appear makes a lasting impression. Wear golf clothing that is comfortable to play golf in, but also projects your professional image. A nice pair of golf slacks or shorts and a polo shirt work well. Wear your company's logoed golf shirt or hat, but don't wear too many logo items. Clean your golf shoes and clubs before your round of golf. Make sure you play with white golf balls, rather than pink balls or X-outs. Mark your balls with a permanent marker so you'll be able to identify them, especially if others in your group are playing with the same type.

Avoid Using Cell Phones and Pagers

For some of you, having access to your cell phone and pager is the only way you can escape from the office. Before you leave the office, you should update your e-mail and voice mail greeting announcing that you will be in a client meeting most of the day and will not be available to return messages until late in the day or the next morning. If you have a contact for emergencies, give that person's name and contact information as part of your greeting.

If you need to keep in touch with your office, be sensitive to how cell phones and pagers can intrude on the relationship you are trying to build on the golf course. Consider the golf course a sanctuary of a lesser sort, and leave your cell phone and pager in your car or at least set them on the silent mode. Or you can use a text pager with a silent mode that takes messages that you can reply to with a text message or defer to callbacks after the round.

. . . .

Before you step onto the golf course, turn your cell phone and pager off, or set them on vibrate or silent mode.

. . . .

Remember, you're trying to enjoy the beauty and serenity of the golf course and a day away from the office. The ringing of a cell phone can disturb one of your playing partners during his or her golf swing. It's also rude to take a phone call when you're trying to build a relationship with your golf partners. Just as you would hold your calls in the office during a meeting, do the same on the golf course. A few private clubs have even prohibited the use of cell phones on the golf course.

Beware of Betting

Don't suggest a wager on the round of business golf. Even the smallest bet often adds an unwelcome competitive atmosphere to the round, which can interfere with getting to know each other better. However, if your playing partners suggest a wager, agree and consider asking the reason for the bet. Does a bet help them stay more focused? Do they enjoy the competition and like to win something if they play well, regardless of the amount? This helps you get to know your guests' personalities and business styles.

If your group decides to bet, wager an amount you can afford to lose. I suggest you ask, "What's the maximum I can lose?" Then, assume you've lost the bet. This helps you focus on building business relationships rather than winning. You'll be more relaxed and will enjoy the round without worrying about your score.

In Chapter 5, I describe some of the common betting games and the pitfalls of betting.

Remember That Business Golf Is Business

Just as you would during a business meeting or lunch, watch your alcohol consumption, language, and jokes. You want to have a good time with your playing partners, but it's still business. Someone once told me the story of a colleague who played with a salesperson before they had signed a contract. The salesperson made the mistake of thinking the deal was already signed and the golf round was a celebratory outing. He used inappropriate language, drank too much, and then wondered why his prospect decided not to do business with him. Don't let that happen to you.

Focus on Building Relationships

To learn more about your playing partners, ask questions about their backgrounds just as you would in an office meeting: How long in the industry? What attracted you to your company or industry? Where were you born and raised?

Also ask about their golf games: Why do you play? Who introduced you to the game? Do you consider it competition against yourself or others? Do you play to relax and have fun? How often do you get to play? Would you say your golf game relates to how you do business? If so, how? What's your favorite golf course? Do you take golf vacations?

Conversation during the round is desirable, but it's also important to understand that silence between you and your playing partners will naturally occur. Although you're building rapport with one another, having some silence as you're riding in the cart or walking in between shots is just a short break in your conversation. Remember, you have almost five hours together, so you have time to pace your conversations. No one likes a chatterbox.

Be a Team Player

Whether you're in sales or are an attorney, you want others to know that you work well with people and intend to provide quality client or customer service. You can show that level of attention to others while you're on the golf course. For example, help your playing partners track their shots and look for lost balls. Offer to tell them distances if you're near yardage markers. If you've finished playing a hole and your playing partners have left clubs on or near the green, pick up their clubs for them. Replace the flagstick more often than you would in a casual round of golf. Manage the golf cart with your cart partner.

If you're familiar with the layout of a golf course and your group is walking, suggest places where they can leave their bags, and take the clubs they need for the next hole. They will likely appreciate a break from carrying their bags when they can pick them up as they walk to the next hole.

You can also take this a step further by cheering for your partner when he or she hits a good shot or makes a nice putt. A positive "Nice shot!" from you, along with an occasional high-five, go a long way toward cementing a "we're-a-team" atmosphere. Like everything else, though, don't overdo this.

Be an Enjoyable Playing Partner

Here are even more ways to be an enjoyable playing partner:

- Hit it and move on! If you're not playing as well as you know you can, don't let it affect your mood and interaction with your partners. Remember, it's not your score that is important. People don't like to play with others who are not enjoying the round. Play ready golf and keep up the pace. Pick up if you're having a bad hole or if you're slowing your foursome. Don't apologize or give excuses for your shots or if you're not playing well. Another saying, "Miss it quick!"
- Stay aware of your playing partners! Know where everyone is at all times, who's hitting and where their balls and ball markers are. This will help you avoid getting in anyone's line, whether on the fairway or the putting green.
- Compliment good shots and empathize if your playing partners are upset about their bad shots. A simple "Nice shot!" or "Bad break." is enough. Some players don't like to have their shots overembellished. It's safer to be understated with your comments. You'll get a sense of how they feel about their shots by watching how they describe your shots.
- Never give unsolicited advice about your playing partners' golf swings. If they're struggling with their game, use humor to try to help them relax or say nothing since they probably feel bad enough.
- Likewise, be wary about accepting advice directed to you. The driving range is the place to practice, not while playing on the course. You can graciously accept advice, though, by saying for example, "Yes, that's an area I need to work on when I practice next."
- Take care of the golf course: Fix your divots and ball marks on the green. After hitting out of bunkers, rake the sand and replace the rake in the bunker.

- Shake hands after everyone has left the eighteenth green even if you're headed for the nineteenth hole together. Tell your playing partners that you enjoyed playing with them. Remember to post your score. And check to see if your playing partners are going to change into their street shoes and put their clubs away, so you can do the same. You're then ready for the nineteenth hole.
- Watch your behavior, attitude, and body language on the golf course and afterward. Behavior that's inappropriate in a conference room is also inappropriate on the course. In Chapter 5, I discuss what you can learn about your playing partners by observing how they play golf. Be aware that they're likely watching you as well.

Nineteenth Hole Tips

After playing a round of business golf, expect to continue the good feelings in the nineteenth hole and also by concluding the day with some business discussions. If you played with more than one person, don't sit at the bar; it's easier to talk to one another at a table. If you were the host of the day, plan on buying refreshments and food for your guests; if a guest, offer to pay for the first round.

If a wager was made during the round and you lost, it's time to pay up! You don't want a reputation of not honoring your word by not paying your bets. If you won, don't gloat. Share your winnings and buy some refreshments and snacks.

A word of caution about drinking alcohol immediately after playing. Your body can get dehydrated after playing a round of golf, even if you were riding a cart, so drink at least a glass of water before having any alcohol. I've felt the effects of only one beer after a round. Remember, it's business and you want to keep your professional composure.

· ·

You can lose up to a gallon of perspiration during a round of golf. While playing eighteen holes of golf, you should drink up to a gallon of water. On very hot days, you should drink water before you tee off so you don't become dehydrated while playing.

· ·

Golfers love to relive and talk about their good shots. Bring up a good shot or a hole by your playing partners. They'll enjoy talking about it, and they'll likely bring up your good shots. Even if you don't feel you played as well as they did, accept their compliments graciously. It's also the time to find out if their playing style reflects their business style. For example, you can ask, "I noticed you laid up on the fifth hole, rather than trying to go over the water. Do you tend to be more conservative in your business decisions as well?"

As the talk about golf winds down, you or one of your playing partners may raise a business topic. If a playing partner made a business comment during the round, now is the time to ask him or her to elaborate. If a detailed business discussion doesn't seem appropriate because the mood is jovial from golf or everyone is feeling fatigued, then still consider your business golf outing a success. As you're concluding your outing, exchange common courtesies, and mention that you would like to follow up with a call within the week to set up a meeting to discuss business.

Follow Up after Your Round

Sending handwritten thank you notes seems to have become a lost art. I always take notice when someone takes the time to thank me with a handwritten note, and I certainly enjoy sharing my appreciation for a person's effort and consideration. As a guest, make sure you send a thank you note. But even if you were the host, send a note to your guests. It's another chance for you to get your name and company in front of them. And it shows you value their time, as well as the opportunity to know them better.

If you prefer not to send a handwritten note, at least follow up with a thank you e-mail. This gives the person an opportunity to send you a quick reply with his or her own acknowledgment and comments. Your e-mail can also suggest a follow-up time for a phone call or meeting.

You played golf together to deepen your business relationship. If you mentioned that you intend to call or follow up within a week after your outing, by all means do so. You've created the setting for your call to be taken or immediately returned. Even if you were thanking a client for past business, you've reinforced your business relationship and can reasonably expect to continue working with him or her.

Work Smart and Play More

I hope that after reading this chapter you've seen how easy it is to play a business golf round, and that you're intending to play more business golf. If you are experiencing a slow period at work, consider playing more business golf to deepen existing business relationships, brainstorm with colleagues on how to increase business, or possibly meet new clients. Rather than react with fear to an economic downturn, take action and create new opportunities for your business.

As you saw from the ways some businesswomen have used golf, you can enjoy different types of success from playing business golf. And even if you don't have a noticeable "win" soon after your round of golf, such as signing a contract or gaining a new client, you still enjoyed the FREEDOM benefits of playing for your professional and personal well-being.

Staying On Course

_____ Understand that when you can hit the ball consistently and can play with proper etiquette and an understanding of the basic rules of golf, you're ready to play business golf.

_____ A business golf round can only be nine holes at an executive course. Play with those who have encouraged you to learn to play and who understand that you're a beginner.

_____ Set up business golf practice sessions at the driving range. You'll deepen your business relationships and can practice your swing and putting.

_____ Set a goal for your business golf round. Whether it is to say thank you, network, brainstorm ideas, or meet prospects, remember the goal during your golf outing.

_____ When hosting a foursome for a business golf round, consider your goal for the round, the personalities, the golf experience, and common business interests of your prospective guests. Remember, you can invite one, two, or three others to play. Consider who should share a golf cart with whom.

_____ When inviting guests, let them know your playing ability, that you play with proper etiquette, and know how to play ready golf.

_____ Select a golf course that is challenging, yet not too difficult for you and your guests. Mention to your guests any clothing and spike requirements.

_____ Choose a tee time convenient for you and your guests. After lunch or late afternoon tee times let you and your guests work half of the day. Make sure everyone has time for refreshments after the round in the nineteenth hole.

_____ Confirm your outing with your guests several days in advance of your scheduled date. Send a note or an e-mail with specifics on the date, time, the golf course's name and location, and where you're meeting at the course.

_____ Arrive early at the golf course to pay green and cart rental fees.

_____ You may play from different tees than your guests. Of, if your game warrants it, consider playing from the same tees as your guest. Explain that you want to get to know them better, it's easier than stopping at the forward tees, and that you'll pick up when necessary. Don't worry about your score. Instead, you want to make sure everyone has a good time playing together.

_____ If you've been invited to a business golf round, clarify your playing ability and whether you should expect to pay your green fee. If invited to a country club, confirm that you can play on the day of your outing, and the dress and spike requirements. Be aware of etiquette particular to country clubs.

_____ Keep your business conversation to a minimum while playing. If you must talk business, do so during the middle of the round—between holes six and thirteen. Take cues from your guest or host on whether to discuss business topics.

_____ Your business golf round is business. Appear professional—from your clothing to your equipment. Turn your cell phone and pager off or set them on vibrate or silent mode. Watch your language, alcohol consumption, and jokes.

_____ Focus on building relationships, and on being a team player and an enjoyable playing partner.

_____ Keep the good feelings going in the nineteenth hole. If you lost a bet, make sure you pay the winners. Use the nineteenth hole to discuss business and establish ongoing contact.

_____ Whether a host or guest of a business golf round, send a thank you note. It's another chance to make contact with your playing partners and follow up with any unfinished business.

CHAPTER 5

Avoid Getting Teed Off

Women attending my presentations often mention that they are intimidated by playing with strangers, especially men. As you start to play more, you'll have a variety of experiences playing with both women and men—some good and some otherwise.

This chapter gives you a preview of what commonly occurs during a round with men and women. Just as with starting a new job or visiting a foreign country, you may be nervous and anxious about your encounters with strangers, regardless of your confidence and abilities. This chapter prepares you for what might occur to lessen any apprehension that you might have about playing golf. You'll also have a chance to consider how you would handle a particular situation should it arise in the future.

Are You Wanted in the Foursome?

Playing with Men

Many of the businessmen that I spoke with wish that more women played golf, especially for business reasons. They've experienced how playing golf has helped them in their businesses and careers and would like women to share these benefits as well. Some said that they enjoyed playing with women more than with other men because it is often a more relaxed and less competitive round of golf. They get tired of having to compete with the other guys—whether it is the distance of their drives or their scores.

Several men also said that they enjoy watching women play golf. Some like seeing women's athleticism and confidence when playing. Other men find it sexy to watch a woman play, especially if she's a good player. One male golfer's comment proves my point when he jokingly asked me on the second tee whether I would marry him. The gentleman said, "You're every male golfer's dream. You're attractive, smart, and can play golf well. When can we get married?" I'm still single and searching for Mr. Right, but you get my point.

Unfortunately, there are other men who still believe that GOLF stands for "gentlemen only, ladies forbidden." They're dated in how they think, since women constitute the fastest growing segment of new golfers. With more women playing (especially after reading this book) and more golf course owners and equipment manufacturers targeting women, perhaps men with that mentality will become enlightened in the near future.

You may meet some of these gentlemen on the first tee and not be given the most gentlemanlike welcome. You may see them roll their eyes, flash a look of annoyance, or, in their most extreme reaction, they may return to the starter and demand to be put in another foursome.

Assuming that you've never met these men before, they're obviously behaving this way only because you're a woman. They don't know you, so they have no other reason not to want to play with you. Some men are afraid that you'll play slowly, or don't know the etiquette. Or, they may wish they could simply play without having to worry about a woman in earshot of their swearing and jokes.

Let's say you're at the first tee and you get a sense that the players are less than pleased to be paired with you. Here are some suggestions on how to handle the situation. As you would with any players you've never met, introduce yourself and give each player a firm handshake. Then, say something along the lines of, "I'm a beginner, but I know how to keep up the pace. I'll pick up when I need to." Don't sound apologetic; say this in a matter-of-fact tone. You can also announce that you'll be playing from the forward tees.

By letting the players know your skill level and golf knowledge, you should allay their fears of slow play and put them at ease about your joining their foursome. After watching you play a hole or two with the proper etiquette and pace of play, they'll likely forget their worries about playing with you and you'll have an enjoyable round together.

Even if you are playing with etiquette and keeping up, it's still possible that they may never warm to the fact that you're playing with them. You might notice that they don't include you in their conversations or compliment your shots. Or, if your foursome is walking, they might forget that you're playing from the forward tees and walk ahead before you hit, or they might not walk with you. What should you do? First, make sure you don't hit them with your drive. If they walk in front of you before you hit, jokingly announce, "Player on the tee!" That should catch their attention. Then, to include yourself in the group, ask your male partners questions. Or, if you're feeling introverted, you can imagine that you're playing by yourself, yet remain cordial and play appropriately. It's more likely, though, that they'll eventually ask you questions about who you are and what you do.

In any case, I certainly wouldn't take their behavior personally. It's their loss if they don't want to get to know you. Besides, you probably aren't missing much if they're behaving in such a manner. If it's really uncomfortable for you, then play only nine holes with this group and at the turn check with the starter to see if you can join another group behind you that is only a threesome or call it a day.

Playing with Women

It's doubtful that you'll get this type of brush-off if you join a group of women. They'll probably be thrilled to have you join them. If you have a reputation for being a slow player or of not knowing the rules, however, you may feel some tension in the air about your joining them, just as you would with men. Or, if you're considered too talkative, they might not enjoy playing with you. Part of enjoying the game is knowing when to be silent and to take in the serenity of the course.

Do You Have to Be a Good Golfer?

Playing with Men

In Chapter 1, I talked about the fear many women have about needing to be a "good enough golfer" before playing with strangers or for business purposes. By now you know it's more important to play appropriately, rather than being able to drive the ball long. At a minimum, you should be able to hit the ball consistently.

It may surprise you to learn that most men have fairly low expectations about how well women can play. They understand that most women started playing recently and were likely not raised playing sports. Men really don't expect women to be able to play well or know much about the game. It seems that women's fears are self-created about how well they need to play—perhaps out of this perception that women aren't welcome on the golf course. Instead most men seem to be pleasantly surprised if a woman can make good contact with the ball.

. . . .

Median Handicap Index: men, 15; women, 28.

Source: USGA

. . . .

By the way, when talking about their wish for more women to play, many men said most men aren't good golfers either, and women shouldn't even worry about having to play well. Instead, they should just go out and play!

Playing with Women

If you're a beginner and join a foursome of more experienced women golfers, they'll understand if you aren't able to hit the ball as far or have to take a few extra putts. But experienced women golfers, like any experienced golfers, will likely become impatient with you if you take three or four practice swings, or if you don't know the etiquette. You can have a preshot routine of taking aim and preparing to hit, but keep it brief. If experienced women golfers know you are a beginner, they may ask if they can offer you some tips on proper etiquette or how to play ready golf. If it will help you play more appropriately, be open to their comments. You might make some new friends to play with in future rounds.

Advice Giving

Playing with Men

When women aren't playing well, some men offer unsolicited swing tips. If you're practicing at the driving range before going out to play, you may have men, perhaps your clients or prospects, offer you pointers such as: "You should grip the club this way," or "You're standing too far away from the ball." Then, while playing on the course, you'll get a couple of suggestions that contradict what you were told on the driving range. The problem with receiving all these tips is that often they're wrong or confusing. And, while you're on the golf course, you should *not* be thinking about different swing tips; you should be focusing on hitting to certain targets and your overall enjoyment of the round.

. . . .

No one can make you feel inferior without your consent.

Eleanor Roosevelt

. . . .

It's frustrating and distracting to have your swing critiqued on every hole. If you encounter advice givers, whether strangers or clients, assume that they only mean well in wanting to help you improve and play better. They offer advice because they've been playing longer, read the latest golf magazines, or perhaps they're simply hardwired to want to help women. When men are playing golf with other men, you'll seldom hear them give another male player swing advice.

Rarely should you take any kind of swing advice on the course, especially when the golfers aren't very good themselves. Instead, it's best to thank them politely and hope they stop after their first suggestion. If they continue with their generosity, then you need to casually say, "I really don't like to change anything in my swing without talking to my golf professional. If I have a question about my swing, I'll ask." By saying this, you should put an end to their advice giving. If not, then you may have to be more assertive the next time you decline their advice.

Playing with Women

Rarely will a woman give unsolicited swing tips to you, and few would ever consider giving a tip to a man. Perhaps it is because most women have gone through the frustration of being told what to change in their swing, and they would never subject another to that type of harangue.

What if You're Too Good?

Playing with Men

Businessmen have said that they are impressed if they know a woman plays golf, regardless of how well she plays. They sense that a woman golfer must be comfortable with being around men as well as with her physical abilities, and that she has a high level of confidence about herself. If you're a good golfer, most men will enjoy seeing you outdrive them or sink a long putt. They'll respect you as a golfer and that respect will likely carry over into the business arena.

However, some male egos may be threatened if a woman can outdrive them. For example, Meriby is a long hitter off the tee. She often plays from the middle tees, rather than the forward tees. When playing as a single, she is usually paired with men, who play from the back tees, since she is playing from the middle tees. As the day progresses, Meriby can hit the ball off the tee even longer. By the end of the day, she is outdriving the men from the tee, and it frazzles them. They'll swing faster and harder, trying to hit the ball longer than Meriby. But the harder they swing, the worse their games fall apart, while Meriby laughs to herself as she hits her ball down the middle of the fairway.

If you're playing a round of business golf with a male associate and you're playing better than he is, hope he doesn't become competitive and upset. That would defeat the purpose of your golf outing, which was to build a better business relationship. If you see that he's trying to swing harder or is getting frustrated, make a comment in a joking manner to try to diffuse the situation: "Hey, let's not worry about our golf shots, let's just enjoy that we're out of our offices." A comment such as this should help him put the round in perspective and lighten up about how well you're playing.

Playing with Women

Most women will be thrilled to see another woman play well. If you're a better golfer than most women, many will likely tell you that they wish they could play as well as you can. I've had several women say to me, "In my next life, I want to be able to play like you." They wish they had the strength or age on their side, or the advantage of starting at a young age. As the stronger player, it's helpful to make other women players feel comfortable playing with you and not be a competitive threat. Rarely will women think another woman golfer is too good. Most women don't seem to be as competitive against one another as men are.

Psyching Each Other Out

Playing with Men

"Golf is a mental game." What people are referring to is that you'll play well if your mind is not interfering with your physical abilities. For example, some people have what are called the "yips" when they attempt to make short putts, especially if it's a pressure putt for the win. Rather than taking a smooth swing, they jerk their putter and miss the short putt because they're nervous. Or, when they need to make a shot over a bunker, they'll tighten their grip and not take a relaxed swing, so they hit the ball into the bunker.

When playing with men in your foursome, don't be surprised if you hear them goad each other on or try to psych each other out. Male golfers who play together often, and likely have a wager on the round, will play mental games with their playing partners hoping they'll make each other miss their shots. For example, an attorney was playing with one of his friends. At the tee, the friend hit first and drove the ball well. He then turned to the attorney and said, "Let's see you outdrive that one!" He was challenging the attorney—hoping to make him swing harder and miss his shot. Instead, the attorney hit a great drive and his ball went beyond his friend's drive.

If a playing partner hits a bad shot, his male friends may laugh out loud and make sarcastic comments about him and his shot. The most humiliating shot a male golfer can make when playing with his buddies is to drive a ball that doesn't reach the forward tees. He'll get tremendous grief for hitting such a lousy, weak drive!

. . . .

You swing your best when you have the fewest things to think about.

Bobby Jones

. . . .

Another way of psyching out a playing partner is to call his attention to the hazard that he should avoid hitting into on his next shot. Let's say there's a lake or out of bounds (OB) that he could hit his ball into. A playing partner might casually say, "Don't hit into the lake over there," or "Watch out for the OB on the left!" Rather than being helpful, the playing partner is actually trying to get him to focus his thoughts on the lake or the OB to make him hit a bad shot into the lake or OB.

Let's say that I said to you, "Don't visualize an elephant." What do you immediately see? An elephant! So, be careful about what you say before someone hits his or her ball. If you want players to avoid trouble, tell them what they *should do*, rather than what they should not do. For example, if a hazard is on the right side of the fairway, then you can say, "Hit it down the middle." To be safe though, it's best not to say anything before someone takes a swing.

When men do this type of jabbing at one another, it's usually all in jest and fun. Everyone is fair game, and it is part of their ritual when they get together and play. Don't worry though—if you're playing with them as a single, they will likely spare you their torment.

Playing with Women

Women who are beginners and don't play a lot of competitive golf don't try to psych each other out. Instead, they're usually very supportive and sympathetic about their golf games. For them, playing golf with other women is a social experience and a chance to get some fresh air and exercise.

More experienced golfers, those who play in tournaments or on their golf club's team, tend to be more competitive, and some will play mental games.

For example, I played in a match with my father as my partner against two women. One of the women would hit first off of the tee, and then I'd hit after her. On several holes after she hit, she would say, "I'm glad that I cleared the bunker," or "I stayed away from the trees," as I was stepping onto the tee to hit. I suspect she was trying to play mind games, so I would hit into the bunker or trees. Or, some women will try to encourage you to hit a good shot when they're insidiously playing mind games. They'll say in a sweet, sympathetic voice, "Oh, don't worry, I know you'll hit it over that lake."

If someone plays these games with you before you take a swing, refocus on your target, and make sure you relax your hands and arms. You'll hit a good shot—and it'll only be sweeter because you know what you had to overcome!

Friendly Wagers

Playing with Men

Joking and psyching each other out among men usually occurs because they have a bet on the round. In general, men tend to wager on the course more often than women do. Why do they bet? Some men say betting helps them stay sharp and concentrate better because something is on the line. Others say it's just more fun. The wager doesn't have to be large. It can be a $1 a hole, lunch, or drinks afterward.

There is a myriad of golf betting games. Some foursomes create their own games, ones that you've never heard of. Here are a few of the more common betting games that golfers play:

- *Low net.* The player who shoots the lowest eighteen-hole score less his or her handicap is the winner.
- *Low gross.* The player who shoots the lowest score is the winner. Handicaps are irrelevant in this format, so it's most often played by players with more or less equal and low handicaps
- *Nassau.* In this game, there are three bets: (1) The lowest net score for the front nine holes, (2) the lowest net score for the back nine, and (3) the lowest net score for eighteen holes. Let's say, for example, that the foursome is playing a $5 Nassau. The most someone could win or lose is $15, or $5 for each of the three bets. Or, someone could win or lose as little as $5.
- *Skins.* In Skins, each hole is worth a certain amount of money. If the group is playing $1 Skins or $1 per hole, then the player with the lowest net score on a hole wins $1 from each player. If there is a tie and no one wins a particular hole, then the $1 Skin is carried over to the next hole,

which is now worth $2. Skins can be quite exciting—and quite nerve-wracking. Standing over a putt with $1 on the line is one thing; standing over a similar length putt with $10 or $12 on the line is something else.

- *Bingo, Bango, Bongo.* Points are awarded for:

   The first ball on the green, which is bingo.

   The closest shot to the flagstick, which is bango.

   The first player to hit the ball in the hole (or the player who sinks the longest putt or who sinks his or her first putt), which is bongo.

The winner is the person with the most points at the end of eighteen holes. The wager is an agreed on amount per point based on the difference between the player with the most points and the total points of each player. Bingo, Bango, Bongo is a good game for foursomes with a mix of low and high handicap players because it tends to give everyone a good chance to score points.

If you're playing as a single and are asked to join in on a friendly game with strangers, should you bet? If you're new to the game, and you just want to enjoy playing without the added pressure of a bet, then decline betting. If you're up for a bit of additional pressure, then you should consider it.

A word of caution: You need to be aware that some golfers are called *sandbaggers*—they have higher handicaps than their playing ability would otherwise suggest and you may not be able to verify their handicaps. They have inflated handicaps, so they can get more strokes and improve their chances of winning.

. . . .

According to a USA Today survey, 65.5 percent of those who responded believe when golfers misrepresent their handicaps, the error is to inflate their handicaps.
Source: USA Today, January 13, 1999

. . . .

Before anyone tees off on the first tee, you may hear haggling over each player's handicap, whether or not it is too high, or someone will give reasons why he should have more strokes (he hasn't played in a month or his back is tight, etc.). Recall that your handicap on a golf course depends on your index and the slope of the course that you're playing. However, it's also likely that the people you're playing with don't adjust their handicaps according to their index and the slope.

Given all of this, I would ask for the rules of the game they are proposing and the maximum amount you can lose under the format that they're playing. If you're comfortable with the amount, then go for it! Otherwise, just enjoy your round and let the other players deal with the machinations of keeping track of their bets.

If you're playing with friends and the wager is small, then join in on the bet. Some women have said that by not betting, they have felt left out of the foursome. The other players who are betting joke with one another and there's a sense of camaraderie even though they are opponents. If the wager is small and you're comfortable with losing that amount, then bet and join in on the fun. If betting gets you uptight and too serious about your game, then assume you've lost the bet, so you can relax and have a good time during the round. By doing so, you will probably play better and win.

If you're playing in a business golf round, however, discourage betting. The smallest wager can bring out competitive tendencies in players and create a win–lose atmosphere. Since your goal during the round is to get to know one another better and build rapport and trust, betting may defeat your purpose.

If someone insists on a bet, then limit the wager to a small amount and suggest one of the team formats below. By playing as a team, a defeat or win isn't as personal and there is camaraderie created between the two partners. Here are a few team formats that you can play:

- *Low net of the team.* The highest and lowest handicap players are paired as a team against the two middle handicap players. The team with the lowest net total of the team scores is the winner.
- *Change partners.* You start with one partner for the first six holes, then you have another for the second six holes, and the remaining player is your partner for the final six holes. The longest driver on the first tee decides which player is his or her partner. Then on the seventh hole, the person with the longest drive chooses his or her partner, and so on. You never have the same partner twice. You receive a point if you are on the team with the lowest net score for each hole and the player with the most points at the end of the round is the winner. Even though you're playing in a team format, the winner is an individual.

Here's another word of caution: Avoid accepting a *press*, which is a bet added in an ad-hoc fashion somewhere in the round. Some players who are behind on one bet want to make a press bet in an attempt to win back the amount they might lose—and then some. Press bets can become complicated to keep track of, and they can significantly increase the amount that you could win or lose.

Always remember that if you lose a bet, you need to pay off the bet in the nineteenth hole. If you win, great! You can graciously share your winnings and offer to buy refreshments for everyone.

Playing with Women

Women aren't as likely to bet against one another as men are. They probably don't because they play to enjoy the game and socialize with friends. For others, it's too much of a bother to figure out the points and bets when they need to focus on counting their strokes.

Playing by the Rules

Playing with Men

Some golfers are purists. They don't believe in mulligans, gimmes, or rules that change with the seasons. There are no such things as "Winter Rules" or "Summer Rules." (By the way, you play the ball down under "Summer Rules" as you would following the rules of golf.) The purists play by the thirty-four rules of golf and see no reason not to do so.

Gary is a mortgage banker and a golf purist. He thinks that if you don't play by the rules, then you're not playing golf. During his business golf rounds, he watched other players bump their balls to improve their lie. He finally asked a few of them why they did so, knowing, of course, the answer in advance. Rather than make a scene, Gary decided to play a couple of rounds under *their* rules. He said, "I hated it. It didn't make a bit of difference in how I played. If anything, I played worse knowing that I wasn't playing according to the rules of golf."

Gary is in the minority of most recreational golfers. According to Mark Russell, the PGA Tour Rules official (Golfweb.com, April 18, 2000, interview), an estimated less than 2 percent of the 26.7 million casual golfers actually understand the rules. Beginners and those not serious about the game tend to focus on their swings. They don't take the time to learn the rules, so they don't play by them. As you play more, I believe it's important for you to know the basic rules of golf. You'll play according to them or at least know when you're not, and you'll know when someone isn't playing by the rules when they should.

Serious male golfers who bet often or play in competitions seem to be more aware of the rules and the need to follow them more carefully. Here's what golf purists would consider as not playing by the rules:

- *Gimmes.* Some men can be very generous in giving and even asking for gimmes—the short putts that it's presumed you'll make. One problem with accepting too many liberal gimmees is you lose practice in making short putts. Then when you need to make one in competition, under pressure, you won't feel comfortable and may be more likely to miss. Also, if you take too many gimmees, you're underestimating your score and that may lower your handicap inappropriately.

- *Bumping the ball.* As Gary saw, some men bump the ball to improve their lie. Bumping can significantly help a player with his or her shot— especially if the ball has landed in a divot.
- *Kicking the ball in bounds.* If a ball is out of bounds, then the player is supposed to hit another ball from where he or she just hit and take a one-stroke penalty. Some players may use the *foot wedge* or *shoe wedge* and kick the ball in bounds.
- *Counting strokes.* You're supposed to count all strokes and add penalty strokes for each hole. Some men give themselves a score that they *should have had*, rather than their actual score, plus penalty strokes. Or they may inadvertently forget to count every stroke.
- *Inaccurate handicaps.* You may play with someone who claims to have a low handicap, yet his score when you play together is much higher than his handicap. If he's a good golfer, you can usually tell by his swing that he is having an off day. Several women told me that they have played with men who claim to have low handicaps. Then, when they played together, they realized that these men couldn't have such low handicaps. The men lowered their handicaps to make themselves look good. Meriby plays with one man who doesn't keep score. Yet, when he plays an easy course, he posts a 97, and if the course is more difficult, he posts a 98. The chance of his handicap being accurate is about the same as having a hole in one!

Playing with Women

Since many women are new to the game, they probably have not taken the time to learn the rules. Therefore, women beginners may violate the rules out of ignorance. Women golfers who have been playing since they were young or play in tournaments often tend to know the rules better.

Some women can take the rules too far, however. I was told about a woman at my club who had a reputation for being a stickler about the rules to the point of being ridiculous. If you were playing a match with her and were trying to determine whose ball was farthest away to hit first on the putting green, she would take out a measuring tape. Needless to say, she wasn't well liked and had a hard time getting a game. Eventually she left the club.

There is a cartoon that says it all. Four women are on the first tee; the caption reads: "Shall we play by men's rules, or will we count every stroke?"

Stogies, Swearing, and Scotch

Playing with Men

Stogies

Some men smoke cigars while they're playing because they're probably not allowed to do so at home. It's part of the pleasure of playing for them, even though they might not really enjoy the cigar. Linda, the telecommunications consultant, doesn't smoke, but she'll give male prospects or clients cigars before teeing off if she knows they'll enjoy them. You can usually buy cigars at the pro shop, snack bars, or on the beverage carts, or bring them with you if you've purchased them elsewhere.

It would be considerate if men asked before lighting up their cigars if you would mind the smoke, but if they don't, simply try to avoid the smoke. This is fairly easy to do since you're outdoors and the course is so spacious. If you're walking with a cigar smoker, walk on the upwind side. If your cart partner lights up, ask if he could hold the cigar outside the cart. If you're allergic to the smoke, then certainly tell your partner so, and most likely he'll offer not to smoke. Otherwise, ask him not to do so.

. . . .

They call it golf because all of the other four-letter words are taken.

Raymond Floyd

. . . .

Swearing

Bad golf shots can bring out the worst in people. Even those who ordinarily are calm and mild mannered can get frustrated and upset while playing. So don't be surprised if you hear a few swear words. Understand that such fury is only directed at themselves and is unlikely to have anything to do with you.

You may also hear a few jokes that you find offensive. I am not a fanatic of political correctness and will likely not confront someone about a joke that I find inappropriate or tasteless. If I don't like a man's sense of humor, I just consider it a reflection of who he is as a person and don't get personally offended.

If a man's swearing or offensive joke really bothers you, then you can bring it to his attention tactfully and see how he responds. Katherine, a financial advisor, did so with a colleague and he immediately stopped his inappropriate behavior.

Scotch

Some men also enjoy imbibing spirits while they play, especially when in a tournament. Having a beer or two is common during a round of golf. Some might go so far as to have a flask of scotch or tequila in their bag. Robin is the president of a Silicon Valley company. During one round, the men she was playing with offered her a cigar and some scotch. She accepted because she loves a good cigar and scotch. She was even tested to see if she smoked the cigar correctly (I don't know from experience, but I've been told that you slowly twirl the cigar as you inhale to get an even burn at the end.). She said she was one of the boys, and the scotch and cigars were just part of the game and conversation.

If you're playing a round of golf for business, you obviously need to watch whether you can handle your alcohol on the golf course. Keep in mind that your body may be dehydrated from playing, so you will feel the effects of the alcohol much more quickly.

Speaking of fluids, I think it's worth warning you about how men handle their fluid management when drinking. On newer golf courses and resort courses, the course designers (thankfully) have built bathrooms, or at least installed portable toilets, on the golf course, say, at the fifth and the thirteenth holes. At older golf courses, however, you'll likely find bathrooms only at the clubhouse, pro shop, and at the turn. Except for these central locations, you'll seldom have bathrooms located on older courses. At these courses, men in desperation may resort to the trees and bushes to do their business.

If you're with a group of men on an older course, you may suddenly notice that one of the guys is missing from your group. Rather than ask his whereabouts or worry that aliens have abducted him, just know that he had to sneak into the bushes to relieve himself. The awkward moment for you will be on the eighteenth green when you're expected to follow tradition and shake hands with each of your playing partners. You know where at least one guy's hands have been, so what should you do? Since you should wash your hands after playing anyway, be a sport! Be polite and shake hands with him, then you can go to the ladies' room to clean up.

Playing with Women

Stogies

Although most women, unlike Robin, do not enjoy a cigar, some women smoke cigarettes on the golf course when they otherwise don't smoke. Perhaps, while on the golf course, they can relax and enjoy their cigarettes.

Swearing

You'll hear some women swear like the guys on the golf course, yet you'd never hear them utter a swear word off the course. As I said, sometimes the golf course can bring out the worst in people.

Scotch

I've seen few women drink even a beer on the golf course. I don't drink alcohol on the golf course, since I can quickly feel the effects of one glass of wine or beer nowadays. Women who have had drinks while playing said that they did so during a golf tournament that had a margarita table on a hole. Otherwise, it seems less likely that a woman will have any alcohol during her round of golf. After golf in the nineteenth hole, however, it's certainly common for some women to drink.

As for fluid management, I suggest that you ask the pro shop staff if there are bathrooms on the course. By knowing about the facilities in advance, you can limit your fluid intake, drinking less water than you ordinarily would while playing, or you can plan to stop at the turn to use the bathroom.

Discover for Yourself

You have been given an introduction to how women and men differ in playing styles. As a friend said, men are from Mars and women from Venus applies not only in relationships but also in how they play golf. You'll have varied and different experiences as you start playing golf. As long as you play appropriately and conduct yourself in a professional manner, you'll stay out of trouble—whether you're playing a round with friends or business professionals or at a country club or public course.

Staying On Course

_____ Welcome opportunities to play with both men and women; it's no different than how you interact in the business world.

_____ Don't take it personally if a man doesn't want to play with you simply because you're a woman—it's his loss. You'll find most golfers enjoy playing with others who know how to play appropriately, regardless of their gender.

_____ If receiving unsolicited swing advice bothers you, try to ignore the tips or make sure you tactfully put a stop to it.

_____ If a male playing partner becomes upset and competitive because you're playing better than he is, make a lighthearted comment to diffuse the situation about how he must bring out your best game.

_____ Be careful of what you say before someone takes a swing. You don't want your comments to be misconstrued as trying to "psych out the player." If someone says something inappropriate to you, refocus, relax, and hit the ball well.

_____ If someone wants to bet, make sure you're comfortable with the maximum amount you can lose, the game being played, and consider the wager lost—you'll relax and play better. In the nineteenth hole, pay off your bets!

_____ As in any business and social settings, personalities, morals, and attitudes all differ. Handle any awkward or uncomfortable situations in a professional and businesslike manner.

CHAPTER 6

....

Leveraging Golf to Develop Business Relationships

Body Language Speaks Louder Than Words

Communication experts estimate that nearly 90 percent of how we exchange information with others is unspoken. Your body language, gestures, facial expressions, and tone of voice can reveal more to a listener than your actual words.

Think about meeting someone for the first time at a business meeting or networking event. You exchange names and perhaps a description of your work. Thereafter, what do you notice about that person? When you shook hands, did you pay attention to the firmness of her handshake? Is he dressed professionally and appropriately? During your conversation, did she make eye contact with you? Did he exude confidence or timidity? Understanding these silent communications will tell you more about that person than his or her title or occupation.

A corporate recruiter once described to me her litmus test when hiring a person: Would she want to spend a ten-hour flight sitting next to that person? Regardless of a person's excellent credentials for a position, if the recruiter doesn't like the candidate's personality and unspoken cues, she wouldn't hire that person. The recruiter's decision is based on gut feelings and intuition about the candidate rather than on his or her resume, regardless of how stellar it might be.

In a similar way, how a playing partner plays and behaves on the golf course can also be very revealing to you. In Chapter 1, I countered the lack-of-time objection for not playing golf with what I call the FREEDOM benefits of playing golf. Recall that the second E in FREEDOM stands for "Examining the Personality of Your Playing Partners." During a four-hour round of golf, you'll learn valuable information about that person's personality and character, and, most important, how he or she is as a businessperson.

This information is the key reason it's worth your time to play business golf. For example, when exploring whether I want to do business with someone, I'd prefer to know as much as I can about that person's personality or character shortcomings before we join forces. Partnerships or alliances take time and energy—it's an investment. Still, it's more expensive in terms of time, energy, and money to unravel a professional relationship *after* you've discovered that your business styles or values are incompatible. If you play a round of golf together during an exploratory stage, you will likely discover whether you enjoy spending time with that person. If you don't enjoy your round of golf together and wouldn't want to play another round with that person, you probably wouldn't want to do business with him or her either.

. . . .

You can discover more about a person in an hour of play than in a year of conversation.

                                                                    Plato

. . . .

Remember that playing golf can be a double-edged sword. Just as you can learn about your playing partner's personality and character for off-the-course negotiations, he or she can detect personality information about you. It behooves you to be aware of what you might unwittingly be saying on the golf course.

In this chapter, I describe some common golf scenarios. How your playing partner responds or handles these situations on the golf course may give you some insight about that person. These are generalizations; a person can act differently in business situations than when playing golf. However, your encounters on the golf course can be a precursor to your business-related interactions. After a round of golf, I suggest that you jot a few notes about your playing partners' characteristics and reactions exhibited on the golf course to see if they are consistent with how they conduct business.

Confidence On and Off the Course

Imagine that you're interviewing for a financial advisor to help you manage your investment portfolio. In selecting an advisor, you'll probably consider a variety of factors, including each candidate's experience, the reputation of the firm, the type of investments recommended, and, of most importance, whether you have confidence in his or her ability to manage and grow your hard-earned money.

You've seen someone with confidence and someone who hasn't yet obtained it. There's a difference in his or her voice when answering your questions—a tone that exudes experience and certainty or a pitch that squeaks with self-doubt. You know by whether the person looks you in the eye, or turns his or her face away as if embarrassed that he or she doesn't know the answer.

You'll also see a person's confidence level while playing golf. You'll notice how he or she approaches the tee. Does the person walk in full strides with club in hand, tee the ball up, take one smooth practice swing, and then hit it well? Or, is he hesitant as he walks up to the tee, debates which club to use as he looks down the fairway and at the club a couple more times, takes a jerky practice swing, and then makes a nonaggressive swing at the ball? Does she step up to the tee box when she can safely hit, or does she always ask or need to be told when she can hit next? You'll get clues as to whether a person has confidence in how he or she plays golf, and perhaps confidence as a person.

. . . .

Self-confidence is the first requisite for achieving great things

Samuel Johnson

. . . .

Here's an example of how showing a lack of confidence on the golf course can possibly translate to lost business. Bob is a community affairs vice president for an international food company. He plays regularly with two male golfers, one of whom is a better golfer with a lower handicap than the other golfer. Assuming everything else being equal, however, if Bob had to do business with either, he'd select the higher handicap player because of the difference in their confidence levels.

Bob noticed that when the better player is preparing to putt, he tightens up, is nervous, and is unsure of his putts. In contrast, the higher handicap player stands over his ball, aims, and putts confidently. He might not sink the putt (more often than not he doesn't), but before he hits the ball he thinks the ball will go into the hole. He's relaxed, having fun, and expecting good things to happen. The lower handicapped player is pessimistic, and is surprised when he hits a good shot. Bob says he'd rather work with someone who is optimistic and expecting a positive outcome than someone who is constantly second-guessing himself.

Watching someone else for his or her confidence level applies to you as well. You want colleagues and clients to see your confidence and assertiveness in how you handle yourself and your challenges, whether they're in the boardroom or on the golf course. Having an arrogant-free, self-assured style provides a comfort level when you're a leader of a project team or handling your clients' matters.

Regardless of your handicap, you should play golf with that same sense of confidence, command, and control. If you're fairly new to the game, your handicap might be high as you gain muscle memory and timing in your golf swing. As you take lessons, practice, and play more, your handicap will likely go down.

Your handicap doesn't show your confidence; it's how you conduct yourself on the golf course. A good start to playing with confidence is to understand the basics of the game, as described in chapters 3 and 4, and to play according to the basic rules of golf described in Appendix A. After reading this book and playing more frequently, your confidence as a golfer will likely increase. You'll begin to have an understanding of the dance of etiquette and the timing of that dance between you and your playing partners. Here are some additional ways you can show that you are a confident golfer, even as a beginner:

- Assume your group is playing ready golf. For example, if another player is farthest away from the hole and should hit first but can't because of danger to the group ahead and you can safely hit your ball, tell your playing partners that it's safe for you to hit and then do so. They'll appreciate that you know how to play ready golf.
- While waiting for others to hit, decide which club to use and where to aim, then be ready to take your stance (take at most two practice swings) and hit your ball when it's your turn.
- If the player whose ball is farthest away is not ready to putt and you're ready to putt and your turn is next, then offer to putt first. This gives the person a chance to read his or her putt and helps your foursome keep the pace.

- When riding in a golf cart, communicate with your cart partner about managing the cart. For example, if your cart partner's ball is on the putting green, and you are a short distance from the green, tell your cart partner that you'll take the clubs you need and that he can drive the cart ahead to the putting green. You'll keep your foursome moving and get some exercise as well.

Risk Taking

Depending on your profession, you may want to know the risk tolerance of your co-worker, client, or prospect. Playing a round of golf together may give you some insights that you might not otherwise obtain by talking or having lunch with him or her.

For example, I discovered the risk tolerance of Ed, a high-tech executive, who at that time was the best golfer I had played with and not a member of my club. On one particular dogleg left hole, I mentioned the shortcut that long ball hitters often took. Ed said he doesn't play what he called "show-off golf." When I asked him to clarify, Ed explained that if he made the show-off shot and it was successful, he could save a stroke or two. But, if he hit the ball badly, it could be in the trees, out of bounds, or lost and cost him a shot or two. He said the risky shot had a greater probability of failure and wasn't worth taking.

During lunch, I asked Ed if he is as conservative and methodical in making his business decisions. He confirmed that his golf-playing style and business tactics are very similar. He weighs the probabilities of success and failure and decides if the risk is worth taking. He does not consider himself a risky, reckless player, whether in golf or in business matters. After having watched his course management throughout the round, I wasn't surprised by his response.

You should know, though, that there are times when a player takes a risky shot for the fun and challenge of doing so. For example, I'm fairly conservative in how I conduct business and play golf. Still, if I'm playing a practice or casual round, I might try to hit a shot that has a low chance of success. I'm selective, however, in when I take a higher risk shot. If I am playing in a tournament, then I'd hit a safe shot.

By watching how someone plays golf, it might give you an idea as to how he or she will respond when faced with a choice of solutions for a given situation. Are they strategic, calculating, and methodical in their decision making, or do they let emotion, ego, and bragging rights determine their next move?

Reasonable Expectations?

As a practicing attorney, I always knew whether my clients had reasonable expectations about the outcome of the negotiations that I was undertaking on their behalf. Similarly, financial consultants that I have worked with stress the importance of managing their clients' expectations with regard to the potential increase or loss in the value of their portfolios.

During a recent presentation, a financial consultant who is a business golfer shared a very revealing story about one of her clients. The client is a mover and shaker in a small northern California business community. (In fact, the consultant refused to even mention the town for fear that her client's identity would be apparent.) Her client is highly regarded in the community, always well dressed, and professional in her demeanor.

The consultant invited her client to play in a golf tournament that was a fund raiser for a local charity. On one hole, the client asked to borrow the consultant's 5-iron. Without any hesitation or thought as to why her client didn't have her own club, the consultant gave her client her 5-iron. The client took a couple of practice swings with the club, aimed, and hit the ball. The shot wasn't her best, which was understandable since she was using an unfamiliar club. But, in an unforgettable moment for the consultant, the client became enraged, raised the club, and broke it over her knee! (This probably explains why the client didn't have her own club!) As you can imagine, the consultant was incredulous about the client's behavior.

I asked the financial consultant what she had discovered about her client as a result of this incident. She realized that she had no idea that her client was so unreasonable in her expectations and could be that hard on herself if she didn't perform up to her own standards. The consultant worried that if her client had such unreasonable expectations for herself, then she had them for others as well, notably, the performance of the consultant and the portfolio that the consultant managed. Thereafter, the consultant was even more diligent in explaining to her client not only the possible returns for any investments, but the potential risks.

Breaking a club or even throwing a club is pretty extreme out-of-control, immature behavior. If it should occur, you have valuable information about such a person. It is more likely that if a player has unreasonable expectations, you'll see less obvious signs, such as banging the club head on the ground or belittling comments made after a poor shot. You'll have to gauge the player's overall behavior to determine if he or she has unreasonable expectations. A one-time comment may be just venting of frustration, but if self-criticism continues throughout the round, you can be fairly certain of high self-demands.

Here are some other factors to consider when determining whether some-one has high or unrealistic expectations:

- How long has he or she been playing golf?
- How often does he or she play?
- When was the last time he or she played?
- Was the ball in a difficult lie, such as in a divot or on the side of a hill, where it's reasonable that the player's shot is not his or her best?
- Is the player experiencing any physical or emotional circumstances, such as being tired or stressed or having allergies, that may affect how he or she is playing?

If someone is a beginner, hasn't played recently, or is suffering from jet lag, it would be unreasonable for that person to expect to hit good shots each time or to play well.

A Team Player or a Selfish Loner?

Golf is unique in that you can play with other people, but, unless you are play-ing in a tournament with a team format or wagering, your score doesn't affect anyone but yourself. Nevertheless, how you conduct yourself can give your playing partners some insight as to whether you're a team player.

· ·

Eighteen holes of [golf] . . . will teach you more about your foe than eighteen years of dealing with him [or her] across a desk.

Grantland Rice

· ·

Denise is a sales account representative for a wireless technology company. She played in a trade association golf tournament with a male cart partner whom she did not know. She described the round as being one of her most frus-trating, but not because of how she played. Instead, her frustration was with her cart partner, who left the cart behind when he should have driven it forward. On many holes, she said, "I would tell him that I have my clubs and putter, and he could drive the cart up because I would walk to the putting green." After hit-ting her approach shot, however, she would look back to see that he had left the cart and was at the green waiting to putt, so she had to walk back to get the cart.

Denise's cart partner was oblivious to the need to manage the golf cart and ignored her comments about it. Denise said that she would never consider doing business with her cart partner. His behavior showed that he was too self-involved and couldn't help a partner on his team when he was asked and it was appropriate to do so.

Here are other examples of a person not being a team player and what you can do to show that you are a team player:

- Looking for another player's ball. It's courteous to watch where other players' balls land, especially if a ball is heading toward some trees or out of bounds. If you can't see a player's ball in the fairway or rough, you should help look for the ball as you are walking to your ball. A selfish player will just walk down the fairway and not help his or her playing partners look for the ball.
- Pulling and replacing the flagstick. If your ball is closer to the pin than your playing partners' balls, then you should pull the flagstick. Or, if you sink your ball in the hole first, then you should replace the flagstick after the others have putted out. An attorney colleague shared a story about two playing partners: One player said to the other, "Hey, do you know how much a flagstick weighs?" The other player thought about it and responded that he didn't. The player sarcastically answered, "I know you don't. You haven't picked up the flagstick once today."
- Playing slowly. If your foursome is falling behind the group in front of you, every player should try to play faster and pick up the pace. The techniques set forth in Chapter 3 will help you do so.
- Never replacing divots or repairing ball marks on the green. At a minimum, each player should replace his or her own divots and repair ball marks. People who do not are rude and inconsiderate.
- Leaving the green and teeing off at the next hole. You should wait for the other players to putt out before moving to the next tee. Unless your group is falling behind and needs to speed up, it's inappropriate to leave the green to tee off first while others are still putting.

Handling Challenges

When playing a round of golf, most players will be faced with situations that reveal how they handle pressure and challenges. For example, can your colleague hit a shot over a lake or a bunker? Can your client sink a simple 2-foot putt to win a bet? Some players simply can't handle the pressure. Suddenly, shots that they ordinarily would make without the adverse conditions are hit badly. Players become tight, nervous, and erratic.

. . . .

You gain strength, courage, and confidence by every experience in which you really stop to look fear in the face. You must do the thing which you think you cannot do.

Eleanor Roosevelt

. . . .

A golf teaching professional once described a woman student who, if faced with a shot over a bunker onto the green, would consistently hit her ball into the bunker. Yet, if she had to make a similar shot *without* the bunker in front of her, she would be able to hit onto the green nine times out of ten. She simply couldn't handle the mental pressure of the bunker. Was it because she focused on the bunker rather than on what she needed to do to get the ball over the bunker? When faced with off-the-course challenges, I wonder if she does the same—worry about the problem, rather than focus on getting around or overcoming the obstacle in an effective way so she can succeed.

In contrast, Linda tells a story about playing with her boss and two friends. Her boss and another player placed a large wager on their match. They were playing the eighteenth hole and the match was tied. Her boss was 50 yards off the green, and his opponent's ball was on the green close enough to sink the ball in two putts. Everyone knew that her boss needed to sink his chip shot to win, or at least get it close to the hole to tie his opponent. He addressed the ball as he normally would and, sure enough, he chipped it in! Sure, there may have been some luck to the ball rolling in. But he also showed how he typically handles pressure—whether on the golf course or in business. He takes control and takes care of the business at hand.

Knowing how a colleague or business partner performs when faced with a challenging predicament may be important to you. When I'm working with others, I want to know that they can stay calm and work effectively under most circumstances.

Perhaps a player is not accustomed to handling pressure. One woman golfer noticed that career businesswomen tend to handle challenging shots better than women who have never worked in high-stress jobs. A businesswoman who has experienced success in challenging business situations may be better able to transfer her mental toughness to golf shots.

When a player can't handle the pressure of a shot, it's likely because he is thinking ahead about the positive result—he's cleared the water safely—or dreads the negative result—he's in the water. Rather than having either emotional reaction before the shot, it's best to stay in the present, calmly consider your options, and decide what you need to do to overcome the challenge.

For example, if there is a lake in front of you, consider whether you can hit the ball to one side of the lake where it can land safely and still leave you with a good next shot. If you decide that you have to hit over the water, then consider hitting more club, so you can take a relaxed swing and have the extra distance to clear the water. It also helps to take a deep breath before you swing, and even loosen your grip slightly to make sure your hands and arms are relaxed, so you can make a smooth swing. Also don't say to yourself, "Don't hit it into the water." Remember, your mind doesn't recognize the word "don't." By doing these few things before a challenging shot, you'll likely find that the shot isn't as formidable and you'll make the shot that you want.

Making Excuses or Taking Responsibility?

You probably know a few co-workers who have a plethora of excuses for missing deadlines: "I didn't get the numbers from the other department," "I was waiting for Smith to call me back with his information." They have plenty of people to blame—everyone but themselves.

. . . .

The least thing upset him on the links. He missed short putts because of the uproar of butterflies in the adjoining meadows.

P. G. Wodehouse

. . . .

Some golfers also look for anything or anyone to blame for their bad shots. In the beginning of the round, you'll likely hear how long it has been since he played, how his back is stiff, or that he had an important call before he left and didn't have time to warm up. As you continue playing, the bad shots will be due to the lie of her ball, the car driving by when she was about to hit, or someone else hitting a poor shot and she saw it. Soon you'll begin to realize that you better hold your breath each time he or she hits, or you'll be blamed next! Whatever the reasons, after a few shots, this running commentary of excuses can become comical or annoying.

Karen, a Silicon Valley executive recruiter, likes how her boss responds when he hits a bad shot. He doesn't dwell on the bad shot or even acknowledge that he just hit a bad shot. Instead, he refocuses and moves to the next shot. She said he has the same style when working with her. If she's working on a problem, he doesn't look for whom to blame for the situation. Rather, he focuses on the issue, encourages her, and helps her to find a workable solution.

If your playing partners can't accept responsibility for the results of hitting a stationary golf ball, will they be able to do so when they fail to meet a deadline at work or when a new business venture doesn't meet the financial projections?

If you hit a poor shot, don't overanalyze how you could have hit such a shot. Analyzing your golf swing should be left to you and your golf swing instructor on the driving range. Even pro golfers don't hit every shot perfectly. Remember my mantra, "Hit it and move on!" No one expects you to hit every shot well, so there's no reason to give an excuse. Instead, relax and focus on how you can hit the next shot well.

Uptight or Have a Sense of Humor?

When someone isn't playing well in a casual round of golf, often he or she may get quiet, tense, and uptight. Suddenly what was supposed to be fun is no longer a pleasant experience not only for the uptight golfer but potentially for the entire foursome. I've been fortunate not to have played with anyone who throws clubs when playing poorly. Those who have, however, describe the round as being a powder keg; you don't know if he is going to miss another shot and throw his club.

That person has ruined the round not only for himself, but also for his playing partners and will most likely not get an invitation to play again, let alone do business with them. Even when playing poorly, the goal of playing should be to have a good time and get to know one another. If a player can't enjoy the satisfaction of playing well, then at least she should enjoy the company and the beauty of the golf course.

When Tiger Woods was playing in the 2001 U.S. Open, one of four golf tournaments known as Majors for the PGA Tour (the others being The British Open, The Masters, and The PGA Championship), he was struggling with his game in the first round. Even someone who makes a tremendously good living by hitting the golf ball must admit an absolute truth about this game: "Sometimes things don't go your way. And there's nothing you can do about it. Sometimes you just have to laugh at yourself." If Tiger can laugh at his shots, we recreational and business golfers can certainly laugh at ours.

. . . .

The Majors for the LPGA Tour include The Kraft Nabisco Championship, The U.S. Women's Open, The McDonald's LPGA Championship, and The Weetabix Women's British Open.

. . . .

I'll never forget a shot made by my uncle when playing at his country club. He had only recently joined the club and was a fairly new golfer. We had just finished nine holes and stopped at the turn to get a bite to eat at the snack bar. On the tenth tee, he was ready to hit first, and teed up his ball. He took one practice swing. Then he stepped up to the ball, swung his driver, and I saw a shot that I had never seen before. The tee flew forward several feet, and his ball made a complete loop in the air and flew about a yard or so backwards! I was absolutely speechless. During that awkward moment, I was thinking, "What can I say to my elder, who invited me to his country club, and clearly hit the worst shot I have ever seen?" Thankfully, he quickly broke the silence and said while chuckling, "That was a pretty horrible shot, wasn't it?" Of course, we shared a great laugh together, one that we still talk about years later.

. . . .

Shared laughter creates a bond of friendship. When people laugh together, they cease to be young and old, master and pupils, worker and driver. They have become a single group of human beings, enjoying their existence.

W. Grant Lee

. . . .

Remember that you're playing golf to build rapport and relationships and, just as important, to have some fun, and get some fresh air and exercise. Our livelihood isn't determined by the quality of our golf shots. Use my mantra to help you enjoy the game and keep your perspective that the game is just a game. If you hit a bad shot, there's no need to get uptight and belittle yourself; just move on to the next shot. If you hit an especially bad shot, there's no harm in laughing out loud at yourself. It'll give your playing partners a chance to laugh with you (rather than *at* you) and share a light moment together.

Gloating Golfer

Instead of excuses for every shot, you may encounter the opposite scenario of someone who is not able to handle compliments for good shots. If someone hits a good shot, it's common for golfers to say, "Nice shot," or "Good hit." A simple "Thank you," or "Thanks, I like that shot, too," are appropriate responses. Thereafter, everyone moves on to the next shots. Then, maybe during the typical recap of the round over drinks in the nineteenth hole, the exceptionally good shots or a hole played very well will be talked about again. Since golf is such a humbling game in which you can shoot your best score one day and then shoot your worst the next, most golfers graciously accept the praise and then concentrate on the next shot.

One golfer, Larry, told me about John, who simply can't let go of his good shots. If John hits a good shot, which isn't necessarily that spectacular (even though John thinks it is), he continues to talk about the shot several holes later and even throughout the remainder of the round. Then, during drinks, he'll constantly turn the conversation back to his shot. Larry describes it as being with a five-year-old who constantly needs approval and a pat on the head. According to Larry, when John finally does hit a good shot, you don't even want to say anything because you know you'll never hear the end of it.

Unfortunately it sounds like John has bigger issues than just how well or poorly he plays a round of golf. Although Larry is sympathetic toward John, he doesn't enjoy playing with him because of his constant need to talk about his good shots. I would imagine it would also be a challenge to work with John since he always needs approval and has to talk about his successes all the time. I also doubt if he would know how to share credit for his success with others.

If, on a given day, you play better than you typically do, thank your playing partners for making the round a pleasant and relaxing one, which enabled you to play so well. Although I believe in not blaming anyone if I don't play well, I do think the behaviors and attitudes of my playing partners can affect positively (or negatively) how well I play. If I'm enjoying the conversation with my playing partners and I'm relaxed, I have a better chance of playing well. Similarly, if someone in the foursome is uptight or unpleasant, and, although I try not to let it bother me, it often is distracting and affects subtly how I play.

Cheating: Must Win at All Costs?

Except in professional golf tournaments, you do not have officials on the course to enforce the rules of golf. You're expected to assess a penalty on yourself if you violate a rule of golf. The game is based on integrity and honesty, which is why I suggest that you become familiar with some of the basic rules in Appendix A.

If I'm playing with a beginner who is cheating, I will give the person the benefit of the doubt and simply make a mental note of it. Perhaps he or she hasn't taken the time to learn the rules yet. It would be better, however, if the beginner asked a playing partner or me what to do under the rules. I often also ask a beginner if he or she would like to learn the appropriate rule and then show him or her how to apply the rule.

However, if the player is experienced, should know the rules, and is cheating, I question the person's trustworthiness and consider carefully whether I would want to work with that person. And, if we already do business together, I'd certainly keep my eye on him and take note of his lack of integrity.

Kimberly knows how to do business quite successfully with people who cheat at golf. Kimberly is the president of an international public relations company based in Washington, D.C. She played with two men who both cheated. Although she handled each person differently, she was extremely successful in business as a result of witnessing their cheating.

The first businessman was a service provider to a mutual client. They had discussed a possible strategic alliance of their businesses, and this was their first outing on a social basis. She was a fairly new golfer and had created a foursome to play in a charity golf tournament. She invited three men, one of whom was the potential alliance partner.

They were playing in a practice round prior to the tournament the next day. She wasn't playing well, but she was taking her poor performance in stride. She hit into the trees near the green and was looking for her ball. As she was searching, she noticed the potential alliance partner. He was looking around to see if anyone was watching him. He also had hit into the trees beyond the green. Thinking no one was watching, he picked up his ball and threw it onto the green. She ducked behind a tree as he shouted, "Wow! Look at my ball! It's on the green!"

She was amazed that he was that desperate to look good. It was a casual round of golf with no pressure to perform well. She realized that if he was that afraid of not doing well on the course he would not react well in business situations. She decided not to pursue a strategic alliance with him. Her instincts were right; six months later she learned that his business practices were not ethical and he was forced out of business.

Thanks to playing a round of golf, Kimberly saw this businessman's unscrupulous behavior and heeded the signs. She knew that if he would cheat in an insignificant round of golf, he'd likely do the same in business.

Kimberly's next encounter with a cheating golfer was while on vacation in Mexico. She and her boyfriend were paired with another golfer and a London business executive, who claimed to be a scratch golfer. The London executive's wife was walking along with them, enjoying the fresh air.

After golf, in the nineteenth hole, the London executive's wife asked if Kimberly knew that her husband had been cheating throughout the round. Kimberly said that she was quite aware of it. When the woman asked Kimberly why she hadn't said anything, Kimberly said, "I'm a beginner, and if your husband has to cheat when playing with me, it shows how much he needs to win. I don't care if he wins or not."

Six months later, long after Kimberly had forgotten the incident, the London executive called to confess. The executive explained that his wife had told him that Kimberly knew that he was cheating throughout the round. He apologized and insisted that Kimberly visit him and his wife the next time she was in London, which Kimberly did. What were the results of her visit and their round of golf together? She landed his business, as well as sixteen other companies referred by the executive. Kimberly now has an international company with an office in London.

I asked Kimberly if she had been leery about working with him. She felt that since he had the guts to call and apologize, then he would be able to admit his faults and mistakes. She knew he would be a difficult client at times, but at least he would be honest and a straight shooter. And, if he were wrong, he'd call to apologize, even though it could be months later.

Since most golfers don't know the rules, it can be difficult to tell if a player is cheating intentionally or out of ignorance. So that you'll recognize when a player may be cheating, here are some common ways golfers can cheat:

- Taking a mulligan. Mulligans do not exist under the official rules of golf. Every shot counts. Some golf purists consider taking a mulligan as cheating. At most, a mulligan should be limited to the first tee in a friendly relaxed round.
- Improving the lie or playing "Winter Rules." Traditional golfers play the ball down, that is, exactly where the ball lands after they have hit it. Improving the lie or cleaning a wet or muddy ball under "Winter Rules" is not sanctioned under the official rules of golf. Traditional golfers consider it cheating to improve the lie or to play "Winter Rules."
- Gimme putts. Under the official rules of golf, gimmes do not exist, and purist golfers would consider it cheating to take them. Also, some players give themselves gimmes, which is the height of inappropriateness!
- Not counting all strokes, including penalty strokes. A player who takes a lower score than his or her actual strokes, including all penalty strokes, may be cheating.
- Asking for advice. Remember that you would be penalized two strokes if you asked or received subjective information to help your game, such as what distance your ball is from the green.

When playing a business golf round, I suggest that you follow the rules as they apply to your ball to show your playing partners that you know the rules. If you're still learning the rules, then, on the first tee, say to your playing partners, "I'm still learning the rules, so tell me if it looks like I'm about to break one." Your playing partners will understand that you know there are rules, but you don't know them all yet.

If your client or prospect is new to the game and doesn't yet know the rules, then don't follow the rules to the precise letter such that it takes the fun out of the round. You might mention, however, that if he or she were playing in a competitive round of golf, then the rule would require him or her to do something or take a penalty. (This will serve as a gentle reminder of the rules.) Remember, your goal of the round is to have a good time and get to know one another. You can take note if an experienced golfer cheats and then consider how you want to work with that person in business.

Let Your Client Win?

Attendees of my presentations often ask if they should let a client or prospect win. Since the game is based on integrity, I'm adamant against *letting* someone win.

. . . .

She has honor if she holds herself to an ideal of conduct though it is inconvenient, unprofitable, or dangerous to do so.

Adapted from Walter Lippmann

. . . .

If a person is that desperate to win or can't lose graciously, that's important information for you to know if you're working together in business. Moreover, I'd be afraid of his reaction if he discovered that I missed the putt on purpose to let him win. I would be insulted if someone lost a match to me in hopes that I would then want to do business with him or her.

Robin was in an awkward situation when a salesperson asked her not to play so well, so his boss could win. She was playing with a male colleague and his boss, a woman. During the round he asked Robin not to play so well. Robin asked why and he told her that his boss wanted to win. Robin suggested they play in a team format. It was a win–win solution because the female boss became more relaxed, and, since she was paired with the better player, she was on the winning team! Afterwards, they had a great time in the nineteenth hole.

Robin found a great solution so the female boss could have the satisfaction of winning without compromising Robin's game or integrity.

What You Can Learn

I've presented some common situations that can arise on the golf course and the information you might gain by watching how a person responds. Obviously, a one-time occurrence may not be a good basis for drawing a conclusion about a person's personality. However, if you see a pattern in a person's behavior, you will likely witness similar behavior in the conference room or during negotiations. And always remember to make sure that you don't behave on the golf course in a way that may discourage someone from wanting to work with you.

Staying On Course

_____ Playing golf can be a double-edged sword. Just as you're assessing your partners, they are evaluating you. Handle yourself on the course as you would in a business meeting.

_____ Exhibit the three Cs—confidence, command, and control—when you're on and off the course.

_____ Set realistic expectations for your game. If you're not pleased with your progress in learning the golf swing, schedule a golf lesson with your instructor.

_____ Courteous behavior requires awareness of your playing partners, their shots, and location of their golf balls. Be a team player!

_____ When faced with a challenging shot, assess your options, focus on the present shot, and take a smooth relaxed swing.

_____ If you hit a bad shot, "Hit it and move on!" Avoid the temptation to overanalyze your golf swing while on the golf course. Humor and laughter are important to remind you that the game is just a game.

_____ Cheating is a violation of personal and business ethics. If you're uncertain about the rules of golf, ask your partners and apply the rule you believe is correct. You can check your rule book after the round.

PART THREE

Expanding Your Golf Opportunities

CHAPTER 7

....

Playing in Tournaments: Clubs, Charities, and Corporate Events

If you want to use golf to connect with clients or to meet new people (which I strongly suggest!), you'll find golf tournaments an easy way to do so. Charities, churches, chambers of commerce, trade conferences, and corporations across the country sponsor golf tournaments. Whether to have participants network, raise money for a good cause, create client goodwill, or launch a new product, eighteen-hole golf tournaments have become the hottest venue in drawing together people with a similar interest or intent.

Playing in tournaments can be very memorable. Some golfers plan a year or more in advance to be able to play in their favorite tournaments. Tournaments offer fun golf, the ability to play good (even private) courses, great prizes, and usually delicious food. What's more, they're relatively simple, usually team events, and have a single all-inclusive fee. This entry fee usually includes your cart rental, tee prizes (which are usually logoed golf items as a souvenir of the event), food and drinks, and a chance for you and your team to win prizes.

In this chapter, I give you the ins and outs of playing in a tournament. I start with helping you decide which tournaments to enter and how to find golf tournaments that you might want to play in. I also give you the pros and cons of playing as a single or creating a foursome. Don't let your fear about being good enough to play stop you from entering a tournament—the team formats are beginner-friendly to encourage anyone who wants to play.

. . . .

We must be willing to get rid of the life we've planned, so as to have the life that is waiting for us.

Joseph Campbell

. . . .

I also give you some tips on how to network during the after-golf activities. I close with a couple of ideas on how to follow up after the tournament.

Which Tournaments to Play?

Corporations, charity or civic organizations, trade associations, and women's golf clubs often sponsor golf tournaments. Knowing who typically plays in these tournaments can help you decide which tournament you should play in.

Corporate Tournaments

If you've been invited to play in your corporation's golf tournament, you will want to play in that tournament. Upper management will likely be playing, and you'll get a chance to meet them away from the office in a more relaxed setting. If you don't already know or have a personal relationship with many in upper management, then this is a great opportunity to make a positive professional impression outside the conference room. At many corporate tournaments, you'll also have a chance to say thank you to your top clients, since you may be asked to invite one or two of them as your guest.

You might recall Peggy from Chapter 1. Peggy is a vice president of a credit card company. She credits playing in a corporate tournament with a promotion that she received. As a result of her playing, the promotion decision makers had a chance to see her outside the office. They especially noted her confidence in her golf game and her ease in being around her male clients. She was no longer just a name with statistics on meeting her quotas; they had much more information about who she is to base their promotion decision.

Charity or Civic Fund-Raising Tournaments

More and more organizations are using golf to increase awareness of their causes as well as to raise lots of money. There are a plethora of charities from

breast cancer research, boys and girls clubs, to memorial scholarship founda-
tions, and many more to support. In addition to charities that sponsor their
own tournaments, a chamber of commerce or a civic group may select a charity or foundation to raise funds for by sponsoring a tournament. If you are a
member of the chamber or a civic group, you can play in its golf tournament
as a way to support the organization and have fun with golf.

Another way to participate in fund-raising tournaments is to ask your top
clients about the charities they support and play in those tournaments. It's a
unique way to say thank you for past business and show that you care about
your clients and their causes. Michelle is the president of a general contracting
company and she uses this technique very successfully. As Michelle begins
work with new clients, she asks if they have a particular charity or foundation
that they support. If so, she asks if the organization has a golf tournament because she would like to enter a foursome to play in it.

If Michelle wants to develop a relationship with a prospect, she checks to see
if the prospect is involved in any local golf tournaments. Many golf tournaments are advertised at golf courses and in local newspapers. The ads often list
the tournament sponsors. If she sees that the prospect is sponsoring a charity
tournament, she'll call the tournament planner to request a list of the previous
year's players. She wants to see if her competitors, whom the prospect has
awarded contracts to in the past, have played in the prospect's sponsored tournament. If her competition isn't playing, she'll enter the tournament as a way
to introduce herself to the prospect. It has worked for her!

Trade Association Tournaments

Many trade associations sponsor golf tournaments. For example, real estate
brokers and mortgage bankers have tournaments in the San Francisco Bay area.
If you're in the meeting planning industry, then you should know about the
Meetings Industry Ladies Organization (MILO), which is based in Bethesda,
Maryland. They have golf institutes and tournaments for women in the meeting and hospitality industry, all designed for members to use golf to enhance
their business opportunities. Check to see which trade associations have a local
golf tournament. You'll be able to network with colleagues and perhaps you'll
even find a referral source or an associate to become a strategic partner.

Women's Golf Club Invitationals

When I explained how to get a handicap in Chapter 3, I suggested that one
option is to join a women's golf club at a local course. Those clubs often have

invitationals, when members of the club invite one to three women playing partners for a one- or two-day team event. During the invitationals, you'll play a team format and have a chance to win prizes, such as gift certificates for the pro shop, golf merchandise, or some nongolf items, such as a spa package, a gift basket of wine and cheese, or other goodies. As part of the invitational, they'll also often have a raffle for prizes with the proceeds to help a charity.

Benefits of Tournament Golf

One of the benefits of playing in a fund-raising golf tournament is that they're often held at exclusive country clubs. Some country clubs have prestigious reputations and ordinarily you need to be invited by a member to play as a guest at such clubs. Playing in a tournament held at such a country club gives you an insider's view to the golf course and its facilities that you otherwise may not have the opportunity to enjoy. You might pay more to play in these tournaments, but it can be an experience worth the price.

Tournament location is particularly important when inviting customers or clients. People are busy; the need to take off at least a half a day or more to play a tournament is daunting to many business people. A tournament at a prestigious country club, however, usually is a strong incentive for enticing key customers and prospects to join you.

If a tournament is not held at a country club, then you'll likely play at an upscale daily-fee public course or a resort course. Many of the newer public courses have a country club feel and atmosphere. Besides, recall that Pebble Beach Golf Links is a public course, albeit, it's the most famous (and the most expensive) one in the world!

If your tournament is on a public course, when inviting customers or prospects, play up the other benefits of the tournament: the prizes, the special dinner afterward, possible celebrity or other unique tournament participants, and so forth.

Enter as a Foursome or as a Single?

In most tournaments, you can enter as a single or create your own foursome. Denise, the senior account executive for a wireless company, entered her trade association tournament as a single so that she could enjoy the Opportunities Galore benefit of the FREEDOM benefits of playing. She wanted to meet and network with others in her industry. By playing as a single, she had no idea whom she might meet and how they might work together. Remember, her method worked when she played with someone who ultimately became a $1 million client.

One word of caution about signing up as a single: Some tournament planners will automatically put you in a foursome with three other women. I find this slightly condescending. I enjoy playing with men and women. If there is an opportunity to play with some men that I don't know, then I would like the chance to do so. If you prefer to play with men as well, then simply call the tournament planner well in advance and ask that you be placed in a group with both men and women. You should also make a note of your request on your entry form.

Alternatively, you can also invite up to three others to create a foursome to play in a tournament. Kimberly, the president of the international public relations company, strategically decides whom to invite to play with her in tournaments. She considers the personalities of the players and chooses players who want to have a good time and are not focused on winning. She often invites a prospect, a client, and a strategic partner to play in tournaments. If a prospect is considering whether to retain her services, she also invites a client who has had exceptional success and increased earnings as a result of her public relations services. To allow Kimberly and her prospect to learn more about each other in a nonthreatening sales environment, she shares the cart with the prospect.

You want to avoid inviting competitors or business rivals for your foursome. That could be very awkward for everyone. However, you could invite two clients whose companies are in the process of merging. It's a good way for the clients to meet in a nonthreatening casual atmosphere.

One important issue about playing in a tournament is the cost. A golf tournament can cost $100 or more per person. Besides the green fee, you're paying for the cart rental (most tournaments require you to ride), food, prizes, and a contribution to a charity. If your boss or company believes in using golf to build goodwill with top clients, ask for company authorization to pay for the entry fee for you or a foursome.

If you run your own business or have a marketing budget from your company, you should consider allocating the cost of golf in your marketing plan annually. Michelle budgets $3,000 to $4,000 for seven to ten golf outings per year. Lena, the president of a building restoration company, also factors the cost of golf in her annual marketing costs. She sets aside 25 percent of her marketing budget for golf, since an outing can cost $1,500 for a foursome as a tournament sponsor. Her investment in golf, however, has paid off. She has seen a greater return on her investment from playing golf with clients and referral sources than from advertising in the Yellow Pages or the real estate journal in the state of New York. She said her top 10 to 20 clients are rewarded with golf outings, and they love it!

What If You Can't Play?

If you want to support a cause or charity but can't play in the tournament, you can still use golf as a networking tool. (You know by now that feeling that you are not good enough to play won't cut it.)

Let's say you can't play for some reason, such as an injury. You can still show your support and use the tournament as a networking venue in a variety of ways. One way is to volunteer to assist in the running of the tournament. Tournaments require many volunteers—duties can range from checking in the players, to driving the beverage cart, to handing out prizes during the awards ceremony.

Some clients have expressed concern about volunteering to drive the beverage carts, however. They are women in senior management and want to maintain their professional credibility with those playing in the tournament. One client, Barbara, said when she couldn't play in a tournament because of repetitive stress in her arm, she chose to check in golfers. She said it gave her an opportunity to introduce herself to players that she might want to follow up with after the tournament regarding business matters.

If you can't play in the tournament, then you can also sponsor a tee, a hole, or one of the many contests that are held as part of the tournament, such as longest drive for men and women, closest to the hole, straightest drive, longest putt, and others. As a sponsor, the tournament planner will have a sign with your name and company on the tee of the hole where you are sponsoring a contest, and you'll be mentioned in the program.

. . . .

In addition to the team competition, most tournaments have contests for individual players. Here is a list of some of the more common contests:

- Closest to the hole. *This contest is held on par 3 holes. A player who hits a tee shot onto the green and near the flagstick measures how far his or her ball is from the hole. There is usually a marker near the green where a player writes his or her name and the distance the ball is from the hole. If you are the first player to get onto the green, write your name and the distance since it may be the closest shot throughout the day. Make sure you measure your ball before you putt.*

- Longest drive. *This contest is held on either a par 4 or a par 5 hole. The player who hits the longest tee shot that lands in the fairway places the marker at the spot of the player's ball and writes his or her name on the marker. If men and women are playing the tournament, there should be a longest drive contest for each.*
- Longest putt. *On a particular green, the player who sinks the longest putt is the winner. Again, make sure you measure your ball before you putt.*
- Straightest drive. *The golf course staff paints a white line down the center of a fairway of a par 4 or a par 5 hole. The person who hits a tee shot closest to the line places the marker at the spot of the ball and writes his or her name.*

. . . .

If you're a tee sponsor, most tournament planners allow you or your representative at the tee to greet golfers. Obviously, I'd rather have you playing in the tournament, but at least as a tee sponsor, you'll have more face time with the players, so you can introduce yourself to them and learn more about them.

If you sign up as a sponsor, ask the planner to give you a list of players with their contact information. You should also ask for a pairing sheet, which gives you the names of each player in a foursome and the holes that they started playing from, so you can see if some are hotter prospects than others. You'll learn in the next section about what's called shotgun starts and why everyone doesn't start playing at the first hole.

If you can't play golf, you can join in the after-golf festivities. Most golf tournaments have presentation of prizes and recognition of the notables involved with the tournament and charity during an after-the-round cocktail party and/or dinner. You can purchase dinner-only tickets and network with golfers during this time. To break the ice with people you meet, you can ask the condition of the course, how their team played, and other golf-related questions. You can also donate raffle prizes (which can have logos of your company), sponsor the beverage cart, or provide giveaways which are often given to all contestants as part of their package.

Shotgun Starts

Tournament planners often choose a team format to encourage many golfers of different playing experiences to enter—the more players, the more money they can raise. Rather than have only 72 players on the course at one time (a foursome on each of the eighteen holes), the tournament planner usually will attempt to have a full field of 144 golfers. Planners are able to have so many players on the course because of two factors: first, they have two foursomes start on each hole; second, they use a shotgun start where foursomes on each hole are ready to tee off at a given time, usually 8 A.M. or at 1 P.M. The reason for using shotgun starts is simple: everyone starts at the same time, and everyone finishes at basically the same time. Scoring and after-golf festivities can then begin soon after everyone is off the course.

Here's how shotgun starts work. Let's say a tournament has a shotgun start at 1 P.M. You should plan on arriving at the course by at least 11:30 A.M. When you check in, you'll be told the hole that you will be starting on. Someone will likely take your golf bag and put a tag on it with your name and starting hole, and place it on a golf cart for you. The cart will have a placard with the name of your cart partner and the hole that you're starting on. For example, if the placard has your name and your cart partner's name and an 8B on it, then you're starting on hole number eight, and you'll be in the second group playing that hole. The 8A foursome will tee off first, then your foursome will start after them. You'll also be given a bag filled with tee prizes, which can include logoed items such as a sleeve of golf balls or a towel, a bottle of water, snacks, or suntan lotion. You'll often also be given a box lunch consisting of a sandwich, chips, and an apple that you can eat while playing. If you have an early morning shotgun start, a continental breakfast will probably be served before you play.

If you've invited a foursome, then you'll want to greet your guests. Or, if you're a single, you might try to find your playing partners or you can wait until you've warmed up. Since you're likely playing an unfamiliar course, you will probably want to practice at the driving range and the putting green. You may not be able to take the cart to the driving range, so you'll have to carry your golf bag or take a few clubs, your putter, and some balls. The tournament sponsors usually provide complimentary range balls at the driving range. There may also be a putting contest, which raises more money for the charity, so bring some money with you to enter.

You'll want to be back at your cart at least twenty to twenty-five minutes before the shotgun start. You may want to visit the ladies room and have time to introduce yourself to your playing partners. Fifteen minutes before the shotgun start, an announcement will be made about enjoying the day, and then you'll be allowed to drive to your starting hole. Golf course personnel may escort you to your starting hole to avoid confusion. The carts are staged, so there is an orderly process in how foursomes drive to their holes. If you're driving, make sure that you follow the order. Remember to stay on the cart paths as you drive to your starting hole.

Friendly Formats

To encourage many players to play, tournament planners use team formats that are good for both experienced and beginner golfers. The advantage of using a team format is team building among the players; individual scores are not counted. Hence, the fear of not being a good enough player to play shouldn't be a factor. You won't be asked your score since the tournament is a team event.

I describe how different tournament formats work so you know what to expect when you play in a tournament. After describing the formats, I give you some tips on how to play with your playing partners in the formats.

The most common tournament format is the *scramble*. In a *four-person scramble*, the team chooses a captain of the foursome. Typically, the best player of the foursome is chosen as captain. Each player hits a drive, and the captain decides which drive is the best. The other three players' drives don't count, and they can pick up their balls when they get to them. Each player then plays the second shot from the best drive's position. The captain decides the best second shot, and each player hits his or her third shot from this location; the play continues in this manner until the hole is completed. Typically, tournament rules require each player to contribute at least two drives during the course of an eighteen-hole round. Thus, the team with a very good player doesn't have an unfair advantage. On the green, when a player putts out, the team has putted out.

Here are some tips for when you play in a scramble format:

- If you're playing in a scramble that requires your team to use two drives from each player, then you should tell your team captain when you've hit a drive that is probably one of your best. If your teammates are unsure of when you've hit a good drive, they may wait until near the end of the round to want to use your drives. By speaking up, you can let them know when a drive is a good one for you, and you'll avoid unnecessary pressure on yourself.
- Don't be surprised if your teammates ask you to hit first. In a scramble, the steadiest player who will most likely hit the ball safely down the middle of the fairway should hit first. The drive may not be long, but it will be safe. You could be the steadiest player, so be prepared to have honors. By having one safe shot in the middle of the fairway, the rest of the team can try to hit their drives longer or take a high risk shot on a dogleg.
- Likewise, your teammates may ask you to putt first. In a scramble, the team with the fewest putts usually wins. Everyone will read the putts and

give his or her opinion about how much break there is in the green. By having you putt first, you show your teammates the putting line. The idea is that they learn from your putt how the green breaks and the speed of the green, and are able to hole their putt. Here's a warning if you putt first: In a scramble, when the first player putts his or her ball into the hole, then the other players are not supposed to putt and the team has completed the hole. If you putt first and the ball is only two inches away from the hole, don't automatically tap the ball in like you would in a nontournament round of golf. Instead, mark your ball and let your teammates try to sink their putts. Also, don't think that by playing first, you shouldn't try to make the putt. You should! But as the first putter, you also should make certain that your ball rolls at least to the hole, if not slightly beyond. Why? By leaving a putt short, you fail to show your teammates how the putt breaks near the hole.

• Before your tournament outing, practice your short game and putting. Women tell me that they let their male teammates and more experienced players hit their balls long, but they were stars of their teams because they could pitch the ball close to the hole or sink the long putts. If your team wins, they'll be thanking and remembering you for your short game and the long putts that you sank.

The other format that a tournament may use is referred to as *two best balls*. Each player plays his or her own ball. Depending on whether the format is best ball gross or net, the team score is the lowest score of the four players gross (without handicap) or net (with handicap). It's more likely that the format will be net best ball, so handicaps are factored into the scores. The team score is the total of the two lowest scores in the foursome.

One variation of this best ball format includes selecting the longest drive as in scrambles. Each player hits his or her drive from the tee. The team decides which drive is the best and from that location each player hits his or her second shot. Thereafter, each player plays his or her own ball until he or she completes the hole. The format may require your team to use two drives from each player, but your team will usually benefit from having a player that can hit the ball long off the tee.

The most important thing for you, if you're a beginner, is not to worry if you have a bad score on a hole. You have three other teammates who are part of your team. Let's say you score ten on a hole and your net score is eight, while the rest of your teammates have lower net scores. That's great! That's why you have teammates. Don't become discouraged about how you're playing. On the next hole you might have a net one or net two because of your handicap strokes, and then your team will love you for it! Besides, keep in mind your goal of why you are out there; it is to have fun and get to know your teammates better, not to win the tournament.

The same is true in the scramble format. Make a bad shot? Forget it, and concentrate on making your best shot possible on the next one. Tournaments can have a slow pace of play, so make sure you and your foursome play ready golf and keep up the pace. And, never apologize to your teammates for your bad shots or holes! All of you are trying your best to play well, so there's no need for an apology.

After-Golf Festivities and Awards

You've finished playing eighteen holes of golf and, it is hoped, you had a great time with the members of your foursome. Now it's time to go inside the clubhouse. First, you have to complete your scorecard and turn it into the scorers. The tournament planners or the golf course staff are checking the scorecards for accuracy and writing the scores on the leaderboard as foursomes get off the golf course. Make sure your foursome turns in your scorecard before you go to your cars and unload your clubs or clean up, so you don't delay the scoring (or lose the scorecard—it's been known to happen!).

While scores are checked and posted on the leaderboard, you'll have drinks and lunch or dinner, depending on when you started the day. If you played as a single in the tournament, you also have a choice to make as to whom you want to sit and eat with. If you really didn't have a good time during your round of golf with your playing partners, then you can consider exchanging business cards with them, saying, "Thanks for the round. I had a good time out there." You can then join another group for lunch or dinner, since it's common that some players will need to leave before lunch or dinner starts. For example, when Denise has played a tournament as a single, she will play and have a drink with her playing partners, and then have dinner with another group.

If your teammates were three guests whom you invited, then of course you continue to act as their host. You can offer to buy the first round of refreshments. It's more likely, though, that one of your guests will offer to do so as a way of reciprocating for your invitation to the tournament. It's during this time that your team will probably recap the memorable shots or holes of the day. Since you'll probably be sitting at a table with another foursome, it's a chance for all of you to meet those players as well. You can consider it an additional networking opportunity as part of playing in the tournament. Again, you never know whom you'll meet. It may be a new client or a fabulous referral source. Don't be bashful; hand out your business cards in a casual manner.

Before and after the meal and awards presentation, you'll have time to do some networking. If you see someone from a company that you've wanted to contact or a person that you've wanted an introduction to, this is a perfect chance for you to introduce yourself. Everyone is usually in a good mood after playing and is open to meeting new people. If you're approaching a business-man, make sure you have a business card ready to give to him; give him a firm handshake, so he doesn't misconstrue the reason for introducing yourself. You can say something like "Hi, I've been wanting to introduce myself and my company to you. I'm glad we could meet at this tournament. Can I have your card and give you a call in a couple of days?" When you do call, you'll imme-diately have the commonality of playing in the tournament and can easily move into the business reason for your call.

After lunch or dinner, the winners of the various contests and the tourna-ment will be presented. It's fun to watch which man and woman hit the longest drive and hear how far they hit the ball. You'll also learn who hit closest to the hole, and watch him or her be heckled by others as to whether he or she made the birdie putt. You'll also discover whether your team played well enough to take home a nice prize. The first-place prizes can be gift certificates worth $100 or more for merchandise in the pro shop, a golf club, a putter, a golf bag, or some other nice prize. Some tournaments are played because of their reputa-tion for giving quality prizes.

During some fund-raising tournaments, a silent auction for prizes may also be held. You'll probably find items that are related to golf, such as a set of golf clubs donated by a company, a round of golf for three with a member of a prestigious country club, a golf bag, or lessons from a local golf professional. You may also see spas, vacation packages, or even legal and accounting serv-ices. The donors of these prizes consider it an opportunity to advertise to a tar-get market of better-than-average wealth and a chance to support a charity. Denise plays in lots of tournaments and is often the high bid on golf packages, so she can get access to country clubs for more client golf outings. She claims that for the price of playing at high-end public courses, she can play at some exclusive country clubs and have a chance to play with a member as well. After the auction is closed, the sponsors will announce who the high bidder is for each item.

After Tournament Follow Up

If you were invited as a guest to play in a tournament, send a thank you note to your host. Consider how you can reciprocate for your host's generosity. If your host mentioned a newfound interest in a place, a thing, or someone, consider sending a book, audio tape, or CD-ROM on the topic. Or if your company has logoed golf shirts, towels, cap, or golf balls, create a nice gift package for your host.

If you played as a single in the tournament, send a brief note to each of your playing partners letting them know how much you enjoyed playing with them and ask them to think of you if your services or company could ever be of help with their business needs. Include a couple of business cards with your note—you never know if your playing partners may become a referral source for you or a new client.

Because most people don't think of women as golfers, you sometimes have to go out of your way to show that you do play. At many tournaments, a photographer takes pictures of each foursome as a souvenir of the tournament for each player. Michelle puts these pictures from all of the tournaments that she has played in on a bulletin board in her office. Since most of her clients and prospects are men, they immediately talk about her game and build rapport by their common interest or love of playing the game.

There are many ways to benefit from playing tournaments. By playing often, you'll discover more ways to leverage your golf contacts into business relationships.

Make Your Golf Dates

This chapter should inspire you to learn about the tournaments that you can play in. Whether to support your own charity or your client's, a golf tournament is a fun outing that you can use to meet new people or play with clients and prospects. You'll have a good day of golf and camaraderie, as well as a chance to win some great prizes. Check your local golf courses, newspapers, or organizations for announcements about upcoming golf tournaments and mark them in your calendar.

Staying On Course

_____ Enter tournaments as a single player or create a foursome. Support your favorite charity or your client's.

_____ Consider tournament sponsorship opportunities, such as tee signs, logoed item giveaways, and the like to promote yourself and your company.

_____ Before the tournament, practice your swing and especially your short game and putting. In a scramble tournament, let your teammates take care of the long shots—you can contribute with your stellar short game.

_____ Participate in pre- and posttournament activities for additional networking opportunities besides those in your foursome.

_____ Follow up with your playing partners after the tournament. If invited to a tournament, create a thank you gift for your host.

_____ Keep tournament souvenirs in your office as a conversation starter and to let others know you play the game.

_____ Add golf expenses as a line item in your marketing plan. Plan on playing in your favorite charity or association tournaments.

CHAPTER 8

··

Hosting and Organizing a Golf Tournament

If you've already played in a golf tournament, you know how much fun you and everyone else can have at these golf outings. You probably also have had some business successes thanks to playing in a golf tournament—a new client, a hot prospect, a great referral source, or maybe a playing partner for a future golf event. You've seen first hand how sponsors of a golf tournament can benefit by either raising money or promoting their company, products, or services. Perhaps you're even thinking now of how your company or organization could profit from hosting a golf tournament.

Behind the scenes of running a golf tournament require enormous attention to detail. If you're considering a golf tournament to enhance your company's business image or to raise funds for a charity, proper preparation and planning are essential. A great tournament will make your company shine. A poorly run tournament may tarnish your organization's image.

A tournament will be successful when all the minutest details have been considered. With so much work, planning a golf tournament isn't a job for one person. You can have committees for choosing the golf course, marketing and public relations of the tournament, obtaining sponsors, selecting prizes, fund raising, and much more. Although committees can gather the appropriate information, prices, and provide suggestions, one designated person should be authorized to make the necessary decisions.

Before you commit to organizing a tournament, read this chapter to make certain that you have the time, persistence, and resources to get the job done

171

right. In this chapter, I discuss how to host a tournament successfully. You'll learn when you can use a golf tournament for business as well as what to offer nongolfers during the event. I give you pointers on managing a budget, which golf course to select, how the golf course staff can help you, and when to seek a professional who is trained in planning golf tournaments to help you with your tournament. You'll get ideas on how to make your tournament a success!

Why Have a Golf Tournament?

You've probably seen a variety of companies and associations sponsor golf tournaments. Why do they spend the time and money on tournament sponsorships? Tournaments are great venues for people (employees, clients, prospects, vendors, etc.) to meet one another, have a good time, and play golf. But there is also an underlying business reason for every golf tournament. Some common objectives for business golf tournaments are:

- Customer appreciation. Thank customers and clients for past business.
- Employee outings. Use golf as a venue for employees to mingle and get to know one another.
- Product launches. Introduce a new product in a fun and relaxed atmosphere, rather than a typical tradeshow launch.
- Charity or fund-raising events. Make money and increase the exposure of a cause, charity, or foundation.
- Sales incentives. Reward top performers with a day on a beautiful golf course.
- Membership networking. Use a tournament as a venue for members to get to know one another and their businesses.

Michelle, the president of a construction company, has hosted golf tournaments for the past six years to thank customers. She says a golf tournament allows her company to spend more time with clients, rather than just the usual party during the holidays. She starts planning the tournament in January and holds the event in late August or September.

Andrea is a director of business development and a self-described new golfer. After playing in a few golf tournaments and experiencing the interactions between players in a foursome, she volunteered to organize a tournament for her colleagues in a fast-growing high-technology company. She had discovered that most employees only knew colleagues who worked in the same department and perhaps a few in other departments. She created foursomes comprised of players with different golf experiences and from different departments. No one played on the same team as his or her boss. Andrea noted that the golf tournament was a great way for employees to meet one another outside the work environment.

Tracy is the regional director of sales for the largest golf course management company in the United States. She works with companies and organizations that want to hold golf tournaments on one of the many golf courses that she represents. Some clients have launched new products during a golf course tournament. One sponsor of a product-launch tournament was a car manufacturer. To showcase the cars, a new car was parked near the entrance to the clubhouse and near each of the par 3 holes. The manufacturer invited car dealership personnel, the media, and corporate customers to a round of golf and to view the latest car models.

As you can see, a golf tournament can be a productive way to accomplish business while providing a way for people to have fun. I'm sure your company can find many reasons to hold a golf tournament.

What About Nongolfers?

If you're thinking about sponsoring a golf tournament, some co-workers or management may disapprove or even resent the idea of using golf as a way to conduct business. Some people have outdated opinions about the game, thinking it's for the elite country club set. In the past, that may have been true, but with the heightened popularity of the game and the increase in the number of golf courses, the game is accessible to almost everyone. Some people also think that playing golf is simply a way to get out of the office on company time and at company expense.

You may need to provide the business benefits of playing golf to these golf opponents. Stress the value of spending nearly five hours of uninterrupted time with a client or prospect, or how many calories they can burn if you think those reasons will motivate them to want to play. Talk about who plays golf for business—sales executives, management executives, decision makers, presidents of companies, and the like. Give examples of colleagues or friends who have had tremendous success as a result of playing golf with someone. Explain that these executives play golf because they know the game is an international language of business; it truly can be a conversation icebreaker and a relationship and rapport builder.

Consider introducing the nongolfers to the game with a teaching clinic during the golf tournament. While others are playing in the tournament, the nongolfers can attend a seminar on the benefits of playing, how to play a business golf round, and business golf etiquette and rules. After the seminar, they can learn the basics of the golf swing, putting, and pitching from golf swing instructors. Show the nongolfers the rapport-building opportunity that they're missing out on by being on the sidelines of the golf course and turn them into excited golfers for next year's golf event. After their clinic, they can enjoy the after-golf festivities with the players.

. . . .

An investment banking firm spent about $40,000 to send forty-eight women executives to a golf clinic. Why? The firm considers playing golf with clients an advantage when closing deals.

. . . .

Whom to Invite?

Depending on the objective of your golf tournament, you can have as few as 12 to 20 employees for a golf gathering or a full field of 144 golfers for a large-scale business golf outing. You'll want to look at your invitation list for outside clients, vendors, and other people and businesses with whom you have existing business relationships. Budget is always a consideration when considering whom to invite. Michelle invites 120 to 130 clients, referral sources, subcontractors, and others who have contributed to building her business, as well as her key employees. Mitch, the president of a golf tournament planning company, said he recently worked with an insurance company to host a golf tournament for its top 100 clients.

In addition to the outsiders you invite, you need to consider which employees within your company you want to include in the field. Sales executives, account representatives, and senior management executives should attend the golf tournament and invite their top clients. Senior management people should be available to meet and talk with those guests invited to the company's tournaments. They should act as hosts of the event, rather than simply playing.

The executives must be careful not to offend anyone by spending most of their time with one client. For example, Michelle doesn't play golf in a foursome during her company's tournament. Instead, she drives a cart to visit with every foursome. She might play one hole with a group and chat with them, then she's off to another foursome. The insurance company president drives a cart to each foursome and hands out cigars, chocolates, and beer to players. Both Michelle and the insurance company president are acting as they should: as hosts for the day, making sure all players have what they need and are having a great time.

In your invitations to a golf tournament, make sure you specify dress and spike requirements, especially if your tournament is held at a country club. You don't want a guest to arrive in inappropriate attire. Most courses have staff available to change spikes for a fee.

Pairings

If you're planning a company event, pay close attention to player pairings. For example, you may want to include at least one company representative in each foursome, since your company is the host. Or if you are inviting hot prospects, then perhaps pair each prospect with a key customer who can provide a testimonial about your company. Be careful when creating foursome pairings: You don't want to pair the president of a company that is a major client of your company's with an inexperienced junior sales representative in your company. The president would likely be offended at the lack of respect given to her by pairing her with such a junior employee.

You should also check with colleagues to find those who are familiar with the backgrounds and histories of your clients, vendors, and the other players in the tournament. An unfortunate pairing, for example, would be to have a company sales representative paired with one of his dissatisfied former clients who remained a client as long as that employee did not work on his account. It could be an uncomfortable situation for all if there is an inappropriate pairing of players.

Some additional tips regarding pairings are:

- Don't put four beginners in a foursome. They may be unfamiliar with the concept of ready golf and slow the field behind them.
- Don't put four women in a foursome. Pair women golfers with men who you know enjoy playing with women.
- For an employee outing, create foursomes with different department personnel who don't know one another.
- Mix players with different experience levels, so no one team has a distinct advantage.

Tournament Format

To make the tournament a fun event for all, a team format, such as a scramble or two best balls, is most commonly used. These formats encourage beginners and experienced players alike to play. They also create camaraderie and a team spirit among the players.

Selecting a Golf Course

When deciding at which golf course to host your tournament, consider these factors:

- Private or public. Private country clubs do allow outside tournaments access to their golf courses, but scheduling is usually limited to Mondays when the course is closed to members. Many companies now prefer to hold their golf tournaments during the middle of the week at 1 P.M., so the tournament doesn't take place just before or after the weekend and some work can be done in the morning. If that is the case, these companies can choose public courses.
- Location. If the golf outing is for employees only, then a golf course near the office makes sense. When clients, vendors, and others are coming from various locations, then a golf course in a central location, close to a major highway or thoroughfare is more suitable. Consider whether air travel and hotel arrangements—possibly at your expense—are necessary as well.
- Golf course difficulty. Consider the golf experience of the players. Most players like some challenge to the course they play, and, if the course is too easy or too difficult, it may deter some players from entering the tournament. If most players are beginners, choose an easier, flatter golf course. Likewise, if most of the players are experienced golfers, choose a slightly more difficult golf course. Remember that the average slope for golf courses is 113. For an easier course, choose a course with a slope less than 113.
- Golf course name. If you want to host a golf tournament with panache, then you want to select a well-known or prestigious golf course, whether a country club or an upscale public course.
- Food and beverage service. Depending on your after-golf program, you may need a golf course with a full-service restaurant to serve dinner and drinks, or at least one with a large banquet room to have food catered.
- Golf-related services. If you're having a full field of players, then you'll likely want the golf course to provide additional services, such as bag drop, cart signage, scoring, leaderboard posting, assistance with contests, and other golf-related services. Ask if the golf course will provide such services and at what additional cost per player, if any.
- Availability of golf club rentals. Determine if the golf course has golf clubs for rent, the cost per bag, the condition of the clubs, availability of clubs for right- and left-handed players, or men's and women's clubs.

- Golf carts. Does the golf course have enough carts for all players? Are they covered for sun protection? Are they in good running condition?
- Condition of the golf course and facilities. Will the golf course or other facilities have any scheduled repairs on your tournament date?

Make sure you visit the golf course to meet the golf course staff *before* the tournament. Several golf course personnel may work with you to put on the event, such as the director of golf or the head golf professional for golf-related activities and the clinic for nongolfers, and the director of food and beverage for after-golf festivities. Be sure to meet everyone and ask who will be personally available on the day of your tournament.

Budget

As you begin planning a golf tournament, you need to look at your budget. A full-field golf tournament can be quite expensive. Michelle spends nearly $40,000 for her tournament of 144 players. While this fee is on the higher end, at a minimum, you will have to pay for green fees and cart rental fees per player for golf, plus food and beverage costs. You'll also want to allocate funds for tee prizes, prizes for teams, contest winners, and other related expenses. If you're planning a golf outing for employees, you may even ask that they pay some nominal amount to help defray costs.

Here's a closer look at what you have to consider when you are planning a tournament.

Green Fees

Depending on when you hold the tournament and its format, the costs can vary for green fees. If you schedule the tournament for when the golf course would be earning its greatest revenue from the public, then you'll have to pay more per player. The highest green fees are charged during prime weather seasons on Fridays or Sundays on a public golf course. Less expensive times are during less favorable weather, such as during the summer in hot climate areas, and on weekdays.

Your green fees also will vary depending on whether you use a shotgun start or traditional tee times. Shotguns are more expensive because the course staff makes the entire golf course available for your tournament. The staff can't let other players onto the course prior to the time it takes groups to play nine holes. Most public golf courses require at least 72 or more players to have a shotgun start with a foursome on each hole. The maximum is 144 players with two foursomes on each hole. For a shotgun start, you'll be limited to early mornings or at 1 P.M. usually, since it can take at least five and a half hours to complete the round. Some courses put one foursome on par 3 holes to speed up play, so the maximum may be only 128 players.

If you don't have enough players for a shotgun start, say, 20 to 80 players, then a golf course may use a *modified shotgun*, where your players start from holes one through nine only. This format allows public play on the course while your tournament is underway.

If you don't have enough players for a modified shotgun, then you have to use the standard tee times, which is the least expensive. You typically pay only the standard green fees per player. The problem with using tee times, however, is the gap between when the first and last groups finish. For twenty players, the wait can be as much as an hour or more. The groups with the earlier tee times have a long wait before others are in the clubhouse for the awards presentation.

The golf course will quote you a tournament package cost per player, which usually includes the green and cart rental fees, money that must be spent in the pro shop on merchandise or gift certificates, a personalized bag tag for each player, a box lunch, and signage on carts and contest holes. The costs vary depending on how elaborate you want the menu and prizes to be.

Tee and Tournament Prizes

A tournament can become popular because of the wonderful prizes that are available for players to win. If you're hosting a fund-raising tournament, then you can look for sponsors for some of the prizes. Otherwise, for a company tournament, you need to include the cost of prizes in your budget. You could, however, ask some of your clients to donate prizes as a way to network with your other clients and give them additional exposure at your tournament. It's likely that you will have credit for prizes in the pro shop. As part of the tournament fee, $5 to $10 per player is allocated to buying merchandise in the pro shop.

Tee prizes are goody bags that tournament players have come to expect. Common tee prizes include logoed items such as balls, tees, towels, shirts, and caps. More unusual and memorable keepsakes (also with logo) are:

- Golf shoe bags
- Wind jackets or vests
- Caddy carrier bags—small zippered pouches with aspirin, divot tool, sunscreen, and so forth
- Backpacks
- Golf books

- Golf throw blankets
- Photo frames with sponsoring company's name displayed

Logoed golf balls are nice, but remember what happens to most balls—they get lost or damaged! In either case, they don't make long-lasting gifts. Choose something in addition to or in lieu of golf balls that people will likely keep and use often.

Contest and Team Prizes

As in most golf tournaments, you will have prizes for particular contests and team winners. Stay away from the traditional engraved trophies; after the excitement of winning wears off, they become dust collectors.

Mitch, the tournament planner, suggests gift certificates from the pro shop as prizes, thus preventing the problem of sizes for clothing or preference in brands for clubs. For full-field tournaments, he suggests this prize structure:

First place team	$100
Second place team	$75
Third place team	$50
Longest drive for men and women	$50 each
Closest to the hole for men and women	$50 each

Mitch suggests these amounts because he has found that if the prize money is much more, then some players get competitive. Just as you seek to create in your business golf rounds, Mitch wants players to have a good time and enjoy the day, rather than focus on winning.

If you prefer giving prizes, consider something unique, such as an engraved crystal vase or bowl, a personalized putter, or a round of golf for each player at an exclusive course. Select prizes that winners will likely use and that will make them want to play in your tournament each year.

The golf course staff will help you to choose the holes for the contests. By the way, even if there is only one woman playing in the tournament, you should have a separate contest for women and men in the longest drive contest.

On-the-Course Activities

Besides golf, you may decide to offer some sort of activity on a par 3 hole where players will likely have long waits for the foursome ahead. For example, you may have a professional photographer take souvenir pictures, massage therapists to help loosen up players' golf swings, or a margarita bar. Rather than grumbling about slow play, the players will enjoy the respite and the surprise you have waiting for them.

Food and Beverage

You have a wide range of choices for food—from box lunches to barbecues to prime rib. Depending on the golf course, you can have a buffet or banquet. It depends on your budget and how elaborate an affair you want to sponsor. Some tournament sites even offer players a choice of entrées, say, fish or beef, instead of the usual chicken dish.

On the golf course, you may want to pay for a beverage cart to offer refreshments, especially if the tournament is held on a very warm day. A word of caution regarding beverage carts: Clarify with the food and beverage coordinator those items that you will pay for. For example, let's say you intend to buy only drinks for players, but there are expensive cigars and food on the cart. If you don't intend to pay for those items, make the necessary arrangements to prevent such a misunderstanding. Some tournament sponsors, for example, provide a raffle ticket to players in their tee prize bag for a free drink on the course.

Tipping

Include in your budget a sum of money for tipping the golf course staff, such as the head golf professional, bag boys, beverage cart drivers, and so forth. A common tip is $5 per player to be allocated among the club personnel. As with any service you receive, if the staff's service was special, then certainly tip more. The food and beverage services typically include the gratuity.

Fund-Raising Element

Companies are willing to donate money, services, or products to a golf tournament that is raising funds for a charity, cause, or nonprofit organization. In exchange, they get a tax deduction and advertising. If you're organizing a tournament for a charity or want to have a fund-raising element, then you should consider these sponsors:

- Tournament sponsors. You can seek a title sponsor for the tournament. If you find a corporation willing to sponsor the tournament and contribute $5,000 to $10,000, then you want to treat that corporation special. You should structure a benefits package for the different levels of sponsorship. For example, the title sponsor should be given the most benefits. You might want to give the sponsor entry for four players, with each entrant receiving a pair of golf shoes, a dozen of the hottest golf balls on the market, swing analysis from a golf professional with champagne on the driving range.

- Hole sponsors. You can sell a hole sponsorship. A sign with the hole sponsor's name is located at the tee box. A nice touch is to have the sponsor's foursome start at the hole he or she has sponsored. Also, you can present the sign to the sponsor as a souvenir after the tournament.
- Contest sponsors. You can have the hole-in-one hole contest, closest-to-the-hole contest, or the longest-drive contest sponsored by different organizations.
- Food sponsors. A company can sponsor a meal or beverages served during the tournament.
- Silent auction. Better prizes, such as vacations, spas, or golf packages can be saved for a silent auction to raise more money.
- Raffles. You can sell raffle tickets for donated prizes.
- Sell mulligans. Although mulligans don't exist under the rules of golf, they do for tournament planners. You can also sell mulligans to raise money and make the tournament more fun, rather than a serious golf competition. You will need to sell tickets. Common pricing for mulligans is one mulligan for $5 or three for $10. Usually for a one-day event, each person is allowed only one mulligan, but it can't be used to win a prize on holes with contests.

In addition to the entry fee and using a variety of these fund-raising methods, organizations can make a sizable profit from the tournament, if that is their objective.

Awards Presentation

The after-golf presentation of awards, introduction of notables within an organization, and dinner should also be well planned. The presentation should start as soon as possible after the golf scoring is completed. If players have already spent five to six hours for golf, they probably don't want after-golf activities to take more than an hour and a half. Make sure this portion of the tournament is done efficiently as well. Often for fund raisers, the awards for golf are presented after the dinner, raffle, and auction activities. To save time, announce awards, raffles, and silent auctions during dessert. You definitely want to have a master of ceremonies, someone who will keep the presentation part of the postgolf event flowing smoothly.

When You Need a Professional Planner

Depending on the course you select to host your golf tournament, its staff will likely offer you suggestions and recommendations regarding the logistics of your tournament. You may lack the time or experience, however, to handle the details of the tournament and prefer to have a golf tournament planner work with you.

These professionals specialize in running golf tournaments and can assist in all facets of the tournament: transportation to and from the golf course, sending of invitations, seeking sponsorships, ordering signage for hole and contest sponsorships, and so forth. They usually have staff at the tournament to make sure things are running smoothly and to work with the golf course staff.

Professional planners can also assist in helping you find a speaker, a celebrity PGA or LPGA golf professional to provide a swing clinic or the master of ceremonies for your event. If you decide you need a professional planner for the tournament, ask the golf course staff or others who have used planners for referrals. Make sure you and the planner are clear about your respective duties and responsibilities for the tournament.

Communication Is a Must

Now you have learned about the inner workings of a golf tournament. As you have found out, there are many issues to consider. If you decide to organize a tournament, you'll stumble on unique situations. It's important that you communicate with the key players at the golf course and with people within your organization. Checklists outlining who is responsible for particular tasks by a given deadline will help prevent any oversights since many people will be involved in the process.

Staying On Course

_____ Consider whether you or your company should host and organize a golf tournament. Objectives can include customer appreciation, employee outings, product launches, charity giving, sales incentive, or a networking event.

_____ Educate nongolfers about the business value of playing golf. During the golf tournament, plan a golf swing clinic and business golf seminar for nongolfers.

_____ Determine budget and time commitments for hosting a successful tournament. Consider whom to invite—clients, vendors, and prospects, as well as executives within your company.

_____ Pay close attention to the pairings of players—avoid uncomfortable or inappropriate pairings.

_____ Choose a golf course that fits your budget, provides the services you want, and meets your tournament objectives.

_____ Select prizes and a menu that will make your tournament memorable and a "must do" each year.

_____ Consider the various ways your organization can raise money with the tournament.

_____ Choose a tournament format so players of all levels have a fun day.

_____ Run the after-golf activities as smoothly as your golf tournament.

_____ Consider whether you need a tournament planner to help make your tournament a success.

PART FOUR

SUGGESTIONS FOR THE MALE GOLFER

CHAPTER 9

....

For Men Who Play
Business Golf
with Women

Perhaps you've picked up this book because you're a golfer. Or, maybe your wife, girlfriend, female boss, colleague, or client gave this book to you. Try to keep an open mind as to what you're about to read. You may be a better-than-average golfer, but your wife or friend may wish you knew some of the following suggestions about how you can make the game more enjoyable for her and any other women you might play with.

In addition, as more businesswomen start to play the game, you may find yourself hosting a business golf round with a woman decision maker. Women are heads of their own multimillion dollar corporations, if not buyers of products and services within corporations. After interviewing businesswomen about what they wished men knew about playing golf with them, I thought a chapter for men would be useful. I hope to give you some things to consider before you next play golf with a businesswoman, so everyone can have an enjoyable round of golf!

....

Women rule! 10.2 million women (20 percent of working wives) earn MORE than their husbands. Consumer spending by women: $3.3 trillion + purchasing agents for government and industry > 50 percent U.S. Domestic Product. Women = 43 percent of Americans with assets > $500,000.

Tom Peters

....

Remember Your Goal

As the vice president of global sales for a rental car company, Bill welcomes the chance to play golf with a female corporate buyer of his company's services. He finds a round of golf a great opportunity to showcase his company and the customer service that she can expect when doing business with him. He sets the goal of making sure she is having a fun, comfortable, and pleasant experience. He doesn't worry about his golf game or his score during this business golf round. Instead, he focuses on what he can do to assure that she enjoys her golf game and that she will be more likely to consider doing business with him.

If you're playing golf with a woman who is a beginner, then you should consider the round a practice round. Don't be concerned about your score or how you play. She'll likely be impressed by how you play even if you consider it an off day for your game.

. . . .

The big issue isn't women's satisfaction with your products and services. It's the women who are turned off to the point of not stopping by in the first place . . . to your company . . . or to your industry.

Tom Peters, Circle of Innovation

. . . .

Inviting a Woman to Play

Are you thinking about inviting a woman business prospect to play? Perhaps you know she plays golf or she's talked about wanting to play more. If she's been playing for a while and talks confidently about her game, then you can easily extend an invitation to play. Some women, however, might be afraid to play with you because they're worried that they're not good enough, or maybe they simply haven't played with men before. You may have to assure these reticent women that you only want to play a congenial round of business golf. For example, you can say, "I enjoy playing with men and women of all different skill levels. Don't worry, we'll just go out and have fun, and talk some business afterward."

A word of caution: If you really *don't* enjoy playing with beginners or women, then it's probably best for you not to try to put on a good face. It's possible that she'll sense your annoyance or impatience, which would defeat your intent in trying to make a favorable impression. Instead, perhaps you can suggest hitting a bucket of balls at the driving range, or practicing your putting and short games followed by a business chat over lunch. Or, you can invite her to your golf club for lunch and use that as an opportunity to gauge her interest and knowledge about the game.

Also, make sure that the other men you invite to join your foursome (if you decide to do so) also enjoy playing with beginners and women. Remember that you may be judged by the company you keep. Even though you're on your best behavior, if one of your playing partners behaves inappropriately, it may spoil the opportunity for you to make a good business impression.

If you intend to have her as your guest, make sure she understands that you'll pay for the green and cart rental fees. When you extend the invitation, ask if she prefers to walk or ride, so she can be prepared to bring her pull cart or be ready to share a cart with you. Also, make clear which course you'll be playing, clarify any dress or spike requirements, and confirm when and where you'll meet at the golf course.

Does she want to hit a bucket of balls to warm up and spend some time at the practice putting green? Does she have time for lunch or refreshments after the round of golf so you have time to talk some business? The woman you're playing with may have read this book and will know how to ask you these questions. If she hasn't read this book, she may not know what to ask, and she'll find it helpful if you offer her this information.

Choosing a Course

If you're inviting a woman prospect to play, ask if she has a favorite local golf course. Keep in mind that even if she accepts your invitation to play, she still may be nervous about playing with you. Choosing a course she is familiar with will probably help her feel more confident about playing golf with you.

If she doesn't have a favorite course, then consider her playing experience and ability. If she's a beginner, you probably don't want to choose a course that has a high slope (average slope rating is 113), is hilly, or has a lot of hazards. Choose a course that is beginner-friendly, perhaps even an executive course. They're more likely to have shorter holes, be flatter, and have less trouble spots.

Also bear in mind bathroom needs. In emergencies, men have the ability to take a bathroom break in the great outdoors. If you're playing with a woman guest, and the need for bathrooms is also an issue for you, then choose a golf course with toilet facilities at different locations on the course, in addition to those at the turn and in the clubhouse. Such a choice is far more appropriate than disappearing for a few minutes in the shrubbery.

At the First Tee

You may always play from the tips or the middle tees and you expect your businesswomen guest to hit from the forward tees (these tees are no longer referred to as women's tees). Rather than automatically making these assumptions, consider her playing ability. For example, if you're playing with a woman who plays often and has a handicap in the teens, she might prefer to play from the middle tees with you, rather than the forward tees. Consider the distance between the middle and forward tees at the course that you're playing. At the club I belong to, it's fairly easy for an above-average woman player to hit from the middle tees, since the distance between the two sets of tees on many holes is only 5 to 10 yards.

Some women don't like feeling rushed to hit from the forward tees after waiting for their playing partners to hit from the back or middle tees. I have also suggested to women that if they feel comfortable playing from the middle tees with three men they should do so. My rationale for this is that a woman is often missing out on parts of the conversation as she moves to the forward tees. If she wants to get to know all of you for business reasons, then she should play from the same tees as you do and pick up later during the playing of the hole, if needed.

Invite your guest to play from the same tees you are. She'll appreciate the gesture and consider it a compliment that you have such confidence in her golf game.

However, if she's a beginner, you have a couple of options as to which tee you should play. If you think you will outdrive her by a great distance if you hit from the middle tees, then consider hitting farther back so that both of your drives will land in the same general area.

Another suggestion is to take shorter clubs and hit from the forward tees with her and consider it a practice round for your irons and trick shots. Or, do as one gentleman does; he plays from the forward tees but uses Cayman balls, which do not fly as far as regular golf balls.

You might scoff at the idea of hitting from the forward tees. I have heard men say they would be embarrassed if guys they knew saw them hitting from the forward tees, or that the round wouldn't be as much fun for them because of the shorter holes. That's fine. I only suggest that this is a business golf round—your ego, manhood, or the quality of golfer you are is not at stake in this round. Of course, you would ordinarily never play from the forward tees, but you're trying to make a business decision maker feel comfortable playing with you in *this* round in hopes of doing business together.

If you are open to the idea of hitting from the forward tees, then ask your guest if she would prefer that you do that: "You mentioned you're a beginner, and to save us from going back and forth to different tees, would you like me to play from the same tees as you?" If you ask in a matter-of-fact way and without sounding patronizing, condescending, or solicitous, you will have made points with your gesture of generosity.

You'll also get a chance to see who she is and how she responds. If she says, "No, thanks for the offer. Play from the tees you ordinarily would," you've learned information about her. She appreciates your ability and may not care how her golf game looks in comparison to yours. She's comfortable and confident in playing her game and in you playing yours. If she says, "Well, thanks, if you don't mind, that would be great," then you have an opening to show how you can provide excellent customer service on the golf course and while conducting business together in the future. And, if she becomes offended at your offer, then you also know the type of woman that you're dealing with. (I know—it's sometimes not easy to be a gentleman nowadays.)

Whichever tee that you and your woman guest have decided to play from, before you tee off, say something to the effect of wanting to have a fun round of golf and not worrying about how you both play. Such an opening will help your guest be more at ease about her golf game. She'll be more relaxed and more likely to enjoy playing with you.

Betting

Unlike most men, women don't bet as often when playing golf. And, if someone does, then she probably will play for only a small wager—drinks or lunch just to keep the game interesting for everyone. As the host of a woman business prospect, I recommend that you not suggest a bet. If she's a beginner, it may be her first bet and it will probably make her nervous about her game and playing with you, which isn't what you want. But if she asks about betting, and is a beginner without a handicap, then be creative about the bet. Perhaps you can count who is on the green first or who has the fewest putts.

If she has a handicap and wants to bet, then you might suggest a Nassau bet, rather than low net, so there isn't pressure on every hole. Remember, the idea is not for either of you to win, but to build rapport and learn whether you'd enjoy working together.

If you are playing with two other men in addition to your guest and all of you want to bet, then don't exclude her from the bet. Invite her to bet, even though you think she might not want to join in on the game; just make it clear that she doesn't have to bet. As long as women are comfortable with the maximum they can lose and they understand the rules of the bet, they should be encouraged to bet to become part of the dynamics within the foursome.

Playing from Different Tees

Suppose you are playing from the tips and she is playing from the forward tees. Since you're playing from different tees, you should know about the first of two things that women golfers—both beginners and experienced players—find most annoying when playing with men.

I speak to women in corporations and associations about playing business golf. They frequently share their frustration about men who hit their tee shots and then drive or walk by the forward tees, forgetting that the women still have to hit. I have had similar experiences and I understand their frustration. Once in a scramble tournament, I played with three men. When the two guys drove by the forward tee the first and second time, it didn't bother me. They apologized, and I assumed that they were having a good conversation and/or didn't play with women often. By the seventh time they did this, however, I was getting very irritated and didn't even bother to stop them as they drove ahead. When they finally realized that they couldn't hear my cart behind them, they stopped and turned around. In spite of this, we used twelve of my drives that day since they were the best drives!

Needless to say, it's rude and disrespectful if you drive by the forward tee without stopping to let your playing partner hit. It's not a way to impress your prospect about how much you value her and her business.

A generous gesture is for you to get out of the cart and stand on the forward tee with her. She won't feel as rushed as having three guys waiting in the carts for her to hit. She'll also focus on her swing, rather than where her ball lands, since she knows you'll help watch her ball. And, by being on the forward tee with her, you are more likely to refrain from talking while she's hitting.

How You Can Help

Besides feeling like they're not part of the game when men drive by the forward tees, the biggest annoyance for women playing with men is men who give them unsolicited swing advice. Women understand that men hate to see them struggle and simply want to help them play better. Nevertheless, it's annoying for women to receive swing tips because they're usually bombarded with them. (It's particularly annoying when the male player isn't that good or has an ugly swing.)

If she does ask for help on her golf swing, keep your advice simple and at a minimum. Tell her if she's aiming too far right or if she's not looking at the ball before she hits it, but don't talk about her swing plane and her X-factor. She probably won't know what you're talking about, which will frustrate her even more. You should wait until she asks again for help before you offer another tip.

One way you can help, though, is to have her gain confidence by focusing on what she's doing well. Perhaps she's having trouble driving the ball, but if her short game is great, tell her so. Or maybe you've seen her hit her 5-iron well, but she can't get off the tee with her 5-wood. On the next tee, hint that she should try her 5-iron since you've seen her confidence with that club and how well she can hit it. After a few good shots off the tee with her 5-iron, you can suggest she try to hit her 5-wood the same way she hits her 5-iron. In other words, reinforce the strengths of her game, and tell her not to worry about the other aspects—she might be having an off day or she can talk to her golf professional about it.

Here are some other suggestions on how you can help:

- Be flexible about scoring.   If she's getting uptight about her high score, stop keeping score. Instead suggest that she keep track of her good shots and focus on taking only two putts.
- Be flexible about playing by the rules.   Although you may usually play by the rules, when playing with a beginner, it sometimes helps to bend the rules. She might know the rules and prefer to play as it lies. Or, she may not know the rules and you can offer her the option of moving her ball or playing by the rules. It's a good idea to let her know the appropriate rule, though, so she doesn't think that is the way the game is played ordinarily. In addition, she gets a chance to learn the rules. Let's say your guest's ball is behind a tree and on hardpan; you could suggest that she drop the ball into the rough or find a patch of grass where she has a clear shot. Or, if she hit her ball into a lateral water hazard, tell her what relief she is entitled to under the rules, but also suggest that she drop another ball on the other side of the water hazard. Even suggest that she tee the ball up in the fairway if that will help her make good contact with the ball.
- Don't tell her which club she should use.   Your guest might ask which club you think she should use, assuming that since you're familiar with the course or are a better player you would know. The problem, however, is you don't know what distances she hits her clubs. The best you can do is to tell her the approximate distance, factoring in things such as elevated greens and wind (I know it's a violation of the rules). Or, if

there's a hazard in the fairway, suggest that she lay up her ball if she isn't sure she can hit over the hazard. You can also suggest that she use the club she feels most comfortable hitting.

- Don't tell her to keep her head down.   When speaking at corporate outings, I also attend the golf swing clinics that are part of the business golf event. I've heard several golf professionals ask women, "Have you been told, 'Keep your head down?'" Most of the women reply yes and nod their heads vigorously. The problem with telling women—or any beginner—to keep their head down is they keep it down such that they can't follow through completely. Try it! Swing your club with your head down throughout your swing—you'll only be able to partially follow through. Instead of suggesting that she keep her head down, recommend that she keep her eye on the ball until she hits it. That's more likely the solution to her topping the ball or missing the ball completely.

- Tell her to slow down.   Most women are afraid that they play too slow and are holding up the foursome or the field. You've probably played with some women who run to their ball or rush to hit without taking the time to aim and think about their shots. If you're playing at an appropriate pace and you notice your guest is rushing, say that your group's pace of play is fine and she can relax. Tell her that if your group starts to fall behind, then you'll say something to her. Otherwise, help her relax and enjoy her game.

- Avoid being overly complimentary.   Let's say a fairly good woman player has hit several "wormburners" in a row and can't seem to hit the ball into the air. Finally, she hits one in the air for 100 yards using her 3-iron. Don't say, "There you go!" or "Good shot!" She is still likely disgusted with her shot and your comment may humiliate her even further. She probably normally hits her 3-iron 150 yards, so your gesture to be supportive may be only a reminder that she's not hitting the ball well. It might be safer not to make any comments about her shots until you have a sense of how she plays. In the meantime, the best thing to do when she's struggling is the same thing you do with a male partner who isn't hitting the ball particularly well; talk about something other than golf that you both might enjoy.

Staying Focused on Your Goal

Your goal of this business golf round is for your woman prospect to get to know you and your company, and vice versa. If you're not playing your best game of golf, don't worry about it. If you're playing from the forward tees, have fun with it, and practice your irons and even try some trick shots. Consider this round as a practice round for you. If you've got a competitive streak in you, then focus on your short game and keep track of your putts. Set a goal of sinking all putts within a certain distance or hitting your chips and pitch shots within 10 feet of the pin.

Etiquette

If you've invited a businesswoman to play and are playing with two other men, don't forget that you're the host and she's your guest. Although it's easy to walk with the guys because you may be playing from the same tees and hit about the same distance, remember you've invited her to play. Don't make her feel left out by walking ahead with them before she's even had a chance to put her club away or spend most of the round talking to them.

Here are some other etiquette tips that your guest will appreciate:

- Be quiet. Even though she is a beginner, she also appreciates hitting her ball without whispers and noise as any player would.
- Watch her ball. Although she may hit the ball shorter than you do, knowing you're watching her ball may help her to keep her eye on the ball and not look up too soon.
- Pick up her clubs. If she's put her pitching wedge, sand wedge, and glove on the green to putt, help her get her clubs and glove after she's putted out.
- Pull and replace the flagstick. Make an effort to take care of the pin more than you ordinarily would during a round. More experienced players usually have a better sense of who pulls and tends the flagstick. If she doesn't pull the flagstick for you, certainly ask if she could do so.
- Offer tips if they seem to be wanted. If you notice she does not know the ins and outs of etiquette and ready golf, ask if she'd like you to share some tips with her. Most beginners—men and women—would like to know more about the finer points of the game, but they haven't had anyone show them. If you keep it simple, she'd probably appreciate the tips.
- Manage the cart with her. If she's a beginner, she may not know common practices in managing the golf cart. For example, if your foursome is falling behind, tell her that you'll leave the cart for her, walk to your ball, and that she should drive the cart to you or to the green. Or, she may need to be educated about the 90-degree rule.

- Turn off or set on silent your cell phone and pager. Avoid interruptions during your business meeting on the golf course. You can check for urgent messages at the turn or before nineteenth hole festivities.

Off-Color Jokes and Foul Language

Obviously, if you're trying to impress a prospect or someone you don't know well—man or woman—you need to be cautious about telling jokes and using expletives. Once again, since you're playing for business reasons, think of the golf course as your office during the round. If an expletive should slip, simply apologize, and remember your goal for the round so it doesn't happen again.

Stogies and Scotch

Perhaps you enjoy smoking a cigar and drinking alcohol while you're playing with your friends. Before you light up, ask your guest if she would mind the cigar smoke. Some women (and men) find cigar smoke too strong and offensive. If she hesitantly says she wouldn't mind if you smoked a stogie, then be cautious about not having smoke blow in her face. As to drinking alcohol, again this is a business meeting, so watch your alcohol consumption.

Quit Before Finishing Eighteen

If you're a diehard golfer like I am, you probably would never think of quitting before finishing eighteen holes. But if your guest is a beginner, midway through the round she may be getting tired or bored with the game. Since you paid for the round, however, she will likely be hesitant about asking you to quit on, say, the twelfth hole. If you are getting the sense that she has had enough golf, offer to quit and go back for an early lunch or refreshments. Just as you wouldn't want to overstay your visit during an office meeting with a prospect, you don't want your guest to feel that she's obligated to finish the round no matter what. She'll appreciate your sensitivity and generosity in offering to quit before finishing eighteen.

You might be disappointed in quitting early. But you may actually be scoring points. I'm sure she'd prefer to work with someone who is patient and sensitive to her needs, rather than with someone who is only focused on what he wants.

Read the Rest

If you've enjoyed reading this chapter, I hope you'll read the earlier chapters as well. Unlike other countries where golfers must pass playing and written tests on the rules and etiquette of golf, golf courses in the United States have extended golfers the unrestricted freedom to play without any training or education. As a result, slow play and inconsiderate behavior on the golf course seem to be occurring more often than ever. Aging demographics, the "Tiger factor," and the increase in using golf for business have all brought new players who are enthusiastic and eager to play, but unfortunately without the knowledge of how to play appropriately. And, since it's impossible to know what you don't know, you might glean a tip or two, which might be helpful, especially if you play business golf.

Giving the Gift of Golf

You might manage or mentor businesswomen or have women you know that you wish played golf. I've found that some women need a gentle nudge from a friend or relative or their boss to help them get into the game. Many companies have paid or sponsored clinics for women employees to learn how to play golf in a business environment. Or, a boss will pay for a couple of women to attend group golf lessons from a local golf professional.

As you know, the golf swing is only one component of being a golfer. Just as important, if not more so, is playing with appropriate etiquette and knowledge of the rules. If you know businesswomen who can benefit from playing golf in their careers and personal lives, then I hope you will help them get *On Course for Business* with this book.

Staying On Course

_____ Women are business owners, buyers, and decision makers. Invite a woman to play business golf as you would your male counterparts.

_____ Your goal is to introduce yourself and your company during a business golf round with a woman. Don't focus on your golf game, but make sure she is having a fun, comfortable, and pleasant experience.

_____ Choose a course that fits her playing level. If your guest is a beginner, avoid a golf course with a high slope rating or choose an executive course or play only nine holes.

_____ Be strategic about which tees you and she should play from. She might join you on the middle tees, or she might prefer that you play from the forward tees with her. Remember, this is a business golf round and you can practice your irons and trick shots.

_____ Avoid betting since it can create a win-lose competitive atmosphere.

_____ If she's playing from the forward tees, remember to stop at her tees and stand at the tee box to help watch her ball.

_____ Refrain from offering unsolicited swing tips. If she asks, keep your tips simple and to a minimum. If she is getting frustrated with her game, suggest she relax and not worry about her score, and talk about something else besides golf.

_____ Behaving as a gentleman is always a safe bet. Watch your language, jokes, cigar smoke, and alcohol consumption.

_____ If your guest is showing fatigue or lack of interest in playing all eighteen holes, offer to stop playing. She'll appreciate your generosity.

_____ Be a golf mentor to women colleagues and friends. You know the benefit of playing golf, so encourage women to play as well. Give the gift of golf.

Our Nineteenth Hole

You're coming to the end of your journey into the world of business golf. By now, I hope you've discovered and experienced the rewards of playing this great game. Perhaps you've had spectacular business successes like Linda finding a high-paying position or Kimberly acquiring a client that made her public relations company expand internationally. These women had their coveted coups thanks to playing a round of golf, and with strangers, no less.

If not business-related wins, perhaps you've met close friends or even a significant other on the golf course. I met a dear friend, Zocko, thanks to our playing in the same foursome at a golf tournament. And Susan, former golf columnist for the *San Francisco Examiner*, fortuitously met her husband while playing as a single golfer (and as a single woman) at a local golf course. You can use the Examine the Personality of Your Playing Partners of the FREEDOM benefits from Chapter 1 not only to get a read on your business colleagues, but also potential life partners. You'll certainly learn more about each other by playing a round of golf together than if you sat in a dark theater watching a movie.

Keeping *On Course* When Off the Course

If you aren't able to play as often as you'd like, you can still use golf to build rapport and deepen relationships with colleagues, clients, and friends. After reading this book, you'll be able to keep up with any conversation about golf on Monday mornings or while in business meetings. You'll have a new perspective when you watch the professional golf tournaments on television, read about tournaments in the newspaper, or click onto a Web site that covers golf. You'll learn about players' triumphs and disasters over the previous weekend.

You can also use golf as a means to stay in touch with people whom you see infrequently. Here are some ideas:

- If you send a newsletter to clients, include highlights of your business golf rounds or your company's sponsorship of tournaments.
- Give your valued business contacts or prospects two or more gallery tickets for a local professional tournament. You can send a day pass or a pass for the entire tournament.
- Send this book or a biography about a favorite golfer to a client as a thank you gift for past business.
- E-mail an article related to golf that has special relevance to the recipient.
- Send a golf-motif note card. People always comment on my personalized golf note cards because of their unique design.

By using golf in a nongolf setting, you'll remind your contacts of the common bond you share. This reminder may also help cure a complaint that many women share about not receiving invitations to play from businessmen. Quite frankly, these people may need a gentle reminder that you play, so they'll think of you when they are creating a foursome.

Golf for Personal Success

In addition to playing for your business or career development, you can also enjoy the personal benefits of playing. Remember the Fabulous Fun and the Exercise for Your Body, Mind, and Spirit benefits of FREEDOM. When we're overcommitted and feeling overwhelmed, that's when we need to take the time and get away from it all. Whether to feel the satisfaction of a shot well hit, or to burn off calories and stress, playing golf can be a healthy outlet. Recall Karen, who plays nine holes by herself on a public golf course—she considers it a vacation.

You can also use a round of golf to examine your personality. As a practicing corporate real estate attorney in San Francisco, I was not just a Type A personality, but a Type AAA! I was constantly stressed, serious, and uptight. Playing golf helped me learn more about myself and made me aware of some unpleasant traits and beliefs that I wanted to change.

Earlier I mentioned the GOD grip—the "grip of death," because I used to grip the club tightly, rather than gently like holding a bird. And, I will never forget the day I missed a short putt for birdie while playing with my friend Zocko. I turned my head in disgust with myself. Apparently seeing the expression on my face, Zocko said, "Woo!" I responded curtly, "What?" She said with a smile, "Lighten up! It's only golf."

She made me realize that I needed to lighten up—not just about golf—but about my life generally. Golf was the arena that enabled me to learn this life-changing, valuable lesson, as well as many other lessons.

Tee Time Is Near

My time to tee off has come, and I hope we will meet one day on the first tee. I wish you tremendous good fortune in your golf adventures—whether for business, social, or personal reasons. This game is so much more than just a game. It's a business tool. A mirror of life. A teacher that constantly challenges you in unique ways. It's a path to new friendships and relationships. It's as much as you want and allow it to be in your life. As Amelia Earhart said, "Adventure is worthwhile in itself." I hope each time you step on the golf course, it's indeed a worthwhile adventure for you!

APPENDIX A

. . . .

Basic Rules of Golf

The USGA and the Royal and Ancient Golf Club of St. Andrews together oversee the Official Rules of Golf. Although there are only thirty-four official rules, most golfers think there are many more because of the numerous subsections and other details.

This is a simplified summary of the rules that you should become familiar with as you play. If you don't know the rules, be sure to ask more experienced players for help. To learn the rules in greater detail, you can consult books such as *Golf Rules Plain and Simple* by Mark Russell and John Andrisani (Harper-Collins, 1999) and the USGA's *Golf Rules Illustrated: 2000 Rules*.

Maximum number of clubs You should have no more than fourteen clubs in your bag.

Play your own ball You must play your own ball throughout the hole. To be able to identify your ball, you should make a distinguishing mark with a permanent ink marker before you tee off on the first hole.

Teeing ground On the tees, tee the ball between the tee markers and behind them but no more than two club lengths.

As it lies Play the ball down or as it lies unless "Winter Rules" are in effect. Remember, "Winter Rules" (which allow you to improve the lie of your ball in the fairway) do not exist under official USGA rules.

No grounding your club If your ball is in a hazard (water or bunker), you cannot *ground* the club—do not touch the ground or sand with your club before you hit the ball.

Water hazard If you hit your ball into a water hazard (marked with yellow stakes that you can move if interfering with your swing or stance), find the point where your ball crossed the hazard. Imagine a line between that point and the hole, and drop another ball behind the hazard anywhere along that line. You must add a one-stroke penalty to your score. If your ball lies within the yellow stakes and not in the water, you cannot ground your club.

Lateral water hazard   If you hit your ball in a lateral water hazard (marked with red stakes that you can move if interfering with your swing or stance), find the point where your ball crossed the hazard. You have three choices where you can drop your next ball: (1) Drop another ball behind the hazard anywhere along the line from the point and the hole; (2) Behind the hazard, you can drop your ball within two club lengths of where the ball entered, but no closer to the hole; (3) Choose a point across the water hazard that is equidistant from where the ball entered and drop another ball within two club lengths of that point, but no closer to the hole. You must add a one-stroke penalty to your score. If your ball lies within the red stakes and not in the water, you cannot ground your club.

Out of bounds or lost ball   If you lose your ball (not in a water hazard) or it goes out of bounds, return to where you hit your original shot and hit another ball. You need to add a one-stroke penalty. If you aren't sure your ball is lost or out of bounds, then tell the other players that you will hit a "provisional ball," so you don't have to go back to the tee if your ball is lost or out of bounds. If you find your original ball, pick up your provisional ball and your strokes for the provisional ball don't count. Out-of-bound markers usually are white stakes and you are not allowed to move them.

Unplayable lie   If you find your ball but can't hit it, then you can declare the ball *unplayable*. You have three choices: (1) Play your shot from where you just hit; (2) drop another ball within two club lengths of your ball's location, but no closer to the hole; or (3) drop another ball any distance on the line behind where the ball lies and the hole. Add a one-stroke penalty.

Pull the flagstick   If your ball is on the green, remove the flagstick before you putt. If the ball hits the pin, you will have a two-stroke penalty.

Loose impediment   If your ball is near a loose impediment (natural objects, such as twigs, pebbles, leaves, etc.), you can remove the impediment *as long as your ball does not move.* You cannot remove a loose impediment if your ball is in a hazard.

Movable and immovable obstructions   If an artificial, man-made object—a cart sign or rake—interferes with your stance or swing, you can move the object. If the item, such as a fence or drain, cannot be moved, you may drop your ball within one club length of where you have a stance or swing without penalty, but no closer to the hole.

Asking and giving advice   You cannot ask or receive subjective information (such as the distance of your ball to the green or what club someone used), but you can ask or receive public information (such as how to apply a rule of golf or the distance according to a distance marker).

Ground under repair   If your ball lands in a construction area or an area marked with white paint, then you can move the ball one club length but no closer to the hole.

. . . .

Resources

Organization Contact Information

Magazines

Golf for Women
800-374-7941
www.golfforwomen.com

Sports Illustrated Women
800-950-5150
http://sportsillustrated.cnn.com/siwomen

Women's World of Golf
800-279-8399
www.womensworldofgolf.com

Women's Golf Organizations

Executive Women's Golf Association
800-407-1477
www.ewga.com

Ladies Golf Professional Association (LPGA)
www.lpga.com

Meeting Industry Ladies Organization (MILO)
301-657-9711
www.clubmilo.com

Recommended Web Sites

To keep up with the world of golf from tournaments to tips on fitness and your golf swing, bookmark your favorite site:

- GOLFONLINE—www.golfonline.com
- GolfWeb—www.golfweb.com
- PGA Tour—www.pgatour.com

To learn more about the rules, the handicap system, and tournament statistics, visit the USGA's Web site at www.usga.org.

For online golf shops and/or information on swing lessons and schools, bookmark your favorite site(s) specifically for women golfers:

- Empowered Women's Golf—www.empoweredwomensgolf.com
- Shegolfs—www.shegolfs.com
- The Women's Golf Company—www.womensgolf.com
- Women on the Green—www.womenonthegreen.com
- Women's Golf Today—www.womensgolftoday.com
- Women's Golf Proshop—www.womensgolfproshop.com

Bibliography

Bryant, Adam. "Duffers Need Not Apply." *New York Times,* May 31, 1998.

Gallagher, Carol, with Susan K. Golant. *Going to the Top.* New York: Viking, 2000.

Peters, Tom. *The Circle of Innovation: You Can't Shrink Your Way to Greatness.* New York: Vintage Books, 1999.

Popcorn, Faith, and Lys Marigold. *EVEolution: Understanding Women—The Eight Truths of Marketing to Women.* New York: Hyperion, 2000.

Richardson, Cheryl. *Take Time for Your Life.* New York: Broadway Books, 1999.

Trump, Donald, with Kate Bohner. *Art of the Comeback.* New York: Times Book, 1997.

Wellington, Sheila, and Catalyst, with Betty Spence. *Be Your Own Mentor.* New York: Random House, 2001.

Glossary

ace A hole in one—a score of one on a par 3 hole.

address A player's position prior to hitting a shot. According to USGA Rules of Golf, a player has addressed the ball when she has taken her stance and grounded her club. In a hazard, a player has addressed the ball when she has taken her stance.

adjust score Reducing the score according to Equitable Stroke Control system for the maximum score a player can take depending on his or her handicap.

aerify Process of boring small holes into fairways and putting greens to improve growth and drainage. The process is usually done once or twice a year.

albatross A double eagle—a score of three under par on a hole. For example, on a par 5 hole, a score of two.

amateur Any golfer who plays the game and does not receive a prize greater than $500 in a golf tournament.

approach A shot from off the green toward the hole. Also the closely mowed area leading up to the putting green.

apron The closely mowed area surrounding a putting green. Also called the collar or the fringe.

army golf A slang term describing a player who is having problems hitting the ball straight. One shot goes to the right, the next to the left, and so forth. Hence, the term army golf.

attend To hold the flagstick and remove it after a player has struck the ball.

away The player farthest from the hole whose turn it is to play.

back foot Assuming a right-handed golfer, the player's right foot, farthest from the target.

back nine   The final nine holes of an eighteen-hole round.

backswing   The motion of moving the club away from the ball. Also known as the take away.

bag boys/bag girls   Golf course staff who assist you in removing your golf clubs from your car and placing them on golf carts.

bag drop   Location where bag boys or bag girls pick up your golf clubs.

bag tag   Used to identify a player's golf bag. Usually customized for each golf course.

Balata   Type of golf ball designed for feel and spin. Beginners should avoid these balls because they are not durable and are expensive.

ball mark   Indentation made when a lofted shot lands on the putting green. Using a repair tool, ball marks should be repaired to maintain the putting green.

ball markers   Used to show the location of player's golf ball on the putting green, usually made in dime- or quarter-size plastic styles with club logo on the top.

ball washer   Found at the tees of holes. Used to clean the golf ball.

banana slice   A shot that has a flight pattern shaped like a banana.

bent grass   Type of grass, characterized by thin blades, found on most courses with varying seasonal climates.

Bermuda grass   Type of grass found on most courses located in warmer or tropical climates. Characterized by thick blades with a grainy surface.

best ball   Usually a team competition in which the lowest score of the players on a team is the team score.

bingo, bango, bongo   A betting game where points are awarded for the first ball on the green (bingo), closest shot to the hole (bango), and the first player to putt out (bongo).

birdie   A score of one stroke less than par on a given hole. For example, on a par 4 hole, a score of three.

bite   Slang term expressed when a player wants the ball to stop on the putting green without a lot of roll.

blades   Type of golf club that is the most difficult to hit because the sweet spot is the smallest. Also known as forged clubs.

bogey   A score of one over par on a hole. For example, on a par 5 hole, a score of six.

box lunch   Usually includes a sandwich, fruit, and chips for players during a tournament.

break   The amount a putt will curve as it rolls on a putting green. The more slope the green has, the greater the break.

bump and run   A type of shot where the golfer aims short of the intended target and allows for substantial roll of the ball after its initial landing.

bunker   A type of hazard consisting of a prepared area of ground from which grass has been removed and replaced with sand.

buried (lie)   In a sand bunker, where most of the ball is below the surface of the sand. See also **fried egg**.

business golf   Golf played with clients, colleagues, or prospects with the goal of developing or deepening a business relationship. May be a practice session at the driving range or playing nine or eighteen holes.

caddie (caddy)   The person who carries a player's clubs during a round of golf.

cart fee   Similar to a green fee, the fee required to rent a golf cart for either nine or eighteen holes.

cart paths only   Term to inform golfers that golf carts must stay on the cart paths at all times. Exceptions may be made for golfers with medical disabilities.

casual water   Any temporary accumulation of water on the course. A marked water hazard is not casual water.

cavity back club   Type of clubhead design where the back of the clubhead is hollowed out.

chili-dip   A shot in which a player hits behind the ball, not moving it very far. Also called a fat shot or a chunk.

chip   A shot to the green with a higher lofted club, such as a 9-iron, pitching wedge, or sand wedge. Ball tends to fly low and roll toward the hole.

chip-out   A shot, generally going only a short distance, to get the ball back in play from a treed area.

chunk   A shot in which a player hits behind the ball removing more turf than desired—the shot is much shorter than intended. Also called a chili-dip or a fat shot.

closest-to-the-line   A contest for men and women during a golf tournament. The player with the drive that is the closest to the line painted on the fairway is the winner.

closest-to-the-pin   Usually a contest on par 3 holes. The player who hits the ball closest to the hole wins.

club face   The side of the clubhead with grooves that makes contact with the ball.

clubhead   The portion of the golf club that makes contact with the ball.

clubhouse   Main building at a golf course that typically houses the pro shop, locker rooms, and the restaurant and/or bar.

club pro   See **golf professional**.

collar   A closely mowed area surrounding the putting green. Also called the apron or the fringe.

commercial putt   Term to describe a putt that is close to the hole.

compression   Measure of how much the ball distorts at impact and can affect the feel of a golf ball. Balls can be 80, 90, or 100 compression. Women usually use an 80 or 90 compression ball.

country club   An upscale (private or semiprivate) golf club, which usually offers other amenities in addition to golf, such as swimming or tennis.

course   The entire area on which a round of golf is played.

course rating   A numerical rating that identifies the difficulty of a golf course. For example, a course rated 72.7 is more challenging to play than one rated at 70.6. A scratch player should expect to shoot 70 or 71 on the course rated 70.6.

cut   A shot, played intentionally, that curves from left to right for a right-handed golfer.

dimple   Depression on a golf ball designed to help the ball become airborne and maintain its accurate flight.

distance marker   An object that indicates the distance to the center of the putting green. Yardage markers are often found at 200-, 150-, 100- and 50-yard intervals from the green. Markers may be trees or bushes along the sides of the fairway or rough or may be plastic, cement, or similar objects sunk in the ground in the center of fairways or on cart paths.

divot   Scottish term for turf removed as a result of contact by the club with the ground. Divots occur as a result of most shots from the fairway or rough. Golfers refer to both the turf removed and the depression left on the ground as a divot.

dogleg   The design of a golf hole in which the fairway curves left or right substantially. If the hole curves to the right, it is referred to as a dogleg right. A hole that curves to the left is a dogleg left.

double bogey   A score of two over par on a hole. For example, on a par 5 hole, a score of seven.

double eagle   A score of three under par on a hole. For example, on a par 5 hole, a score of two. Also called an albatross.

draw   For a right-handed golfer, a shot that tends to curve slightly from right to left in the air.

dress code   Clothing and spike requirements of a golf course for players. For example, many upscale public and private courses do not allow jeans or metal spikes.

drive   The first shot on a hole made from the teeing ground.

driver   Typically the 1-wood used to hit a player's drive. Players that don't use a 1-wood may refer to the 3-wood as the driver.

driving range   A practice area, either at a golf course or on its own, where players practice their game. A range may be as simple as a large mowed field with hitting areas or may be as elaborate as a facility with target greens and practice putting greens.

drop area   An area identified by either paint or chalk in which a player may drop her ball with a penalty of one stroke. Drop areas are found on holes with water hazards and allow the player relief, with penalty, from the water.

duck hook   For a right-handed golfer, a shot that starts straight at the target and curves dramatically to the left of the target.

eagle   A score of two under par on a hole. For example, on a par 5 hole, a score of three.

Equitable Stroke Control   System whereby a very bad score on a hole does not dramatically affect your handicap. Depending on your handicap, you take the maximum score allowed under Equitable Stroke Control.

etiquette   Accepted code of behavior and dress on the golf course. Examples include being quiet while others play, not stepping on another's line of play on the putting green, and so forth.

executive course   A course designed with holes shorter in length and with fewer hazards than most courses—appropriate for beginners to play.

fade   For right-handed golfers, a shot that generally tends to curve slightly to the right.

fairway   Closely mowed area from the teeing ground to the putting green.

fairway woods   The woods, usually 3-, 5-, or 7-wood, used to hit the ball.

fat   A shot in which a player hits behind the ball removing more turf than desired—the shot is much shorter than intended. May also be called a chili-dip or a chunk.

Five-Minute Rule   The amount of time (five minutes) that the USGA allows a player to look for his or her ball. A ball not found after five minutes of searching is considered to be lost, although to keep up the pace, golfers should spend only two to three minutes searching.

flag   Different colors mark the location of the hole on the putting green. For example, depending on the golf course, a blue flag may mean the hole is farther back on the putting green, whereas a red flag may mean the hole is forward on the green.

flagstick   Marks the location of the hole on the putting green. Also known as the pin.

flex   The flexibility of a club's shaft. Depending on a player's golf swing speed, a different flex is required. The faster the swing speed, the stiffer the shaft should be.

flights   Used in golf tournaments to allow players of similar handicaps to compete.

follow through   The portion of the golf swing that occurs after the player has hit the ball.

fore   Warning yelled to a player who may be in danger of being hit by a ball.

forged clubs   See **blades**.

foursome   A group of four golfers playing together.

fried egg   Lie in a bunker in which most of the ball is below the surface of the sand—the ball looks like a fried egg.

fringe   The closely mowed area surrounding a putting green. Also called the apron or the collar.

front foot   Assuming a right-handed golfer, it is the player's left foot, closest to the target.

front nine   The first nine holes of an eighteen-hole course.

gallery   Those who attend a golf event to watch the players.

GHIN   Golf Handicap Information Network. The USGA system used to calculate handicaps.

GHIN number   A golfer's identification number for handicap purposes.

gimme   A short putt, typically the length of the putter grip, that players assume a golfer will be able to hit into the hole. Counts as a stroke.

golf club   A piece of equipment used to hit a golf ball. Also a term to describe a golf course facility.

Golf Handicap Information Network   See **GHIN**.

golf professional   A person whose career in golf is dedicated to helping others enjoy the game—giving lessons, managing operations, running tournaments, and so forth.

good lag   Comment made about a putt that does not go into the hole, but is the correct length.

grain   Direction of growth of the grass. Particularly noticeable on putting greens, the grain will have an influence on the direction and speed of the ball as it rolls.

green   See **putting green**.

greenkeeper   The person responsible for the condition, care, and maintenance of the golf course. He or she may also be referred to as the course superintendent.

green fee   Cost to play nine or eighteen holes.

greens in regulation   Statistic to determine how many holes a player had his or her ball on the green in the prescribed number of strokes.

grip   How a player holds the golf club. Also, the part of the golf club that is held in the player's hands.

gross score   The score that a player has without considering his or her handicap.

ground club   Placing the sole of the club on the ground. Not permitted when the ball is in a hazard.

ground under repair (GUR)   A marked area (usually by paint, chalk, or roping) on the course from which a player may move her ball one club length without penalty, prior to playing her next shot. Common reasons for GUR are areas under construction, damaged turf, and so forth.

group lesson   Learning the golf swing with other individuals from a golf teaching professional. Typically, group lessons are given in a series of four or five lessons for forty-five minutes to an hour. See also **private lesson**.

H-system   Refers to the system of driving the golf cart whereby players stay on the path and then turn 90 degrees onto the fairway to the ball.

hack(er)   Slang, derogatory term given to a player of lesser playing ability.

ham and egg   When two players are competing as a team and one player plays a hole poorly, and the other player plays the same hole well.

handicap   The number assigned to a player's ability level—the number of strokes over the course rating a player is expected to have. The lower the handicap, the better the player. A player's handicap is deducted from her gross score to establish her net score. See **gross score; net score**.

handicap index   The decimal number used to determine your handicap according to the slope of the course played. See **slope**.

hardpan   Area of the golf course (not bunkers or hazards) on which no grass is growing.

heel   The part of the clubhead closest to the shaft.

hit a club   Term to describe the distance a player can hit a particular golf club.

hitting stations   Each player's area to hit balls at a driving range. See **driving range**.

home course   The golf course most often played by a golfer.

honor   The player who hits first on a hole is said to have honors. Honor is gained by having the lowest score on the last played hole.

hook   For a right-handed golfer, a shot that starts to the right of the target and curves dramatically to the left.

hosel   The portion of the golf clubhead that holds the shaft.

initiation   Fee paid prior to joining a private club. An initiation fee may be a few hundred dollars to hundreds of thousand dollars at some elite country clubs.

in jail   Term used when faced with a difficult shot because trees interfere with your ball's flight.

invitational   Type of tournament in which contestants must be invited in order to play. The most recognizable professional invitational is the Masters Tournament held each spring in Augusta, Georgia.

keep the pace   Description of a foursome playing in proper pace in comparison with the foursome ahead.

knock-down   A shot intentionally played to keep a ball low in the wind.

knock-offs   Golf clubs that look like clubs made by brand-name manufacturers but are less expensive.

lateral water hazard   Type of water hazard defined by red boundary stakes. Often runs parallel to the line of play on a hole. The penalty for hitting into a lateral hazard is one stroke.

lie   The position of a ball on the course. A ball in the fairway will typically be considered to have a good lie, while a ball in a divot or high grass will be referred to as a bad lie. Also refers to the angle of the shaft as it goes into the clubhead. When asked as a question, "What do you lie?" it refers to the number of strokes, plus penalty shots, taken so far by a player.

links   Description of a type of golf course design. Also a slang given to any eighteen-hole golf course.

lip   The edge or rim of a hole or a bunker.

lip out   A ball that hits the edge of the hole, rolls slightly into the hole, but does not go in the hole.

lob shot   A high, soft shot, generally played near the green with a high-lofted club or a wedge.

loft   The angle of a club face. The steeper the loft, the higher up a ball will fly, but the less far the ball will travel.

long game   Term to describe shots from the tee and the fairway.

Longest Drive   A contest for men and women during a golf tournament. The player with the longest drive is the winner.

loose impediments   Natural objects such as branches, twigs, sand, or pebbles.

lost ball   A ball is considered lost if it cannot be located or identified after up to five minutes of searching for it.

LPGA (Ladies Professional Golf Association)   Promotes the game of golf to everyone. Provides education and certification to its women golf professional members.

LPGA Tour Organization for female professional golfers that manages tournaments throughout the world in which members play for monetary remuneration.

Major (Championship) One of four of the most prestigious professional golf tournaments in the world played every year. For male golfers, the Majors include the Masters, the U.S. Men's Open, the Men's British Open, and the PGA Championship. For female players, the Majors include the Kraft Nabisco Championship, U.S. Women's Open, the McDonald's LPGA Championship, and the Weetabix Women's British Open.

marker See **ball marker**.

marshal A golf course employee whose duty is to keep appropriate pace of play. A marshal typically drives the course in a motorized cart, identified in some way (flag, sign, etc.), encouraging slow groups to speed up or to allow other groups to play through. Also known as a **ranger**.

match play Type of competition in which the number of holes won and lost is kept. The winner of a match play competition is the side who wins the most holes. An example of a match play score is "3 and 2." The winning team was three holes up (ahead) with only two holes to play. Thus, the match ended after playing the sixteenth hole.

medal play Type of competition in which the lowest total score wins. Also known as **stroke play**.

mulligan A player's shot after a particularly bad shot. Mulligans are common on the first tee during friendly matches and are sold at fund-raising tournaments, but are not allowed under the USGA Official Rules of Golf.

municipal course Type of golf course, usually city or county managed, allowing play by the public, subject to tee time availability. Also referred to as muni.

Nassau A common betting game that consists of a given bet for the front nine, the back nine, and the overall game. A $5 Nassau is a wager of $15 total.

net The player's score less his or her handicap.

nineteenth hole The bar or restaurant at the golf course where players gather after playing a round of golf to talk about their round and possibly business.

Ninety-Degree Rule Refers to the system of driving the golf cart whereby players stay on the path and then turn 90 degrees onto the fairway to the ball.

OB See **out of bounds**.

out of bounds Any area from which play is prohibited and marked with white stakes or lines. The penalty for OB is stroke and distance—player must return to the spot where the original ball was played, hit another ball from that location, and add a penalty stroke to her score.

over par   Number of strokes a player's score is over the par for the holes played. For example, if a player shoots a score of 40 on nine holes whose par is 36, she is said to be four over.

oversized club   Golf clubs designed with a larger sweet spot.

par   Expected score on a given hole based on its length, difficulty, and gender of the player.

par-3 course   A short golf course comprised of all par 3 holes. Par 3 courses are good learning courses for beginners and help better players improve their short games.

par 3, 4 or 5   See **par**.

penalty   Extra stroke or strokes assessed for specific violations of USGA Official Rules of Golf during stroke play. In match play, the penalty may be loss of the hole.

PGA (Professional Golfer's Association)   Organization to promote the game of golf to everyone. It provides education and certification to its male and female members.

PGA Tour   Organization for male professional golfers that manages tournaments throughout the world in which members play for monetary remuneration.

pick up   Term to describe when a golfer has hit his or her maximum number of strokes under Equitable Stroke Control and does not complete the hole.

pin   See **flagstick**.

pitch   A shot to the green with a higher-lofted club, such as a pitching wedge or sand wedge. Ball flies high and bounces toward the hole.

play through   A situation in which the group behind is permitted to play a hole on which the group ahead is playing. The group behind is said to have played through.

pop   Slang for the handicap stroke that a player receives from a competitor.

post   Process of entering your golf score into a computer used for handicaps.

pot bunker   A small but very deep bunker.

press   A new bet in a game. Usually asked for by the player losing at the time.

private course   Type of course requiring membership to play. Guests may play private courses for a fee at specific times when accompanied by a member of the club.

private lesson   A session with a golf teaching professional to learn or improve your golf swing.

professional golfer   An individual who earns a living based on his or her skill at playing the game.

provisional ball   A ball that is played, usually in an effort to speed up play, as a potential replacement for a ball that may be lost or out of bounds. For example, if a player hits her ball toward an out-of-bounds area, but is not certain the ball is out of bounds, she declares she is going to hit a provisional ball in case the original ball is out of bounds. If the original is out of bounds, the provisional becomes the ball in play and she needs to add one penalty stroke to her score. This prevents her from having to return to the position from where she hit her original shot and saves time.

public course A course open to play for all golfers.

pull Assuming a right-handed player, a shot that tends to go to the left of the intended target in a straight path.

punch A shot, played intentionally low, to avoid wind, trees, or other obstacles.

punch-out A shot played from a treed area designed to get the ball back into play.

push Assuming a right-handed player, a shot that tends to go to the right of the intended target in a straight path.

putter Club designed to roll the ball when on or very near the green.

putting green The area of the hole being played that is specifically mowed for putting. May also refer to a practice putting area at a golf course.

putting line The area that a player wants the ball to travel toward the hole.

putt out Said by one player to another to finish putting even though she is not farthest away.

range See **driving range**.

range ball Type of ball used at a driving range. Marked in a particular way, such as a stripe.

ranger A golf course employee whose duty it is to keep appropriate pace of play. A ranger typically drives the course in a motorized cart, identified in some way (flag, sign, etc.), encouraging slow groups to speed up or to allow other groups to play through.

read the green Process a player takes to visualize how the ball will travel on the putting green to the hole.

ready golf Method of playing golf whereby players attempt to keep up with the group in front of them. For example, deciding which club to use while walking to your ball is playing ready golf.

relief Under the rules of golf, a player may drop or place a ball with or without penalty, depending on the situation, such as relief from trees, water, or obstructions.

repair tool Used to repair ball marks on the green.

resort Type of golf course catering to the guests of the resort with which the course is associated. Resort courses may sell limited memberships and may allow public play at specific times.

re-span   Replacing the marker to its original location. See **span**.

rough   Type of grass, bordering fairways, that is higher and generally more coarse than the grass in the fairway. Rough may also be present near greens, tees, and bunkers, depending on the particular course.

round   A typical round of golf, generally eighteen holes, but sometimes nine holes.

Royal and Ancient Golf Club of Saint Andrews   One of the two governing bodies of golf, along with the USGA. Often called the R & A, it is headquartered in St. Andrews, Scotland.

sand trap   See **bunker**.

sandbagger   A golfer who consistently plays to a score better than her handicap indicates that she should.

Scramble   A type of game, played as a team in which all players play from one position. For example, a team of four players each hits a drive. The team decides on the best drive and each player hits a shot from that position. Play continues in this manner until the ball is holed.

scratch golfer   A person with a zero handicap.

second up   The foursome waiting for the group to hit off the first tee.

semiprivate   Type of golf club in which memberships are sold, but that allows public play during specific time periods.

set up   See **stance**.

shaft   The portion of the golf club between the grip and the clubhead. Can be made of steel or graphite.

shag bag   Carrier of many golf balls used for practicing a player's short game.

shank   A shot that is struck in the hosel area of the golf club. The resulting ball flight is generally straight to the right.

short game   Describes shots made from the fairway to the green. See **chip** and **pitch**.

shotgun start   When players begin play simultaneously from different tees around the course. Often used in charity and corporate golf tournaments.

skins   Type of match play game in which each hole is worth a given amount of points or money. Points or money are often carried over in the event of ties, making all subsequent holes worth considerably more.

sleeve   Package of three to four golf balls. Buy a sleeve of balls when looking for a ball that you prefer, rather than buying a box of twelve balls.

slice   Assuming a right-handed player, a shot that tends to start to the left of the target and curves to the right of the target.

slope   A number used to compare the difficulty of golf courses—considers length, hazards, terrain, and so forth. A course with a slope rating of 150 will be far more difficult than one sloped at 100. The average slope rating is 113.

snake putt A putt holed from a long distance.

snap hook Assuming a right-handed player, a shot that starts quickly to the left and angles sharply and further to the left, producing a very short and undesirable result.

snowman Euphemism to describe a score of eight.

soft spikes Generic term given to the plastic spikes required on many courses. These softer spikes are believed to do less damage to the course, especially to the greens. See **spikes**.

sole Bottom part of the golf clubhead that sits on the ground when a player is addressing the ball.

span Moving a player's marker by the length of the putter head to allow another player to putt without interference of the marker.

spikes Metal protrusions on the bottom of golf shoes designed to aid in traction.

stance Position of the feet prior to making a shot. A player placing her feet in position to make a stroke is said to have taken her stance.

starters A member of the pro shop staff who organizes and manages the flow of players starting the first hole on the golf course. A starter may also be found on the first tee at some courses.

stimp Speed of a green after measurement with a specialized piece of equipment (stimpmeter). The higher the stimp reading, the faster the green.

stimpmeter Apparatus used to measure the speed of a green.

stroke: The forward movement of the club made with the intent of hitting the ball.

stroke and distance Penalty assessed for a ball hit out of bounds or for a lost ball. It involves going back to the spot of the original ball, hitting another ball from that location, and adding a penalty shot to the score.

stroke play Type of competition, also known as medal play, in which the lowest score wins.

Summer Rules Slang term given when playing the ball down or as it lies.

Surlyn Durable plastic used for the cover of golf balls.

sweet spot The portion of the clubhead where you want to hit the golf ball.

swing speed The speed a player swings a golf club. The faster the speed, the more stiff the shaft should be.

take away The motion of moving the golf club away from the ball. Also known as the backswing.

tap in A short putt to hit the ball into the hole.

tee The wooden or plastic implement on which a ball is placed prior to the play of the first shot on a hole. The term may also be used to describe the teeing ground.

tee marker   Wooden, metal, or other objects between which the ball is teed prior to playing a hole. There may be several sets of tee markers on each hole for players with different playing abilities.

tee time   Specific time allotted for play on a given day. Assigned by the golf course in eight- to ten-minute intervals usually, tee times are acquired by calling in advance of when play is desired.

teeing ground   The area where the play of a hole starts. It is defined by a pair of markers between which play begins.

tempo   The rhythm of a golf round or a player's golf swing. Also known as timing.

temporary green   When a green is closed for repair or is too wet, the green-keeper may make a temporary green in the fairway. Yardage must be adjusted when playing a temporary green. For scoring purposes, you can only take a maximum of two strokes.

tend   See **attended**.

through the green   All areas of the course, except for the teeing ground, putting green, and hazards.

timing   The rhythm of a player's golf swing. Also known as tempo.

toe   The end of the clubhead farthest away from the shaft. Also used to describe the shot when a player hits the ball on that area of the club.

top   Shot that does not get airborne as a result of a player hitting the top of the ball.

trap   Generic term given to a bunker that contains sand. Also called a bunker or a sand trap.

triple bogey   A score of three over par on a hole. For example, on a par 5 hole, a score of eight.

turn   The halfway point of an eighteen-hole round. A player makes the turn after playing nine holes and heading to the tenth tee.

twilight rate   Reduced green fees at a golf course, typically after 2 P.M. at many courses.

under par   The number of strokes a player has taken relative to par for the hole she is playing. If a player has played the front nine in thirty-four strokes and par is thirty-six, she is said to be two under.

unplayable lie   A ball in a location that is impossible for the player to hit. Examples are balls hit under trees or in shrubs.

up and down   Also referred to as up and in, the situation in which a player misses the green on her approach shot and then makes one chip and one putt to achieve her score.

waggle   Preshot movement in which a golfer moves the club back away from the ball a time or two, usually to relieve tension.

waiting list The number and ranking of individuals waiting to join a private club that has a full membership at the time. Waiting lists at some private clubs may be many years.

water hazard Any relatively permanent and open area of water (sea, lake, pond, etc.) on the course marked with yellow stakes or lines. The penalty for hitting your ball into a water hazard is one stroke.

whiff Occurs when a player swings at the ball and misses it completely.

wind shirt A thin jacket, often made of waterproof material.

Winter Rules Invoked by a golf course as a local rule when the course is very wet and muddy. Not sanctioned by the USGA.

wormburner A poor shot characterized by the ball not getting airborne and simply rolling fast along the ground.

X factor Applies to the differential between hip angle and shoulder angle during a golfer's backswing.

X-out balls Imperfect golf balls marked with an X to cover the manufacturer's name. Should not be used during a round of business golf.

yardage book Provides distances of each hole of a golf course.

yardage marker See **distance marker**.

yips The condition, either mental or physical, in which a golfer misses short putts.

About the Author

Suzanne Woo founded BizGolf Dynamics in 1996 to share her passion and strategies for using golf to build and deepen business relationships and to increase revenues. She is a recovering attorney in the San Francisco Bay area with experience in commercial real estate. The highlights of Suzanne's golf career include having a 12 handicap and hitting a hole in one at her club, Mira Vista Golf and Country Club.

Clientele of BizGolf Dynamics include (Arthur) Andersen, Bank of America, Merrill Lynch, and a host of associations such as Electronic Transactions Association, Texas Credit Union League, and Women in Technology International. Suzanne has been featured in dozens of national magazines and newspapers such as *The American Lawyer, Golf for Women, Worth, The Los Angeles Times, The San Francisco Chronicle,* and *The Wall Street Journal.* She is the also the author of *72 Secrets for Successful Business Golf.*

For more information about Suzanne's books and tapes, to schedule her for a presentation, or to arrange business golf coaching, contact her at

BizGolf Dynamics
2003 Milvia Street, Suite B
Berkeley, California 94704
800-722-8909

Suzanne wants to hear about your business golf experiences, whether good, horrible, or successful. You can e-mail her at Suzanne@BizGolf.biz. Be sure to visit her Web site at www.bizgolf.biz.

Index